# Inside the Sermon

# Inside the Sermon

*Thirteen Preachers Discuss*
*Their Methods of Preparing Messages*

*Edited by*
## Richard Allen Bodey

**BAKER BOOK HOUSE**
Grand Rapids, Michigan 49516

Copyright 1990 by

Baker Book House Company

Printed in the United States of America

Scripture references are from the American Standard Version (ASV); the King James Version (KJV); the New American Standard Bible (NASB), © The Lockman Foundation 1960, 1962, 1963, 1968, 1971, 1972, 1973, 1975, 1977; the New International Version (NIV), copyright © 1973, 1978, 1984 International Bible Society, and used by permission of Zondervan Bible Publishers; the New King James Version (NKJV), copyright © 1979, 1980, 1982, Thomas Nelson, Inc., Publishers; and the Revised Standard Version (RSV), copyright © 1946, 1952, 1971, and 1973 by the Division of Christian Education of the National Council of the Churches of Christ in the United States of America.

**Library of Congress Cataloging-in-Publication Data**

Inside the sermon : thirteen preachers discuss their methods of preparing messages / edited by Richard Allen Bodey.

   p.     cm.

   Includes bibliographical references and index.

   ISBN 0-8010-0982-0

   1. Preaching. 2. Sermons, American. I. Bodey, Richard Allen.

BV4211.2I57   1990

251'.01—dc20                                        90-36846

                                                       CIP

In memory of my father
**Allen Zartman Bodey**
faithful preacher of the Word
for fifty years
and by example
the best teacher of preaching
I ever had

# Contents

# Preface

Nothing fascinates preachers—and students preparing to become preachers—quite as much as learning how other preachers, especially those of note, go about the task of preaching. We all share a curiosity about the secret of their pulpit power. Most of all, we would relish a chance to observe them at work in the study to see how they craft their sermons. Few, if any, of us, however, have ever watched another preacher bring a sermon to birth. Medical students spend hours observing surgeons perform all sorts of operations, from the simplest to the most delicate. But there is no provision for this form of instruction in theological education. Therein lies the reason for this book. In these pages thirteen evangelical preachers—some of international reputation—bring the reader about as close to a homiletical craftsman at work as one can ever get.

This book had its beginning—although I never for a moment suspected it—in a course on preaching I took thirty-five years ago. The professor had recently edited a collection of essays by well-known preachers of the day. Each essay described the preacher's method of sermon preparation and was accompanied by one of his representative sermons. The class found the book intriguing.

Within a few years two other equally helpful books of this kind were published, one in England and one in the United States. All three volumes, of course, have long been out of print. It seemed to both editor and publisher that the time was ripe for a new volume of this kind by preachers of today.

The reader will find considerable diversity of method within these pages. Each contributor has a different philosophy of preaching, and his philosophy influences his approach to constructing his sermons. None of the contributors would pretend that his is the only way, or even the best way, to prepare a sermon. The time-honored homiletical boundaries leave ample room for as many different methods of sermon preparation as there are preachers. The wise preacher will find and follow the method that best works for him or her.

One of the saddest mistakes a preacher can make is to imitate another preacher, no matter how effective that preacher may be. The imitator forces himself into a homiletical straightjacket, and homiletical straight-jackets are frightfully uncomfortable. Worse still, they ruin one's preaching potential. But we can always learn from those who share with us the high calling of proclaiming God's good news in Jesus Christ. All who have collaborated in these close-ups will feel amply rewarded if some of their colleagues find something in these pages—some hint, some procedure, some practice—that will make the task of sermon preparation easier and more rewarding for them.

Students in the preaching class I previously referred to voiced one criticism of our professor's book. We wished he had included a description of his own method of sermon preparation, but he didn't. Because I intend to use this book in my own classes, I reluctantly included myself among the contributors, thereby avoiding this criticism.

I have debts I must, and do most gladly, acknowledge: to each of the contributors for his willingness to share his method of sermon preparation with comrades in the field, and to take time from an already crowded schedule to do so; to the senate, administration, and board of directors of Trinity Evangelical Divinity School for granting me a sabbatical term to work on this project; to Allan Fisher, textbook editor at Baker, who welcomed the proposal of this book with great enthusiasm, and who gave his unfailing encouragement to me through much work and many long delays; to Jim Weaver and Paul Engle, for their help and suggestions; to Linda Triemstra, who oversaw the copy editing; and to my dear wife, Ruth, who relieved me of many of my household chores while the work was in progress, and who—after completing her own full-time job at the switchboard and the computer terminal—devoted many evenings and weekends to typing and proofreading these pages.

Each contributor was granted freedom to choose a Scripture version. Unless otherwise noted, Scripture quotations throughout both sermon and methodology are from the version indicated after the sermon text. The contributors also recommended the books listed in the bibliography.

*Richard Allen Bodey*
Pentecost 1989

# 1

# J. Sidlow Baxter

Born in Sydney, Australia, and reared in England, J. Sidlow Baxter attended St. James' Church of England School and Spurgeon's Theological College, London. He pastored Baptist churches in Northampton, Sunderland, and Edinburgh before coming to the United States. He is a highly respected Bible expositor, having preached and lectured in countries around the world.

Baxter has authored twenty-six books, including *Explore the Book, His Part and Ours, Meet These Men, The Master Theme of the Bible, Studies in Problem Texts, Majesty: The God You Should Know, and Does God Still Exist?* He received an honorary D.D. degree from Central Baptist Seminary, Toronto.

# Reading Till Captivated by a Text

When I think about the preparation and presentation of a sermon, the four components which together form this process immediately come to mind: selection of a biblical passage or theme; study of that passage or theme; organization of the material; and public presentation of the message.

## Selecting a Passage

The first step in sermon preparation is, of course, the selection of a text, passage, or theme. I much prefer the text, or passage, or theme to select me, rather than my selecting it. The only times I make specific selections are when I know that I must adapt my message to some specific need or circumstance. My usual procedure is to let a text or passage capture and compel my own heart and mind.

I have found that by far the most prolific source of sermon suggestion is the continual reading of the Bible. In saying this, I make a sharp distinction between reading the Bible and studying it. Reading the Bible right through, again and again, has value beyond exaggeration. It engenders a vivid sense of the presence of God in history. It begets a profound awareness of divine sovereignty. It gives a comprehensive grasp of divine revelation. It provides a kaleidoscopic picture of biblical unity amid diversity, and exhibits the wonderful progress of doctrine through all the successive parts of Holy Scripture.

In addition to all that, such continual reading of the Bible is endlessly productive of sermon suggestions. Just one word of caution is needed. If we read the Bible *only* to look for sermons, they will be tantalizingly elusive. If we always read it as a hunter stalks deer, we will scarcely ever glimpse the fleet-footed prey, though the terrain abounds with them. We must let the Bible talk to us. If we give it time, it does. We must read enough at a time to get into the throb or flow of it. We must read it daily: long interruptions diminish its impact. We must read it for sheer pleasure. When we are not looking for sermons, but are reading the Bible for our own edification or relaxation, sermons will leap out from their hiding places and pounce upon us like glorious panthers which we simply cannot shake off. The sermons which come in that way are seldom just sermons; they are messages. The truth of the Word itself grips you, thrills you, and you simply must tell it.

Along with that, of course, another rich source of sermon suggestion is Bible study. Whole veins of precious ore in the mine of Scripture truth are opened up by such study. It provides the material for spacious pulpit themes; for instance, the sovereignty of God in Genesis, or blessing through suffering in Job, or the Holy Spirit in Ephesians, or the traits of the born again in John. There is a truly boundless scope for big preaching themes in such systematic study of the Bible. An industrious Bible student never runs out of fascinating preaching material.

Next to that I place Bible commentaries and smaller expository works. You may dub me old-fashioned, but I still maintain that among commentaries on the whole Bible, the most fertile in sermon suggestion for general pastoral use is dear old Matthew Henry's. You would hardly consult him first in matters of textual criticism, but for setting an evangelical minister's mind going on profitable spiritual themes, he is *primus inter pares*. Commentaries yield little in sermon suggestion, however, by being merely consulted: they need to be read. Then, like the little reflector-studs along our highways, which light up at night like stars when our car headlights catch them, we begin to see prospective sermons flashing at us for miles ahead!

I also think that all good books on the Bible and the Christian life, especially those of an expository type, are useful for sermon suggestion in the sense that "iron sharpeneth iron"—often causing sparks of original thinking in one's own mind. Therefore the judicious bookworm will receive many more sermonic ideas than the preacher whose reading is spasmodic or desultory. Many healthy sermon-germs have suddenly penetrated my mind from the marginal notes in the American Standard Version and in Weymouth's New Testament in Modern Speech, not to mention others.

Even magazines can be gleaned, though their use is mainly to supply information on current topics—and topical preaching, I believe, should be occasional rather than continual. An outstanding American psychology professor, when asked by a student which magazines he read, replied, "Young man, if I read as many magazines as most people I would know as little." We preachers need to guard against becoming magazine scavengers.

Books of other preachers' sermons seem to me to be comparatively poor soil in which to find ideas sprouting for sermons of one's own. They tempt us to transplant rather than to originate and cultivate. They may well be read for style and emulation, but they are poor sources of sermon suggestion if we are going to preserve our own originality. To keep adapting (or even adopting!) other men's sermons destroys sanctified originality, genuine pulpit artistry, and all sense of a direct prophetic burden from God. Why keep snooping round in the fenced-off territory of other preachers' sermons when the Bible and scholarly expositions of it keep offering to us "twelve baskets full" for every twelve months of preaching?

The only worthy way to appropriate other men's pulpit products is to imbibe and absorb them, not verbally but in substance, so that the truth in them becomes part of one's own thinking. Spurgeon used to say that he got flour and milk and currants and raisins and sugar and salt and other ingredients from many sources, but he made his own cakes. And that says it "just right."

## Studying the Material

When a text, or passage, or theme either suddenly or more gradually lights up with a magnetic light that tells me that I must preach on it, the first thing I do is to jot down quickly the main idea that has captured or allured me, then the subsidiary thoughts clustering round it, and then the way it seems to assume a preliminary form. Sometimes, if I fail to write those down at once, I lose that first something about the text or theme which makes it live and sing.

Next, I get down to concentrated sermonic preparation. Unless I am using a text merely as a motto or basis for some topic, the first thing I always do is look it up in the original to make sure I give a correct exegesis of it in the message I am building around it. Then I examine the text further in relation to its context. Those two prerequisite safeguards—etymology and context—should never be neglected or separated from each other. They are of first importance in truly biblical preaching.

Usually, after that I make a rough, preliminary outline of the projected message. By the very fact that I have been powerfully drawn to a text or passage, certain dominant ideas are already holding me. These need to be sorted out and jotted down; otherwise they can become "without form and void." So I quickly note all the salient ideas or features and put them in their proper sequence, even though this may be just a rough outline.

Now it is time to turn to the commentaries, a procedure I nearly always find interesting. Who knows? Perhaps I shall find that "all [they], like sheep, have gone astray," or I may find that I myself have erroneously "turned to [my] own way"! But most often each commentary adds its quota of enrichment, offering some new slant, or flash, or facet, even touching some new depth or opening up a new vista.

At the same time I try to look up all other available books that comment on the passage. Often the most valuable contributions come from the least likely references in out-of-the-way territory on my bookshelves. Usually, I reach a point of happy predicament where I have too much material. The hunting period is over. It is time to "divide the spoil."

## Organizing the Material

From my copious cullings and jottings I must now appropriate only those that are germane to my particular theme, resolutely excluding those that are extrinsic, however attractive or beguiling they may be. One of my many faults used to be the inclusion of so many colorful bits and touches that the message became a mosaic. My concern to make it more attractive made it less effective.

This matter of retaining the pertinent and deleting the unessential is more important than some of us may realize, because of the purpose and nature of a sermon. There is a clear-cut difference between an essay, a poem, a drama, and a sermon. An essay has to do distinctively with the intellect, a poem with the imagination, a drama with the emotions, but a sermon expounds God's Word, which (whatever it may have to do with intellect, or imagination, or emotions) calls for a response of the hearer's will and a conforming of his life to the will of God. All that augments a sermon's cogency as a message may well be included, while everything merely adventitious or diversionary should be rejected.

When the material has thus been collected, collated, sifted, and limited to the scope of the message, I am ready to arrange my subject matter. This has always been a most congenial part of preparation for me, yet at times the most taxing. Effective communication of the message to our hearers often depends largely upon its arrangement. In these days, more than ever, over-elaborateness or intricacy must be avoided, yet, on the other hand, a sermon which is merely like an unwinding ball of string can easily fail by seeming to be a meaningless ramble.

When the text itself suggests the divisions, we should follow them. Suppose, for instance, we are opening up Ephesians 1:4, "According as he hath chosen us in him [Christ] before the foundation of the world, that we should be holy and without blame before him in love." The central statement is in the verb, "he hath chosen," and the subject is divine election. Modifying the verb are three adverbial amplifications telling us *how* God chose us, *when* God chose us, and *why* God chose us. If we ask *how* he chose us, or elected us, the first adverbial phrase answers, "in him." If we ask *when* he chose us, the second adverbial phrase answers, "before the foundation of the world (*cosmos*)." If we ask *why* he chose us, the third adverbial addition tells us "that we should be holy and without blame before him in love." In all such instances we should let the text itself determine the arrangement.

In countless instances we still have ample opportunity for sanctified ingenuity. Take Spurgeon's vibrant homily on Jeremiah 1:19, "They shall fight against thee; but they shall not prevail against thee; for I am with thee, saith the LORD, to deliver thee." Spurgeon's stimulating triad is: conflict inevitable—"they shall fight against thee;" defeat impossible—"they shall not prevail against thee;" alliance invincible—"I am with thee, to deliver thee."

Why should there not be elegance and genius in the construction and verbal formulation of a sermon? Even truth is all the more impressive in her best attire. All art and skill which help to grip and hold attention should be prayerfully developed. I recommend that young preachers learn from the printed sermons of C. H. Spurgeon, W. L. Watkinson, and J. H. Jowett, who were masters of sermonic artistry.

For a change, it is often good to let the sermon take the form of four or five or six successive propositions, without need for subdivision. Or one can prepare a message in the form of a cumulative argument, link by link. But whichever form of presentation is envisaged, the sermon should be methodical—never intricate, but amply organized. In the world of preaching, a sermon which is like a wandering river usually "loses itself in the sands." From opening sentence onwards we should give the impression that we are going somewhere worthwhile and that we are going there by the best route.

One of my special concerns is to design prepossessing introductions to my sermons. A weak spearhead always hampers the ensuing attack. A captivating beginning is always excellent strategy. Yet, although this may sound momentarily strange, I usually prepare the introduction last, after I have completed the organization of my material and know fully what it is that I am going to introduce. We can never hold a hearer's attention until we first get it; and the introduction is meant to capture attention at the outset.

As for the use of illustrations I keep in mind the fundamental law that illustrations should illuminate, not merely decorate. I also observe the maxim that illustrations should never illustrate the obvious. A superfluous illustration is like giving an umbrella to a duck.

On the other hand, a telling illustration can immortalize a truth in the hearer's mind, or it can be like the sudden rolling up of a dark window shade and letting the light flash in. Even good illustrations, however, should not be too numerous in any one sermon, for the simple reason that they should not be needed. A superabundance of anecdotes is like serving more stuffing than turkey. A bird needs only one pair of wings to fly well. Why give it five or six more which only flap?

I also give great care to the conclusions of my sermons. There are many hearers, alas, who will never allow us to forget the conclusion. But they are just the people whom we should try to make sorry that there has to *be* a conclusion. We must beware lest our sermons are like airplanes which cannot find the right landing strip! We need to know when we have reached the intended point, then land. Adding a bit more and a bit more only weakens a sermon. Even a fine discourse can peter out like the expiring sigh of a flat tire. I do leave myself room for "the inspiration of the moment." But what if this "inspiration of the moment" does not come? I want to have the best possible conclusion ready in advance, just in case!

## Presenting the Sermon

I have already marked the distinction between an essay, a poem, a drama, and a sermon. The pulpit is not a desk for delivering lectures, nor a platform for making speeches, nor a stage for exhibiting oratorical gifts. The pulpit is meant for the sermon, which, in the time-honored Christian sense, is a message from God, derived from his written Word, under his guidance, through meditation, prayer, study, and the illumination of the Holy Spirit. It may be formulated into a methodical structure, a cumulative argument, even an alliterative device; it may be expressed through skillful explication, illustration, application (being made all the more effective by apt hermeneutics and homiletics); it may flower into impressive eloquence, and even employ legitimate rhetoric; but what makes it truly a sermon is that it is *a message from God.* All other features—analytical, homiletical, oratorical—are only accessories to its transmission as a message from God through preacher to hearer.

That alone is the true concept of a sermon, and that alone, I believe, should determine our pulpit behavior. Furthermore, that concept of Christian preaching will largely decide what we allow or disallow in our style or technique of delivery. It will beget liberty, but never levity; exuberance, but never irreverence; even sanctified humor, but never jocularity. It will engender earnestness without heaviness and seriousness without somberness. It will give us that realism that will rescue us from all hollow professionalism. The more truly spiritual we are, the more truly natural will be our preaching, and this will help to keep us in sensitive touch with our hearers.

I believe it best not to have any fixed practice in the use of notes, for the simple reason that no one practice suits or helps every type of sermon. If I am preaching on a devotional theme such as our love to the Savior, I find that notes hamper and hinder. I need a preparation of heart rather than a manuscript. I will have the outline of my message so clearly in mind that I need not use more than a bare minimum of notes, if any at all. In a message of this type it is the overflow of the heart that must give the lips their eager flow. Trying to communicate an emotionally warm theme through cumbersome notes is like trying to display a rose through prison bars.

On the other hand, if I am discussing some theological issue, or elucidating some finer point of doctrine, or handling some acutely important aspect of our faith, godly reverence prevents me from leaving the entire wording of it to that unpredictable "inspiration of the moment." Granted, some preachers do otherwise, but they must be men of supernormal genius. Lesser mortals like myself dare not take the risk: the truth we attempt to explicate is too vital to jeopardize.

There is a place for notes in these instances, and also when the sermon is a cumulative argument. My own experience is that I must be free enough from notes to maintain eye contact with my audience, yet have just enough memos to ensure that I do not omit any link in the argument.

The subject itself determines the amount of notes I use. I am not ashamed to say that occasionally I have read my sermons from the pulpit, but in each instance I had gone over the sermon so repeatedly beforehand that a mere glancing at my manuscript was all that was necessary in the pulpit. Far more often I have used no notes at all. If your nature is anything like mine, you will find that with some subjects you need notes to restrain you from digressions or from discursiveness, whereas with other themes you will feel that bondage to notes is like preaching in fetters.

I offer the following suggestions as general rules for governing the use of notes: (1) Keep your use of notes to a minimum. Train yourself to that; otherwise you will likely find that you depend more and more on notes. (2) Remember that the bigger the auditorium and the larger the crowd, the fewer the notes. In a small room it does not matter so much if the speaker keeps rather closely to his notes, because he is near enough to the people for them to get some impact from his personality. But with a large crowd, or in a big hall, if a preacher has to keep dipping his head into his notes, like a hen pecking at seeds, he is his own failure. (3) For special occasions like church anniversaries, society rallies, and all other "specials," where vivacity is more appropriate than profundity, a speech or message should be almost entirely free from notes. On such occasions, to read an address often makes it a "*broken* reed."

Whether you use less or more notes in the pulpit, I recommend that your write your sermons. Write them for your own sermonic education. Write articles for magazines. Write letters for the sake of writing. If you always trust to complete verbal spontaneity in the pulpit, you may become stilted in style and probably stunted in vocabulary. Your cliches and undiversified diction will become stale to your hearers. So again I say: write.

And, finally, read. In particular, read the printed sermons of the masters, for they are our best human guides, not only in the formulation of messages, but also in the wording and communicating of them. Among my favorites are Spurgeon for evangelical passion and textual skill clothed in purest robes of Anglo-Saxon wording; W. L. Watkinson of Manchester for masterly homiletical patterns; Alexander Maclaren for choice verbal exactitude; and J. H. Jowett for educative word artistry. Giants like these have taught me much about the art of preaching and challenged me to devote my best efforts to it. They can do the same for you.

# The Sublime Uniqueness
# of Jesus

Jesus Himself . . . [Luke 24:15 KJV]

My subject may be expressed in one word. That word is a name, and that name occurs in the New Testament nearly one thousand times. It is the name *Jesus*. I want to fix your gaze on the wonderful person to whom that meaningful name belongs.   To be more explicit, I wish to exhibit the sublime uniqueness of our Lord Jesus Christ. I shall do this not by trying to say something *about* him, nor even by expounding what various Scripture texts say about him, but simply and solely by collecting and collating some of his own more notable utterances in which he is either self-declared or self-revealed. In reality, our subject is Jesus according to himself.

No one can read (observantly) through the Gospel narratives without noticing the recurrence of three simple yet significant forms of expression in the phraseology of Jesus. Those three are "I am," "I say," "I will." They are so recurrent and characteristic as to be practically idiomatic.

In those three signature forms we see three arresting features. First, in that recurrent "I am," we see a unique and sublime egoism. Second, in that recurrent "I say," we see a unique and sublime dogmatism. Third, in that recurrent "I will," we see a unique and sublime regalism. Yes, indeed, egoism, dogmatism, regalism! In the dictionary meaning and common usage of today, those three attitudes are definitely undesirables, but in the teaching and character of Jesus we see them in a sublime and magnetic form.

## Unique and Sublime Egoism

Think first, then, about the unique egoism of Jesus. Let us be clear as to our use of that term. In philosophy egoism is the doctrine that we have no proof of anything but our own existence. In ethics egoism is the doctrine that self-interest is the root-principle of morality. In common parlance egoism is conceited self-esteem. Let us at once remove those meanings far from that lovely Son of man who said, both by lip and life, "I am meek and lowly in heart."

Ordinarily, egoism is self-assumption accompanied by self-assertive-ness—and both of those spring from the presumings of self-importance based on self-ignorance. But in the case of Jesus we find the unique fea-ture of self-assumption with absolutely no self-inflation; for by all the available data Jesus was of all persons the meekest. Moreover, what he assumed concerning himself is the very opposite of any presuming upon self-ignorance. There is not a psychologist in the world who understands human nature as Jesus did. His mental and moral diagnoses, his ethical and spiritual teachings, his miracles of physical healing, his foretelling the future—all proclaim that he spoke out of a supernatural fullness of knowledge. He was neither egot nor bigot. He was too meek for egotism and too big for bigotry. He spoke from the consciousness of a sincerity which is as evident to us as it was real to him. Listen, then, to the fol-lowing seven occurrences of his majestic "I am" in the Gospel according to John.

"I am the bread of life" (6:35)

"I am the light of the world" (8:12)

"I am the door of the sheep" (10:7)

"I am the good shepherd" (10:11)

"I am the resurrection, and the life" (11:25)

"I am the way, the truth, and the life" (14:6)

"I am the true vine" (15:1)

Did you ever hear of anyone else in history making such august, exalted, profound, and startling claims for himself as those? But was Jesus aware of their immensity? And did he make the claims seriously? Those two questions are easily answered by simply reading those seven "I am"s of Jesus in their setting.

Take the first: "I am the bread of life." To that he added, "He that cometh to me shall never hunger; and he that believeth on me shall never thirst."

Take the second: "I am the light of the world." To that he added, "He that followeth me shall not walk in darkness, but shall have the light of life."

Take the third: "I am the door of the sheep." To that he added, "By me if any man enter in, he shall be saved."

Take the fourth: "I am the good shepherd." To that he added, "I lay down my life for the sheep. . . . I have power to lay it down, and I have power to take it again."

Take the fifth: "I am the resurrection, and the life." To that he added, "He that believeth in me, though he were dead [shall have died], yet shall he live: and whosoever liveth and believeth in me shall never die."

Take the sixth: "I am the way, the truth, and the life." To that he added, "No man cometh unto the Father, but by me."

Take the seventh: "I am the true vine." To that he added, "He that abideth in me, and I in him, the same bringeth forth much fruit; for without me ye can do nothing."

But were those tremendous "I am"s of Jesus substantiated by testimony other than his own? They were. In the fifth chapter of John we find that Jesus, on being challenged, appealed to four other witnesses which corroborated his own: first, the witness of John the Baptist; second, the witness of his own miracles; third, the witness of God the Father at the Jordan baptism; fourth, the witness of the Old Testament prophecies to him.

To those four there may now be added three more: first, his stainless character; second, his bodily resurrection; third, his visible and attested ascension to heaven. Thus his seven "I am"s are accompanied by a sevenfold substantiation.

In Jesus Christ, then, we see the absolutely solitary phenomenon of a supreme egoism in union with utter humility and supernatural knowledge, and endorsed by seven unmistakably divine attestations. It is, indeed, a unique and sublime egoism.

What does it signify? It means that, fundamentally, the message of Jesus is himself. He did not come merely to preach a gospel; he himself is the gospel. He did not come merely to give bread; he said, "I am the bread." He did not come merely to shed light; he said, "I am the light." He did not come merely to show the door; he said "I am the door." He did not come merely to name a shepherd; he said, "I am the shepherd." He did not come merely to discuss the resurrection; he said, "I am the resurrection, and the life." He did not come merely to point the way; he said, "I am the way." He did not come merely to plant a vine; he said, "I am the vine."

Think how all of this relates to us. Jesus is the absolute answer, the final goal of our human heart-quest. I remember, years ago, ploughing through the three main periods of philosophy: the ancient, the middle, and the modern; starting with Heraclitus, Socrates, Plato, Aristotle, on into the modern period, beginning with Descartes and finding a temporary zenith in Kant. But none of them had the abiding answer or the final word for the human heart. Each new philosophical system exposes the fallacies of its predecessors, only to be itself deposed by the next school or theory. Human philosophy is shifting sand.

I remember reading the life and writings of Confucius, the life and theories of Gautauma and his Buddhistic break from Hinduism, the life of Mohammed along with the Islamic Koran, but none of those religious innovators ever dreamed of saying, "I am," "I say," "I will," as Jesus did. By their own confession they were religious philosophers, would-be pathfinders, groping to find the way, the truth, and the life. Jesus said, "I am the way, the truth, and the life."

Is your soul hungry with an emptiness which nothing on earth can satisfy? Jesus says to you, "I am the bread of life: he that cometh to me shall never hunger." Is your mind darkened with a darkness which no philosophy on earth can relieve? Jesus says to you, "I am the light of the world: he that followeth me shall not walk in darkness, but shall have the light of life." Are you seeking the salvation of your soul? Jesus says to you, "I am the door: by me, if any man enter in, he shall be saved." Are you trying to find your life's true leader? Jesus says to you, "I am the good shepherd. . . . My sheep hear my voice . . . and they follow me: and I give unto them eternal life." Are you wanting a sure hope for the other side of death? Jesus says to you, "I am the resurrection, and the life: he that believeth in me, though he were dead, yet shall he live: and whosoever liveth and believeth in me shall never die." Are you trying to find the way to the one true God? Jesus says to you, "I am the way, the truth, and the life: no man cometh unto the Father, but by me." Are you longing to know the secret of true self-fulfillment and fruitfulness? Jesus says to you, "I am the true vine . . . : he that abideth in me, and I in him, the same bringeth forth much fruit."

Listen to the living Savior again as he says seven times over, in answer to your fundamental needs as a human being, "I am."

## Unique and Sublime Dogmatism

But now move on to consider the unique and sublime dogmatism of Jesus. Besides our Lord's recurrent "I am" is his recurrent "I say." No fewer than 113 times in the four Gospel memoirs we find that characteristic "I say" and its implications of an omniscient dogmatism.

That word *dogmatism,* of course, has quite unpalatable associations. In its stricter sense dogmatism simply means the positive assertion of doctrines or tenets in the name of some religious denomination. A dictionary definition of it is, "the laying down of doctrine with authority." In its more common and more objectionable sense it is headstrong self-opinionatedness.

In the case of Jesus dogmatism, like egoism, is given a unique sublimation. If there is one thing more noticeable than any other in the teachings of Jesus it is this: he certainly was not purveying mere opinions or personal views. Nor was he passing on what he had read or studied, or what human teachers had taught him. The dogmatism of Jesus was his declaration of truth with an originality and positiveness which grew out of his own absolute knowledge. Therefore there was no "pride of learning" or show of scholarship; nor was there any necessity for elaborate reasoning. His masterly idiom, "verily, verily," was the signature of a king—a king whose royal dictum cannot be contradicted.

There was a divine royalty about the dogmatism of Jesus. In everything he was certain. Have you ever noticed that Jesus never had to go back and correct himself? He never once had to modify or improve a former utterance. He never once argued. He never once had to reason a thing out. He never drew a mere inference. He never used the word *perhaps*. He never "arrived at a conclusion." He never needed to "arrive" by processes of induction or deduction. He was already *there*. His knowledge was absolute. Therefore, all the way through his life and teachings there is certainty, simplicity, profundity, yet transparency, authority, finality. In a word, there is a unique and sublime dogmatism which two thousand years of testing have only endorsed.

The late Sir Winston Churchill, on his last visit to the United States, said from the platform of a great university that the one and only true hope for our twentieth-century world is a return to the teachings of Jesus Christ. The chancellor of that university said practically the same thing. Who would ever dream of saying that the one and only hope for us is to get back to Confucius? Or to Buddha? Or to Mohammed? Or to any other great figure of history?

Listen again to just a few occurrences of our Lord's "I say." In the Sermon on the Mount he declared, "Verily I say unto you, till heaven and earth pass, one jot or one tittle shall in no wise pass from the law, till all be fulfilled" (Matt. 5:18). Fourteen times in that mighty sermon his "I say" rings out. Read them again, and how can you help exclaiming along with those astonished crowds in ancient Palestine, "Never man spake like this man!" "For he taught them as one having authority, and not as the scribes" (Matt. 7:29). No fewer than fifty-two times in Matthew's record, Jesus says with majestic finality, "I say."

But bypassing all of those, consider just one "verily, verily, I say" from the Gospel according to John: "Verily, verily, I say unto you, he that heareth my word, and believeth on him that sent me, hath everlasting life, and shall not come into condemnation; but is passed from death unto life" (John 5:24). Did such words ever fall from any other lips in all history? Did such a guarantee of salvation for human beings ever come to us elsewhere with such magnificent dogmatism and divine certainty?

## Unique and Sublime Regalism

Finally, think again about the unique and sublime regalism of Jesus. His "I am" and "I say" are crowned by his regal "I will." Over and over again that "I will" comes from those lips in tones which have the sound of supreme kingship.

Nothing is more pathetic than an affected regality—a moving and posing as king, or lord, or master without a compelling power in the personality or kingliness of stature. Moreover, we are living in days which are hypersuspicious of autocracy or regalism of any kind. It is not an admired concept today. But once again, in Jesus we see a regalism unique and sublime. He walks, speaks, acts as one who knows that nature, angels, demons, mysteries, life, and death all pay homage at his feet. He commands the winds and the waves, and they obey at once. He heals all manner of human sickness, and even raises the dead, routs demons, and forgives sins with the authority of God incarnate.

Listen again to a few of his "I will"s, and ask yourself who it is that speaks with such sovereign command. In Matthew 8:3, he says to the pleading leper, "I will; be thou clean," whereupon every taint of the dread disease instantly vanishes. In Matthew 11:28, he says to the whole weary world of toilers and weepers, "Come unto me, all ye that labour and are heavy laden, and I will give you rest." Millions have found that promise true. In uttering such an invitation and giving such a promise, he obviously speaks out of the consciousness that he is "God manifest in the flesh." For any mere creature to make such a promise would be absurd—and no one but Jesus ever has.

In Matthew 16:18 he says, "I will build my church; and the gates of hell (*hades*) shall not prevail against it," and the gates of that underworld never have and never will imprison the blood-bought members of his true church. In John 6:40 he says, "Every one which . . . believeth . . . , may have everlasting life; and I will raise him up at the last day." No grave can resist that voice. Speaking anticipatively of his death by crucifixion he says in John 12:32, "If I be lifted up . . . I will draw all men unto me." As the context shows, he did not mean all men without exception, but all men without distinction. So has it happened. The very cross which slew him, crowned him—crowned him the most majestic king ever known.

Speaking of the Holy Spirit, he said, "If I depart, I will send him unto you" (John 16:7). That is just what he did afterwards, and the divine Spirit is still with his people on earth. And, looking centuries ahead, even to the end of the present age, he said, "I will come again, and receive you unto myself" (John 14:3). Will his promise prove true? Today, after two millenniums, the predicted signs of his return are converging to a focus point, indicating that at last the superevent is imminent.

So, ought we not listen with both ears to those "I will"s? It is no mere human pundit who speaks them. They are the speech of one who knew that he wielded the scepter of sovereign control over all human minds, over death and hades, and over all the ages of history. Yes, listen again to his "I am," "I say," "I will." Do you not recognize him? Ladies and gentlemen, meet the King—the King of worlds and angels, the one true King of humanity, the King divine in human flesh!

Years ago, when the beloved King George V occupied the British throne, he paid a visit to the Yorkshire city of Leeds. Elaborate decorations and other preparations were made for his coming, and excited crowds filled the streets to wave and cheer. At that time there was a large elementary school in Leeds with a playground which ran alongside the railway line. His Majesty graciously agreed to wave to the boys and girls as the royal train passed by on the last day of his visit. The boys and girls, with their teachers, crowded to the playground wall overlooking the railway. Presently, from a long tunnel, the royal train slowly emerged and gradually drew alongside the playground. What do you think? The king actually came outside the royal coach and stood on a small platform where they could all see him. He wore no crown or purple robe, but was dressed in a plain suit, just like an ordinary man. From his jacket pocket he plucked a bright handkerchief with which he waved to the cheering Yorkshire lads and lassies. All too soon the train glided by and disappeared. Then the cheers subsided into silence, except for one little girl who sobbed bitterly, so much so that one of the teachers asked her, "Why are you crying like that, dear?" The little girl sputtered through her tears, "I wanted to see the king, and I only saw a *man*!"

"I wanted to see the king, and I only saw a man." She thought that because he was not wearing his crown and royal robes he could not be the real king. The little incident is both amusing and touching. But there is nothing amusing in the fact that the very same mistake is made by millions of intelligent human beings with respect to the Lord Jesus Christ. If only they had eyes which could really see, they would recognize that he is the King. But because he comes in human guise as "the Friend of sinners," without crown, or scepter, or royal insignia, they see only a *man*. Oh, how blind we can be! How many of you have seen only a man instead of recognizing in him the Savior-King?

Let me rivet your attention just once more on those three signature idioms, "I am," "I say," "I will." Listen again to his "I am"—and gaze at him. Listen again to his "I say"—and learn of him. Listen again to his "I will"—and bow to him. As you hear him say, "I am," see in him your highest Example. As you hear his "I say," see in him your unerring Teacher. As you hear his "I will," see in him your Redeemer-King. In his "I am," see your all-sufficiency. In his "I say," see your everlasting security. In his "I will," see your never-failing pledge of salvation. As he comes to you now with his "I am," worship him. As he comes to you now with his "I say," heed him. As he comes to you now with his "I will," yield to him. If you have never yet done yourself the infinite kindness of welcoming him as your Savior, do so now. If you doubt whether he will receive you, listen to just one more "I will" from his kingly lips. It is recorded in John 6:37. He says, "Him that cometh to me *I will in no wise cast out.*" Let me introduce you to this wonderful, wonderful Savior-King, who never yet refused even the most ragged prodigal who ever came to him.

# 2

## Richard Allen Bodey

After pastoring three Presbyterian churches, Richard Allen Bodey taught Bible at McKendree College and practical theology at Reformed Theological Seminary. He then returned to the pastorate, serving as the senior pastor of the First Associate Reformed Presbyterian Church, Gastonia, North Carolina. Since 1979 he has taught practical theology at Trinity Evangelical Divinity School.

Bodey earned his M.Div. from Princeton Theological Seminary; Th.M. from Westminster Theological Seminary; and D.Min. from Trinity Evangelical Divinity School. He has also done graduate study at the University of Toronto.

He has written *You Can Live Without Fear of Death,* edited *Good News for All Seasons: Twenty-six Sermons for Special Days,* and contributed to *The Encyclopedia of Christianity, The Minister's Manual,* and *The Zondervan Pictorial Bible Encyclopedia.*

# Preaching through the Church Year

Honesty, so the saying goes, is always the best policy. So I begin this homiletical self-unveiling with a testimony and a confession. Nothing in life is for me more exhilarating or more enjoyable—even when it drains all my energies dry—than preaching. There is no place on earth I would rather be than in the pulpit. Many of my happiest moments have occurred there. I wouldn't exchange my divine call to preach for anything. That's the testimony.

Now, the confession. There is nothing in life I find more difficult and even, at times, tormenting, than sermon preparation. I refer more specifically, not to the study of the text and the gathering of materials, which I thoroughly enjoy, but to the actual construction of the sermon. I could count on the fingers of one hand the times that I have glided through the process of sermon preparation. To apply somewhat loosely the words of a hymn, I may never have climbed the "steep ascent" of the pulpit through peril, but I nearly always do so through toil and pain. There you have it—at least in this preacher's experience—the agony and the ecstasy of preaching!

In my development as a preacher, my father was the greatest influence. A preacher of considerable gifts and skills, he taught me by unforgettable example many things about this strange and wonderful art. But the most important thing I learned from him is that the secret of preaching power lies, above all else, in the discipline of faithful, earnest prayer and long hours of diligent, believing study of the Word of God.

To two seminary professors of homiletics under whom I studied I am deeply indebted: Donald Macleod of Princeton and Lloyd M. Perry of Trinity. After listening to me preach in class what I thought was a jolly good sermon, the former struck me down like a bolt of lightning with the blunt and searing comment that I should throw that sermon away, and then proceeded to explain why. It was a moment of devastation and humiliation I shall never forget. But the good professor was right, and to this day I thank God for the beneficent candor of Donald Macleod. In lectures and seminars on preaching I have learned much from pulpit worthies like George A. Buttrick, James T. Cleland, Stephen Olford, J. I. Packer, James S. Stewart, Warren W. Wiersbe, and present colleagues at Trinity, especially David L. Larsen.

For nearly half a century I have relished the opportunity of hearing in person many of the ablest preachers of the day, often in their own pulpits, and have read many of their printed sermons. Some who have impressed me most are Donald Grey Barnhouse, J. Sidlow Baxter, Herschel H. Hobbs, D. Martyn Lloyd-Jones, Clarence E. Macartney, J. I. Packer, David H. C. Read, Paul S. Rees, William E. Sangster, James S. Stewart, and John R. W. Stott. As a teenager I listened quite regularly to radio preachers, particularly Peter H. Eldersveld, Walter A. Maier, Fulton J. Sheen, and a little later, Billy Graham. Still later, television preachers caught my attention.

A practice I found helpful as a young parish pastor was to read a sermon by some outstanding preacher each weekday, often in the evening before retiring. My purpose was not primarily to glean materials for sermons (although this often happened as an extra dividend), still less to imitate their homiletical style, but to observe their methods of handling the biblical text, developing ideas and logical argumentation, illustrating and applying the truth to the hearers, and their manner of expression, especially their use of imagery and their power of description. Favorites include John Calvin, William Clow, Frederick W. Farrar, J. D. Jones, Henry P. Liddon, J. Gresham Machen, Alexander Maclaren, G. Campbell Morgan, Handley C. G. Moule, Charles H. Spurgeon, and in many ways best of all, J. C. Ryle.

I am firmly committed to the view that preaching is Christian only when it is passionately, uncompromisingly biblical, that is, when it sets forth faithfully what the Bible teaches on a given topic. This, I believe, can be done equally well in all four sermon types: expository, textual, topical, and textual-topical. While expository sermons (those that treat an extended unit of Scripture, rather than a single verse or two) deserve a substantial place in one's preaching schedule, topical preaching has its legitimate place too. With many other Reformed preachers, I consider doctrinal preaching, properly applied, the most important kind of all, and most comprehensive doctrinal sermons are necessarily more or less topical.

Beyond this general rubric of biblical preaching, and largely growing out of it, are four more focused questions which serve as guidelines for me in the preparation of my sermons.

First, is this sermon true to the meaning of the specific text on which it is based or from which it is derived? In the case of a topical sermon I want to be sure that the topic is either expressly mentioned in the text or honestly suggested by it, and that it is developed in a way that does not prostitute the text, but is in full harmony with its meaning.

Second, does the sermon explicitly exalt Jesus Christ? I am committed to the christological interpretation of all Scripture, Old Testament and New Testament alike (cf. Luke 24:25–27, 44–47). Just as the Holy Spirit's primary function is to bear witness to Christ (John 15:26; 16:13–15), so the primary function of the Christian pulpit is to display Jesus Christ in the fullness of his glory as divine Savior and Lord, so that those who hear its testimony may come into living personal encounter with him.

Third, is the sermon relevant to the lives of my hearers here and now? Does it relate the teaching of the Bible to their needs? their interests? their concerns? Our task as preachers is to demonstrate how Scripture bears upon the daily life of the housewife, the executive, the mechanic, the salesperson, the teacher, the student, the attorney, the child.

Fourth, is the sermon interesting? This is often the hardest test of all. But its importance dare not be ignored. No matter how biblical, how Christ-centered, how relevant a sermon may be, unless it is interesting to the hearers, it is worthless. The problem, of course, is that I am not always the best judge of what is interesting or not. Because it is interesting enough to me does not guarantee that it will be interesting to the people. That is one reason I usually try my sermons out on my wife (she is very forbearing) before I preach them.

In my preaching I draw heavily on my filing system. The system consists of standard manila folders and plain four-by-six-inch cards, both of which are arranged topically and textually by Bible book, chapter, and verse. The folders contain articles and larger clippings from newspapers, magazines, etc. I use the cards for smaller clippings (attached with permanent tape), notes of personal observations and experiences, brief items copied from resources not in my library, and bibliographic references to my own books. In my reading I make marginal notations of any material I may want to use in a sermon sometime, then enter this reference on one of the cards.

I have also cultivated what Andrew W. Blackwood called a "homiletical garden," with sermons in various stages of development. Whenever I am seized by an idea for a sermon, I write it down at once. I then record the idea by topic or text in one of my sermon notebooks. As I get additional ideas and materials for these sermons, I enter them in the notebook. Once I have accumulated considerable material for a particular sermon, I transfer everything from the notebook to a large mailing envelope. These envelopes are likewise arranged textually or topically. Many of these sermon seeds, of course, fail to grow and eventually are discarded. But others ripen and find their way into the pulpit.

All of life is grist for the homiletical mill, and a wise pastor will train himself to think homiletically, seeing sermons everywhere. I always carry several blank cards or a small notebook in my shirt pocket. When an idea for a sermon pops into my mind or I light on a good illustration or quotation, or anything that may someday be useful in preaching, I jot it down at once. I even keep a card or two on the nightstand and have been known to waken in the middle of the night with an idea for a sermon and write it down. First chance I get, I enter all these materials into my files and sermon notebooks. I have learned that I must write these ideas and materials down at once, or I am apt to forget them and so lose them forever.

Finding time to get the work done each week was my biggest problem in parish ministry. I reduced the problem in part by planning my preaching schedule a year at a time. The method I recommend is to conform the plan to the cycle of the church year, beginning with the first Sunday in Advent and ending with the Sunday before Advent the following year.[1] I think it best to draft the plan during the months of May

1. One of the great advantages of observing the church year is that it focuses on every major doctrine of the Christian faith. Every preacher should be careful to preach on every one of these major doctrines every year.

and June for the church year, which begins with the first Sunday in Advent of the next calendar year. (During May and June 1990, one would design his preaching schedule for the church year beginning on Sunday, November 24, 1991.) This method allows abundant time for the work of exegesis, gathering materials, and designing outlines in advance, without pressure.

I began my plan by choosing texts and topics for each of the major observances of the church year. Using the Common Lectionary in selecting Scripture passages for these sermons can save much time.[2] Next, I chose texts and topics for certain special days on the secular and denominational calendars, and for occasions of special observance or emphasis in my own parish. I then filled in the remainder of the schedule with texts and topics for sermon series and individual sermons.

Throughout the entire planning process I was in constant prayer for the guidance of the Holy Spirit in discerning what sermon(s) God wanted me to preach each Sunday. To ensure a balanced diet, I checked my preaching records for the last several years for any neglected areas of Scripture and Christian doctrine. I identified current issues of concern and particular spiritual needs within my congregation. I also looked through my homiletical garden for ripening sermons and ideas. I sought to provide variety by including, in addition to doctrinal sermons, other types, such as biographical, devotional, pastoral, ethical, evangelistic, apologetic, life-situation, or narrative.

Once my preaching schedule was prepared, I wrote the text and topic for each sermon on a large mailing envelope and placed whatever materials I already had in hand in the proper envelope. I arranged these envelopes chronologically according to the date of delivery. In the course of time, as I gathered more materials, I placed them in the envelopes until I was ready to prepare the message for delivery. I never prepared the full draft of a sermon until the week before I preached it, so that it would be fresh to me. Since I took Saturday as my weekly day off, I had to complete my sermon(s) by Friday evening.

I began my preparation on Monday morning. Again, I began with prayer and carried out the entire process in a spirit of prayer. Before doing anything else, I reviewed the materials I had already collected. If I had not already done so, I looked in my files for materials and references available on the Scripture and topic. On occasion, I found that I had all the materials I needed for a particular sermon in the files and proceeded at once to design the outline. If a suitable outline was there as well, I began to write the sermon. One advantage of a good filing system is that it sometimes yields sermons without further study and research.

Whether I had completed my exegetical study beforehand or did it

2. Pastors in nonliturgical churches can find this lectionary in the Episcopal Book of Common Prayer or in various Service Books.

now, this is the way I worked with the text. I began by brainstorming. I read the text over and over, at least twenty-five to thirty times, in many different translations and versions.[3] I read it aloud as well as silently, because the ear at times picks up something missed by the eye. I also read the text in the light of both its immediate and larger contexts. I then read it in the original Hebrew or Greek, not hesitating to use an interlinear when I encountered some difficulty in translation.

While I read, I pondered and brooded on the text, writing down every idea that came into my mind, until I thought myself empty. I used a separate sheet of paper—more when necessary—for each different idea, but recorded thoughts about the same idea on the same sheet(s). I noted especially all important words, phrases, and syntactical constructions. At times I diagrammed the passage. Never at this stage did I try to impose any order on my notes. I simply jotted down each thought as it came to me, omitting nothing, however inconsequential it might seem. These notes and observations provided the raw materials for the sermon. Most of them were later discarded, but whatever freshness the finished sermon had, it owed largely to these personal notes.

Having concluded this brainstorming on the text, I conducted my preliminary exegesis of it in the original language, checking marginal references and consulting lexicons, grammars, concordances, Bible dictionaries and encyclopedias, word studies, and topical indexes. Throughout my entire study of the text thus far I was seeking to identify its central, unifying theme. By the time I finished my preliminary exegesis I tried to formulate in a single sentence a statement of my understanding of this central message or theme in my own words. At this point I took a break, putting the work aside for at least several hours, while I attended to other duties usually demanding much less intellectual concentration. During this interval, however, as my subconscious continued brooding on the text, I jotted down any additional thoughts that swam to the surface of consciousness.

Returning to the text, I reviewed all the notes I had already made. I then tried to formulate the proposition, statement of purpose (the response I wanted from the hearers, or the effect I wished to produce in them), and a tentative outline. If the outline refused to take shape at this time, I moved on.

I then completed my exegesis by consulting as many commentaries as possible. I began with exegetical commentaries, then turned to doctrinal ones when available, then to devotional ones, and finally, if necessary, to homiletical commentaries. At the end of this stage I finalized my proposition, statement of purpose, and detailed outline. If I needed addi-

---

3. Exceedingly helpful is *The Bible from 26 Translations*, ed. Curtis Vaughan (Chattanooga: AMG, 1985).

tional materials, I browsed in relevant books of biblical studies, theology, and other works, and checked through my files once again.

I was now ready to plan the introduction and conclusion. My main concern in the introduction was to arouse the hearers' interest, bring the proposition sharply into focus, and build a bridge between the hearers and the text. I customarily began with the hearers and their interests, then moved into the text.

The thrust of the conclusion was determined earlier when I settled on the purpose of the sermon. Now I decided how best to clothe that purpose with life and power, driving it home to every individual heart.

The preliminary work finished, I began the actual writing of the sermon in its entirety, taking special pains with the crucial first sentence of the introduction and the final sentence of the conclusion. As I wrote, I tried to keep before my mind's eye several representative individuals in the congregation, as if I were talking to them personally. I wrote with a dictionary and a thesaurus close at hand. Next to the Bible, I used these tools more than any other. I did much of my polishing as I proceeded (a practice I do not recommend, but have never been able to abandon). Once finished, I went over the manuscript with my wife for her suggestions. After making revisions (often the next day), I rehearsed the sermon out loud several times, exactly as I wrote it. Occasionally, I went into the pulpit and rehearsed it there.

On Saturday evening, I rehearsed the sermon again, and once or twice on Sunday morning. I then placed the manuscript, secured in a medium-sized notebook, on the pulpit. Just before going to the pulpit to preach, I offered a final brief prayer commending myself and the message to God for his use in the lives of the hearers to his glory. While I did not memorize the sermon, I did try to preach it in its final written form. Seldom did I depart from it on the spur of the moment, and when I did, I nearly always regretted doing so afterward.

Sometime after the service I would ask my wife for her honest feedback. I also recorded my own impressions, together with any significant comments I received from the hearers. Occasionally, I recorded my sermon and listened to it afterward. I filed each sermon, in its envelope, together with any unused notes I thought might be of value later on. I included notes of any changes I thought should be made in the sermon before future use.

Since I am no longer in a parish, I thought it would be most helpful if I described the method of sermon preparation I used during my years as a parish pastor. Except for some obvious modifications growing out of my changed circumstances, such as formulating a preaching schedule, this is the way I still prepare sermons today.

A few other matters call for comment. I am especially sensitive to the importance of apt illustrations in preaching and have some thousands of them in my files. I try to illustrate every major idea (each point or movement of a sermon normally embraces several major ideas) that seems to require illustration for one reason or another. I believe that the most effective illustrations are generally those which appeal to the preacher himself. The sources of illustrations I draw on most frequently are the Bible itself, the daily newspaper, and my personal experience and observation of life.

Although I do use my personal experience in illustrations, I seldom refer to myself in them (I am aware that I do this in the accompanying sermon). I almost never refer to any member of my family in a sermon. Nor do I think it wise to refer to members of one's parish. I try to include illustrations from a variety of sources in each sermon, so that every hearer will find at least one or two that specially appeals to him.

Nothing in a sermon is more important than application. My use of continual application throughout the sermon or concentrated application in the conclusion is determined largely by the text or topic. When the text or topic lends itself to application in individual points or movements of the sermon, I use the continual method, then pull everything together in one final thrust in the conclusion. When making a single application for the entire sermon, I reserve it for the conclusion. When either method is suitable, I tend to reserve the application for the conclusion. When I wait until the conclusion to do this, the conclusion will most likely be a little longer.

As I indicated, I write out all my sermons in full and take the manuscript into the pulpit. This was my father's method, and this is the method I was taught in seminary. But I believe that for most preachers this is a mistake. Writing is exceedingly time-consuming. I usually spend at least eight hours on this task alone. On occasion I have spent a half-hour or more on a single sentence, only to throw it away the next day. Preachers who write their sermons naturally tend to use literary style. But preaching is done best in oral style, which is quite different. The preacher who writes his sermons should train himself to write in oral style.

Moreover, if one labors long and arduously to express himself to the best of his ability, common sense dictates that he should preach his sermon exactly as he wrote it, or very nearly so. In this case he will almost inevitably memorize his sermon or else rely more or less heavily on his manuscript. In either case, he forfeits some freedom of delivery and misses some of the feedback his hearers are sending him while he is preaching. All in all, I think it best to work with a detailed outline in preparing the sermon. Nevertheless, every preacher needs to write regularly for the sake of mastering and maintaining good style.

I always allow myself twenty hours to prepare a Sunday morning sermon. How can a pastor who must preach more than one sermon a week spend this much time on each? Unless he has a sizeable pastoral staff, he can't. The solution for me was to adopt an informal teaching style on Sunday evening. One can correlate his preaching with his personal Bible study and use the overflow from his sermon preparation in any Bible study group(s) he may conduct. Also, by not writing his sermons a pastor can reduce his preparation time to about twelve to fifteen hours per sermon.

While preaching is an art, a sermon is not a work of art to be admired by wonder-struck hearers. A sermon is food for the soul. My most important concern in preaching is not how much people like my sermons, nor how much my sermons impress them, nor even whether they can remember the outlines six months later. (I sometimes can't recall the main points two weeks later!) Of course, I want them to grow in their understanding of biblical truth. But the most important concern for me is what difference my sermons make in people's lives. That concern depends on much more than a preacher's homiletical skills. It depends primarily on the quality of his own spiritual life—on his daily walk with the living Lord Jesus Christ. That's where true preaching begins, and that is where it always ends.

# The God of Prayer

"Ask, and it will be given you; seek, and you will find; knock, and it will be opened to you. For every one who asks receives, and he who seeks finds, and to him who knocks it will be opened. Or what man of you, if his son asks him for bread, will give him a stone? Or if he asks for a fish, will give him a serpent? If you then, who are evil, know how to give good gifts to your children, how much more will your Father who is in heaven give good things to those who ask him!" [Matt. 7:7–11 RSV]

In 1989, pollster George Gallup reported that 94 percent of American adults—more than 150 million men and women—claimed to believe in God. Interestingly, that percentage has fluctuated only slightly in public-opinion polls in this country for more than fifty years. But as a perceptive Englishman once observed, "There is always a more important question than 'Do you believe in God?' and that is, 'What kind of God do you believe in?'"

Let's apply that insight to prayer. Can you see how the kind of God you believe in makes an enormous difference here? Suppose your God is a celestial tyrant who spends his time snooping around people's lives to see whether they stay in line or not, so he can punish those who don't. How often will you pray to him? What will your prayers be like? Or suppose, again, that your God is a jolly, cuddly, super Old Saint Nick, whose only reason for being is to keep everybody happy by giving us everything we want when we want it. No doubt about it. What we believe about God determines our attitude toward prayer.

In this passage from the Sermon on the Mount, Jesus draws a picture of God that encourages us to pray. The characteristics of God he sketches are so familiar that we usually take them for granted. If we thought about them more often, however, they would transform our prayer life. What are these characteristics?

## God Is Personal

Basic to everything else is the fact that God is personal. Jesus describes him as our Father in heaven. No one who studies the Gospels can fail to see that this was our Lord's favorite name for God. It stands out as prominently in his own prayers as in his teaching. Every time we recite the Lord's Prayer we bear witness to his fondness for it.

God is not a mechanical first cause. He is not a mindless cosmic force or universal life principle. He is not what philosophers call the "logical absolute," the impersonal "ground of all being," the "highest good."

No, the God of the Bible is a divine person. He thinks. He knows. He feels. He wills. He speaks. He acts. Best of all, he loves us and makes himself known to us. When he chose to give us a complete revelation of himself, he came among us as a person. "In many and various ways," wrote the author of Hebrews, "God spoke of old to our fathers by the prophets; but in these last days he has spoken to us by a Son" (1:1–2). In Jesus Christ God so perfectly unveiled himself that our Lord could say, "He who has seen me has seen the Father" (John 14:9). At the heart of our Christian faith there stands not a thing, but a living, loving person.

Doesn't this fundamental truth about God encourage us to pray? What is prayer, anyway? May we not say that prayer, at the heart of it, is just talking with God?

We may praise God for his perfections. We may confess to him our sins and seek his forgiveness. We may thank him for gifts he has given us. We may ask him for something we need. Or we may ask his favor on behalf of others. The type of prayer makes no difference. When we pray, we pour out the inmost thoughts and desires, the deepest feelings and aspirations, of our hearts to God, and listen as he speaks to us.

Suppose we lived, as some people think, in an impersonal universe. Suppose God were a cosmic "it," not a divine person who can say, "I," and be addressed as "you." Suppose he were only a name for a mysterious infinite force. What then? It would make better sense to save our breath and forget about praying.

Paul Tillich, one of the most influential theologians of our time, did not believe in a personal God. Someone asked him shortly before he died if he ever prayed. "No," he replied, "but I meditate." Sad! Very sad, indeed! But consistent. If God is not personal, we can meditate and try to get in touch with the universe. But we can't pray, for there's nobody to pray to. When we come to know the personal God of the Bible whom Jesus called Father, however, we find in that very discovery a stimulus to prayer.

## God Is Accessible

Next, God is accessible. Jesus indicates this when in verse 7 he tells us to "ask," "seek," and "knock."

One afternoon I had to make an important long-distance telephone call. For more than an hour I fought busy signals, no signals, on-hold delays, recorded messages telling me that all representatives were busy, musical interludes which instead of soothing my frustration sent it soaring higher. Several times when I succeeded in making contact with a representative, I was told I would have to speak with someone in another department. Finally, after all this I learned that the office I wanted had just closed for an hour and a half.

God is always available when we need him. He is always ready to listen when we want to talk with him. He is never too busy for us, never brushes us off. He posts no office hours. We never get a busy signal, are never put on hold when we dial him. In prayer he has given us a hotline to his throne that in less time than it takes to blink an eye puts us in direct touch with him. Unhampered by our human limitations, he can hear all the prayers of all the people who call to him at any given moment, wherever they may be. He gives to each of us his undivided attention, as if he were listening to no one else. And he allows us all the time we need to unburden our hearts and spread our concerns before him.

When we speak of God's accessibility to us, we need to remind ourselves that we are touching upon the greatest wonder of the Christian faith. For we are sinners. And God is the all-holy One who hates sin, who recoils from any contact with it, and who will not admit sinners to his presence. How, then, can we enjoy access to him? How can we expect him to listen to us when we pray?

In a passage marked by great intensity and earnestness, the author of Hebrews appeals to his readers, "Therefore, brothers, since we have confidence to enter the Most Holy Place by the blood of Jesus, by a new and living way opened for us through the curtain, that is, his body, and since we have a great priest over the house of God, let us draw near to God with a sincere heart in full assurance of faith" (10:19–22 NIV). Virtually the whole doctrine of prayer is wrapped up in that one sparkling sentence.

Through the cross of Christ, God has removed the sin barrier for every believer, giving us free and open access to himself forever. And through the continuing ministry of the Lord Jesus in heaven as our great priest and mediator, we can now bring our prayers to God's throne of grace boldly and with confidence that he will hear us.

You have seen those TV commercials advertising access to instant cash at automated teller machines around the world, twenty-four hours a day. As Christians, we have something incomparably better than that. Every minute of our lives, no matter where we might happen to be—in a hospital bed, in an airplane hurtling to the ground for a crash landing, in the burning sands of the Sahara or the frozen wastes of the Arctic, even in a space shuttle racing towards Mars, or anywhere else in the immensities of space—through the blood of Jesus we enjoy immediate access to the living God, who is our heavenly Father. Is not the thought of this access, purchased at such incalculable cost, a powerful incentive to us to pray?

## Gid Is Able to Answer Prayer

Furthermore, God is able to answer our prayers. This truth underlies Jesus' assurance in verse 8 that "every one who asks receives, and he who seeks finds, and to him who knocks it will be opened."

Not only is God our heavenly Father, he is also the sovereign Creator and Ruler of all worlds. Put your eye to a microscope or a telescope. Everything you see—from the quark, an elementary particle so tiny it is invisible except in groups, to the biggest sun that blazes in all the galaxies of space—was created by him and remains forever under his control. The universe is his workshop. Wind and rain, light and heat, gravity and motion—all the elements and forces of nature—are his servants. Time is his messenger. History is the unfolding of his eternal plan. So awesome is his power that, in the words of Daniel, "He does as he pleases with the powers of heaven and the peoples of the earth. No one can hold back his hand or say to him: 'What have you done?'" (4:35 NIV).

That power, demonstrated so dramatically in the miracles recorded in Scripture, and above all in the resurrection of our Lord Jesus from the dead, is still released in answer to believing prayer. Take an example.

George Mueller of England, one of the most remarkable men of prayer in modern times, was once crossing the Atlantic by ship, when a dense fog set in and forced the ship to slow to a crawl. Mueller consulted the captain. "Sir," he said, "I must be in Quebec for a speaking engagement on Tuesday."

"Impossible!" replied the captain. "I've been sailing these seas for years. When a fog like this sets in, it stays for a week. It would have to lift immediately for us to make it."

But Mueller protested, "Captain, God made that engagement for me, and I know he intends that I keep it. Let's go to your cabin and pray."

Although he was a Christian, the captain couldn't believe his ears. He had never heard such an off-the-wall proposal before. Can't you see him standing there, gulping in amazement, his eyes threatening to pop out of his head, saying to himself, "What lunatic asylum turned this poor fellow loose?" Reluctantly, he escorted Mueller to his cabin and shut the door. Mueller knelt down and in simple, childlike faith prayed, "Father, I pray that you will lift the fog within five minutes."

When he finished, the captain was going to pray, but Mueller stopped him. "I don't want you to pray," he explained, "because you don't believe God will do it, and because I believe he already has. Open the door and see." The bewildered captain opened the door to discover that the fog was lifting. Mueller arrived in Quebec on time.

Sound incredible? When did you or I last see such a dramatic answer to our prayers? But, then, when did you or I dare to put our faith on the line and trust God that far? "With God all things are possible," Jesus declared (Matt. 19:26). God is the God of the impossible! John Newton was right when he taught us to sing:

> Thou art coming to a King,
> Large petitions with thee bring;
> For His grace and pow'r are such,
> None can ever ask too much.

Can we fail to find in the sovereign power of God one of our strongest encouragements to prayer?

## God Is Willing to Answer Prayer

To know that God is personal, that he is accessible, and that he is able to answer our prayers is encouraging indeed. But we are still not apt to do very much praying unless we also know that he is willing to answer our prayers. It is this very assurance that Jesus is especially concerned to give us.

"Keep on asking"—that is the force of the Greek—"and it will be given you," he says in verses 7 and 8; "keep on seeking, and you will find; keep on knocking, and it will be opened to you. For every one who keeps on asking receives, and he who keeps on seeking finds, and to him who keeps on knocking it will be opened."

As if this assurance itself might not be convincing enough, he reinforces it with a comparison. "If you then, who are evil, know how to give good gifts to your children, how much more will your Father who is in heaven give good things to those who ask him!"

How many parents do you know who deliberately, needlessly disappoint their children? Loving parents, whatever their faults and shortcomings, find one of their greatest pleasures in giving gifts to their children, often at considerable cost and sacrifice to themselves. Young people, remember that when you are tempted to criticize and complain about your parents. Parents do this because God, after whom all parenthood is patterned, has put a drop of his own goodness in their hearts. "If," as John Calvin remarked, "these little drops have such effect, what may we hope to see from the inexhaustible ocean itself? Will God be grudging after thus enlarging the hearts of men?"

"Unthinkable!" says Jesus. And when we remember that the Father went so far that he gave his one and only Son to death for us, can any of us still find it hard to believe that he is willing to grant our requests for things of such lesser value?

Not, of course, that God will give us everything we ask of him. The fog doesn't always disappear. We sometimes lack the persistence in asking of which Jesus spoke and give up too soon. Sometimes we ask for the wrong things. Obviously, God will not give us anything that would harm or injure us. He will not, as James reminds us, cater to our selfish desires and worldly appetites (4:3). Nor again, as James tells us, are we apt to receive anything from him that we fail to ask for in faith, not expecting him to grant it (1:5–8). The psalmist warns us that if we cherish sin in our hearts, the Lord will not hear us (Ps. 66:18). Prayer is not an Aladdin's lamp that brings God running to do our will. Indeed, one of the purposes of prayer is to bring our will into line with his.

Qualifications like these, however, in no way alter the fact that God delights to give us good things. He is especially pleased to answer our prayers for spiritual things. But he also wants us to bring our material needs to him. Earlier in this same Sermon on the Mount Jesus taught us to pray, "Give us this day our daily bread"—meaning everything we need for our material well-being (Matt. 6:11). He went on to promise that if we seek first the kingdom of God and his righteousness—in other words, if we get our priorities right—God will provide us with all these things (Matt. 6:33). Nothing makes our heavenly Father happier than to make us happy by answering our prayers for things that are in harmony with his loving purpose for our lives. There is a prayer that sums up these thoughts well: "Heavenly Father, through your Son Jesus Christ you have taught us, saying, Ask, and it will be given you; seek, and you will find; knock, and it will be opened to you: Give us grace now to ask in faith, according to your Word; to seek only what is agreeable to your holy will; and to knock with patience at the door of your mercy, until our petition is granted and prayer is turned to praise; for the glory of your holy name."[4]

Someone has said that "prayer is not overcoming God's reluctance; it is laying hold of his highest willingness." Another person, who kept a record, testified that he received almost 90 percent of the things he prayed for.

The psalmist did not exaggerate when he declared, "No good thing

4. *Parish Prayers*, ed. Frank Colquhoun (London: Hodder and Stoughton, 1967), 413–14.

does the LORD withhold from those who walk uprightly" (Ps. 84:11). Nor did John Newton exaggerate when he taught us to sing again:

> My soul, believe and pray,
> Without a doubt believe;
> Whate'er we ask in God's own way,
> We surely shall receive.

Because he loves us and wants us to be happy, our heavenly Father is eager to answer our prayers. What greater inducement to prayer could we imagine than this?

In *Knowing God,* one of the great books of our day, J. I. Packer writes that people who know their God are before anything else people who pray. For some of us that may be a disturbing equation. I hope it isn't for you. The secret of a radiant and abundant Christian life depends so much—so very much—upon our faithfulness in prayer.

If you don't have good habits of prayer, make a solemn covenant with God right here and now that you will begin to form them today. Study the Bible to learn those things for which you ought to pray. Examine carefully the prayers recorded in Scripture—those, for example, of Jesus, Paul, and David, remembering that many of the Psalms are really prayers. Note especially the promises God has scattered all across the Bible and claim them in your prayers. Read some of the outstanding books on prayer. Conduct family prayer in your home each day, perhaps at breakfast or at the evening meal, when the family is all together. If your church has a prayer meeting, participate in it, or if it has prayer groups, join one of them. You might even form a prayer partnership with one of your friends. Keep your own prayer diary, logging your requests and God's answers to those requests.

Most important of all, set aside a definite period of time each day—at least ten or fifteen minutes—to talk alone with your heavenly Father, to seek his will, and to bring your requests to him. The best time to do this is the early morning when the day is fresh, and before you are caught up in the traffic of life's pursuits that so easily crowd God out. In every crisis, every moment of special need, turn to him at once. For making prayer a vital part of your life, the character of God should give you all the encouragement you need.

# 3

## Stuart Briscoe

After a successful banking career, Stuart Briscoe left the business world for ministry with the Torchbearers, an organization that ministers to young people worldwide. Since 1970 he has pastored the Elmbrook Church in Brookfield, Wisconsin.

An internationally noted preacher, Briscoe has a television and radio ministry and has written numerous books. Among them are *Discovering God, Tough Truths for Today's Living: A Study of the Sermon on the Mount,* and *Spiritual Life*; and he has also written the volumes on Genesis and Romans in the Communicator's Commentary.

# Constructing a Sermonic "Taj Mahal"

Crafting a sermon is not unlike putting up a building. There are a number of clearly defined stages through which you must pass.

### Deciding to Build

The Taj Mahal, that most distinctive and impressive building outside Agra in India, was built by Shah Jahan as a memorial to his wife, who died in childbirth. The Sears Tower in downtown Chicago was built to meet the insatiable demand for office space in the business section of the Windy City. The objectives in both cases were perfectly stated and the resultant buildings were ideally suited to meet the goals of their builders. The Sears Tower sitting outside Agra would be a monstrosity, while the Taj Mahal in the middle of Chicago's Loop might add to the aesthetics, if not the economics, of Chicago business. In the same way a preacher should always ask the question, "Why on earth am I going to preach this sermon and what do I hope to achieve by it?" If the objective is to challenge people to faith then one kind of approach—an evangelistic message—is most suitable. On the other hand, if the occasion is a funeral service then the approach is quite different.

### Selecting a Site

Try to imagine what it would be like to transport Chicago office workers to India and Indian pilgrims to Chicago. This would have been necessary if careful site selection had not been made in the case of the Taj Mahal and the Sears Tower. If that seems like a bizarre example, it is. But not much more bizarre than some sermons which have been erected on most unsuitable sites.

Assuming the objective of the preacher is to address a subject on the basis of what Scripture has to say about it clearly, the choice of text is profoundly important. Sometimes the preacher may have a subject in mind for which a suitable text must be found. Recently, I was asked to address the subject of materialism and immediately my mind went to the Master's statements, "You cannot serve both God and Money" (Matt. 6:24) and "A man's life does not consist in the abundance of his possessions" (Luke 12:15).

On the other hand it is often advisable to preach systematically through complete passages of Scripture, in which case the site is picked in advance and the only question is, "What kind of building needs to be erected on this passage of Scripture?" So, for example, when I committed myself to preach through Genesis at the rate of one chapter per week, I didn't spend any time selecting a passage of Scripture each week, but I spent a lot of time trying to figure out what significance that Scripture held for people today. Genesis 34 was a case in point! It recounts the sordid story of Dinah's rape, her brothers' treachery, and their father's unwillingness to address the issues. I struggled long and hard over that passage until reading the local paper one morning, I happened to notice that the front-page stories covered almost identical subjects. The overriding theme of both Genesis 34 and the front page of the paper was "violence," and that's what I preached about.

## Drawing Up the Plans

Once the decision to build and the selection of the site have been made, specific plans should be drawn. For the preacher this means having a clear idea of where he wants to go with the subject material as provided in Scripture. My rule of thumb for many years has been to follow the practice of Ezra the scribe and his cohorts. "They read from the Book of the Law of God, making it clear and giving the meaning so that the people could understand what was being read" (Neh. 8:8). Notice the "reading . . . , making clear and giving the meaning," all of which were designed to help the people to understand. It is also worth noting that in addition they gave specific instructions to the people so that they knew how to apply what they had learned. "Nehemiah said, 'Go and enjoy choice food and sweet drinks, and send some to those who have nothing prepared'" (Neh. 8:10).

Charles Haddon Spurgeon said, "Having nothing to conceal we have no ambition to be obscure." I was reminded of this one day when someone said to me after I had preached a sermon, "I thought I understood that subject until you clarified it for me!" When I addressed the subject of "materialism," I drew up the simplest possible plan asking the following questions:

1. What is materialism?
2. What is wrong with it?
3. What should we do about it?

You will note that these three questions address the concerns of Ezra and those who follow in his steps.

## Gathering the Materials

The Taj Mahal is constructed of sandstone and marble but the Sears Tower is made of welded steel, black aluminum, and bronze tinted glass. It is clear that before construction could take place the materials had to be gathered. The preacher needs to take the same approach. Once I know my subject and the text and am clear in my mind about the objective of the sermon, I then try to saturate myself in the text. This means reading and rereading the passage of Scripture until I have almost memorized it. Then I allow it to marinate in my mind as I go about the other activities of the ministry. Depending on how much time I have before the sermon must be delivered, I may take a number of days to allow the truths of the relevant passage of Scripture to infiltrate my thinking so thoroughly that my mind is never far away from them. Then at a specific time I settle down with my yellow legal pad (it must be yellow), my

Bible, and whatever aids to study are necessary and available, and I go about the task, to the best of my ability, of thoroughly grasping what the text is saying. I study individual words, using such tools as Colin Brown's *Dictionary of New Testament Theology* or Gerhard Kittel's *Theological Dictionary of the New Testament* to make sure I have the right meaning. Then I peruse exegetical commentaries to make sure that I am following the train of thought of the inspired author. I write down on my pad every single piece of information I can find, however insignificant it may appear. The result may be two or three pages of scribbled notes which only I can decipher, and sometimes even I can't. This information is the steel and aluminum of my Sears Tower, the sandstone and marble of my Taj Mahal.

## Laying a Foundation

As we all know, houses built on sand tend to topple, while those erected on rock stand. Sermons are no different. The solid exegesis and exposition (another word for doing what Ezra did) of Scripture constitute the rock on which sermons stand. Ditties, perorations, or eulogies no doubt serve their purpose, but they should never be confused with the communication of the Word of God made plain.

Recently, I heard about a preacher who "spoke for an hour and said nothing." We need constantly to pray that we might be delivered from the art of almost saying something. A young boy came up to me in church one Sunday morning and said, "Good morning, Stuart. Have you anything of significance to say to us today?" That's a good question that all preachers should either ask themselves or be asked by someone else. To the extent that their sermon is a proclamation of the Word, the answer is an unequivocal yes. Conversely to the extent that man's best ideas are substituted for God's truth, the answer is an unqualified no.

But there is another side to the foundation laying process. It has to do with leveling the ground between the preacher and the hearers so that the message bridges the yawning (pun intended) gap between pulpit and pew. The preacher must be at great pains to ensure that the erudite statement of truth about to fall from his lips is presented in such a way that the interest and attention of the hearers is grabbed and held. I tried to do this by introducing my "Materialism" sermon by talking about the Wall Street crash and the nefarious activities of Ivan Boesky, who said, "I think greed is healthy."

## Putting Up the Structure

A major part of my sermon preparation goes into the production of a solid outline for both my use and the congregation's, all of whom receive a copy to assist them in following the message. Here is a sample.

## What Is Materialism?

### Matthew 6:19–34

I. What Is Materialism?
   A. Ancient views that material is evil
      1. Asceticism
      2. Epicureanism
      3. Contradicted by creation and incarnation
   B. Contemporary views that material is everything
      1. Communism
      2. Capitalism
      3. Contradicted by Christ (see Luke 12:15)
   C. Common view that material is somewhere in between
      1. A matter of "storing" (v. 19)
      2. A matter of "seeing" (v. 22)
      3. A matter of "serving" (v. 24)
      4. A matter of "seeking" (v. 32)
II. What Is Wrong with Materialism?
   A. It stores the wrong things
      1. Treasures on earth, instead of . . .
      2. Treasures in heaven
         a. 1 Corinthians 13:33
         b. 1 Peter 3:4
         c. Colossians 3:23
         d. Luke 16:9
   B. It sees life through the wrong lenses
   C. It serves the wrong master
      1. Either your materials are your god . . .
      2. Or your God is God of your materials
   D. It seeks the wrong satisfactions
      1. Eating, drinking, wearing, instead of . . .
      2. Matters relating to the kingdom and righteousness
III. What Should We Do about Materialism?
   A. Recognize it—"eyes full of light"
   B. Reject it—"you can't serve God and Money"
   C. Resist it—an ongoing battle
      1. By trusting him, not what he made
      2. By seeing yourself as his, not yours
      3. By handling resources as a steward, not an owner

### Finishing the Building

Since I never preach from a manuscript, it is possible for me to fill out the details of the sermon as it is in progress. This is not a substitute for preparation, because my mind will be well saturated with more information on the subject than I can possibly use, but it does allow for eye contact and flexibility during the course of the message. For example, if I sense that the people are losing interest at any one point, I can move quickly on to the next one or lighten up the presentation by inserting a window. I try to bear in mind Spurgeon's statement: "Often when didactic speech fails to enlighten our hearers we may make them see our meaning by opening a window and letting in the pleasant light of analogy."

The key to illustrating well is to be observant at all times. Read books, watch people, listen to conversations, check the papers, see some movies or television, and either make mental notes or file away the material that strikes you as interesting.

The final word goes to no less a critic of everything in sight than George Bernard Shaw: "Some preaching is like wine: it has colour and sparkle, but does no permanent good; some is like drinking coffee: it stimulates, but does not nourish; some is like carbonated water: a fuss over nothing; some is like spring water: good but hard to get."

# What Is Materialism?

"Do not store up for yourselves treasures on earth, where moth and rust destroy, and where thieves break in and steal. But store up for yourselves treasures in heaven, where moth and rust do not destroy, and where thieves do not break in and steal. For where your treasure is, there your heart will be also.

"The eye is the lamp of the body. If your eyes are good, your whole body will be full of light. But if your eyes are bad, your whole body will be full of darkness. If then the light within you is darkness, how great is that darkness!

"No one can serve two masters. Either he will hate the one and love the other, or he will be devoted to the one and despise the other. You cannot serve both God and Money.

"Therefore I tell you, do not worry about your life, what you will eat or drink; or about your body, what you will wear. Is not life more important than food, and the body more important than clothes? Look at the birds of the air; they do not sow or reap or store away in barns, and yet your heavenly Father feeds them. Are you not much more valuable than they? Who of you by worrying can add a single hour to his life?

"And why do you worry about clothes? See how the lilies of the field grow. They do not labor or spin. Yet I tell you that not even Solomon in all his splendor was dressed like one of these. If that is how God clothes the grass of the field, which is here today and tomorrow is thrown into the fire, will he not much more clothe you, O you of little faith? So do not worry, saying, 'What shall we eat?' or 'What shall we drink?' or 'What shall we wear?' For the pagans run after all these things, and your heavenly Father knows that you need them. But seek first his kingdom and his righteousness, and all these things will be given to you as well. Therefore do not worry about tomorrow, for tomorrow will worry about itself. Each day has enough trouble of its own." [Matt. 6:19–34 NIV]

Ivan Boesky, the Wall Street wizard of insider trading before his dramatic fall from grace, was invited to give the commencement address at the Business School of the University of California, Berkeley. During the course of his remarks he said, "I think greed is healthy. You can be greedy and still feel good about yourself." The students responded to his talk with a standing ovation. On another occasion he said quite openly, "My master is my purse." Reputedly his favorite T-shirt carried the message, "He who owns the most when he dies, wins."

Most people would cringe at the crassness of his remarks, nodding their heads wisely and saying such things as, "Yes, and look where he finished up!" Yet there is little doubt that many would not be averse to subscribing to his theory if they had the chance. Alexis de Tocqueville in his classic book, *Democracy in America*, wrote, "No stigma attaches to the love of money in America, and provided it does not exceed the bounds imposed by public order, it is held in honor."

That we human beings have certain needs which should be met goes without saying. That we humans are both spiritual and physical beings is equally evident. It follows, therefore, not only that some of those needs will be material, but also that material and spiritual concerns may possibly collide and disturb the balance between the two which is so necessary for healthy living. When a human being becomes absorbed with material concerns to the exclusion of spiritual realities, that person has slipped into materialism.

### What Is Materialism?

In ancient times it was not uncommon to meet people who believed that matter is intrinsically evil and spirit is intrinsically good. The ascetics followed this theory to its logical conclusion by trying to divorce themselves (unsuccessfully, of course) from all physical and material concerns, hoping that as a result they would live spiritual lives. On the other hand, the Epicureans, starting at the same point of believing that material is evil, finished up as far away from the ascetics as possible. They reasoned that since material is evil and therefore useless, it doesn't really matter what you do with your body. This rationalization gave them license to do all kinds of unmentionable things. They were some of the forefathers of our modern-day "Eat, drink, and be merry" crew.

But can we accept this view of material things today? Since God created all things and pronounced them "good," it is obvious that matter cannot be evil. Furthermore, given the fact that the Lord Jesus assumed our humanity and lived a totally sinless life in the body prepared for him, it is clear that material cannot be evil. The basic doctrines of creation and incarnation refute the idea that material is evil.

Contemporary views of material things have tended to fly to the opposite extreme. The popular view now seems to be that material is everything. It is ironic that the conflicting ideologies of communism and capitalism should ever be in agreement. Yet on two points they are closer to each other than many people realize. They both tend to measure reality in material terms, and they both seem to believe that there is something about man that guarantees that he will behave properly as far as material things are concerned. The communist doesn't seem to allow for greed which might lead an individual to cheat the state if he gets the chance, and the capitalist, according to Adam Smith's doctrine, believes that an "automatic harmony" will be evident in human economic relations because of man's inherent goodness.

The Christian not only rejects this rosy-eyed view of man but also remembers the trenchant warning of the Lord Jesus, "A man's life does not consist in the abundance of his possessions" (Luke 12:15). But J. Paul Getty, the oil tycoon, said, "The best things in life are things," and the whole structure of our economy, which requires increased production, which presupposes increased demand, which must be constantly stimulated by touching the inner core of human greed, leads us away from the Master's words. For those reasons we need a clear understanding of what materialism is and what to do about it.

If material things are not evil and they are not everything, it would be fair to say that they fall somewhere in between. In the Sermon on the Mount Jesus showed that it is our attitudes to material things that determine whether we are materialists or not.

He said, for instance, "Do not store up for yourselves treasures on earth . . . but store up for yourselves treasures in heaven" (Matt. 6:19–20). The accent is on the storing. The amassing of material things. The bias towards accumulating material things to such an extent that spiritual realities are blocked out. That is materialism.

Jesus also said, "The eye is the lamp of the body. If your eyes are good, your whole body will be full of light. But if your eyes are bad, your whole body will be full of darkness" (Matt. 6:22–23). Here he is referring to the tendency we have to focus on material things. We see and desire and covet and possess until, if we are not careful, we evaluate everything and everybody in purely material terms.

Perhaps the most powerful words Jesus spoke on the subject are, "You cannot serve both God and Money" (Matt. 6:24). Arthur Schopenhauer, the German philosopher, said, "Money is human happiness in the abstract: he, then, who is no longer capable of enjoying human happiness in the concrete devotes himself utterly to money." Those who start out with money as the means to happiness find eventually that money has become the end in itself and that their happiness (or otherwise) is found in it. God is irrelevant. That is materialism.

The Master went on to point out that his disciples should be different from the pagans in their attitude to material things. "The pagans run after all these things," he said, "and your heavenly Father knows that you need them. But seek first his kingdom and his righteousness, and all these things will be given to you as well" (Matt. 6:32–33). The words translated "run" and "seek" are actually the same word in the original language, and they both point to a seeking after things with great ambition and determination almost to the point of obsession. That there is nothing wrong with material things or with possessing them is clear from the Master's teaching at this point, but to be constantly seeking after them to the exclusion of other more important things like God's kingdom and righteousness is materialism.

## What Is Wrong with Materialism?

First, materialism leads people to store up the wrong things. The Lord Jesus differentiated between things on earth and things in heaven, and while he identified the former, he said nothing to help us identify the latter. Perhaps a little detective work might be appropriate here. Paul wrote, "And now these three remain: faith, hope and love. But the greatest of these is love" (1 Cor. 13:13). If the greatest thing in the world is love and it will "remain," it seems (reasonable) to me to assume it has heavenly worth. Think of how many people you know whose families have starved for love while the father sold himself to his business. He started out doing it for his family to make them comfortable and to give them the good life, but he finished with nothing of eternal consequence.He forgot that he would leave his money, but that loving as God intended would remain.

Peter wrote, "Your beauty . . . should be that of your inner self, the unfading beauty of a gentle and quiet spirit, which is of great worth in God's sight" (1 Pet. 3:3–4). Anything which is specifically identified as being of great worth in God's sight must have heavenly value. But in today's world such is the frenetic, frantic competitive search for material goods and advancement that these qualities are all too often sacrificed on the altar of the Almighty Dollar, and lives are impoverished as a result. I have often observed that when a family loses a loved one, it is only a matter of time until the old adage, "Where there's a will, there's a quarrel," proves true. Sad to say, I have seen more acrimony among believers where money was involved than anywhere else.

Eternal rewards are promised to God's people under certain circumstances. It is apparent that those things which merit such divine approval and recognition must also have heavenly worth. Surprisingly, one of these things is everyday work done for the right reasons. "Whatever you do, work at it with all your heart, as working for the Lord, not for men, since you know that you will receive an inheritance from the Lord as a reward" (Col. 3:23–24). When I was a young man growing up in England, I became very friendly with an old printer known affectionately in our small town as Percy the Printer. Percy had a printing press used by Noah in the ark, and he usually dressed in missionary-barrel chic. He rarely charged people enough to make ends meet (his own, that is), and he was always ready to stop what he was doing to talk to people about their concerns and needs. His work was of high quality given his equipment, and his integrity was unquestioned. When—as is often the case in the printing business—his customers wanted delivery of their order yesterday, he would oblige without a word of complaint about their unreasonableness. People, knowing his meek spirit and commitment to righteousness, constantly took him to the cleaners. But when eventually he died, after a long painful illness borne with great dignity, a resident of the town who made no Christian profession was heard to say, "If ever there was a Christian, it was Percy the Printer." To this the whole town said a hearty "amen."

Jesus also pointed out that he wished that his disciples were as smart as some secular people when it comes to the utilization of their resources. In the parable of the shrewd manager he said, "Use worldly wealth to gain friends for yourselves, so that when it is gone, you will be welcomed into eternal dwellings" (Luke 16:9). In other words, it is apparent that the correct investment of material goods on earth can lead to dividends paid in heaven. Those dividends are clearly of eternal value. But the squandering of material assets on earth without a thought for eternal investments in lives and the kingdom is symptomatic of chronic materialism.

Second, materialism sees life through the wrong lenses. In much the same way that a view seen through the wrong end of a telescope is diminished rather than magnified, so life seen through materialistic lenses is totally out of perspective. Of course, if this life is all there is and spiritual concerns are the figment of too fertile imaginations, then the materialist is right. You may as well live life with all the gusto you can because, as those purveyors of profound nonsense, the aging athletes on the beer commercials, tell us, "You only go round once in life." But if there is an eternity beyond time, and if we are spirit as well as body, then life viewed from a materialistic point of view is deprived of richness and texture, of meaning and significance.

I heard of a man who, when asked what he thought about the English Lake district (an indescribably beautiful part of England where, incidentally, I was born!), replied, "Oh, it was nothing but rocks and water." The poet William Wordsworth in similar circumstances rhapsodized about "a host of golden daffodils" and expressed thoughts that often lay too deep for tears when he sensed the wonder of it all. But the crass materialist can see only his goods and his bank balance. Life for him has lost its excitement, its depth, its content, its color, and its significance. Like Ebenezer Scrooge—embittered and muttering, "Bah humbug," as he scratched and scraped his lonely, mean way through life when he could have enjoyed its finer, simpler, richer things—so the materialist is damned to self-imposed impoverishment as he looks at life through the wrong lenses.

Thirdly, materialism serves to make people serve the wrong master. It is a solid rule of thumb that if you don't master matter, matter will master you. A man bought a baby python and played with it until he had taught it to wrap its powerful length around his body. Then he took his act to a circus where the people clapped and cheered as he showed his mastery over the fearsome reptile. But one day on the given signal to release, the python decided otherwise, and the cheers turned to screams as the former plaything played with the former master and crushed out his life. Jesus was addressing this characteristic of materialism when he said unequivocally, "You cannot serve both God and Money." Either God is the God of our material things, or our material things will take over as our God.

Fourth, materialism seeks the wrong satisfactions. There are undoubtedly pleasures in eating and drinking well, and some people derive tremendous pleasure from dressing up and looking nice. All this is perfectly acceptable to the God who created all these things and gave them to us in order that we might enjoy them and give him credit for them. The problem comes when we fall into the trap of assuming that because there is much to enjoy in material things, more material things mean more enjoyment, and that fullness of joy comes from fullness of possessions, whatever that means.

A recent discussion between a number of the most wealthy people in America showed that without exception they believed that "enough" is always a little more than you have at any given moment. One thing that can be said in favor of such television hits as "Dallas" and "Falcon Crest" is that while they portray "the good life," they also show that these people who are so busy enjoying it are actually shriveled people whose hearts are as empty as their wallets are full. Material things can no more satisfy the inner longings of the soul than you can feed an elephant on strawberries. But what is one to do?

## What Should We Do about Materialism?

There are three things that we can do to guard against materialism. The first is to recognize it. Jesus talked about the eye being the lamp of the body, and while he was using a metaphor, we can easily see what he meant. That which fills our gaze eventually fills our life. If our focus is on the things that are significant, our lives will be significant; if not, they will not. The man who has time only for business should not be surprised if his character and his relationships with both God and man deteriorate. The woman who is absorbed in feeling good and looking good instead of being good and doing good should not be taken aback when she wakes up one day and discovers that her looks have fled, and her "get-up-and-go" has got up and gone. All she may be left with is a closet full of clothes that won't fit, an exercise room full of equipment that she can't pedal any more, and a vanity covered with cosmetics that no longer work their peculiar brand of magic. She should have realized earlier that her eye was full of darkness and that she was manufacturing a life of Stygian gloom. Everyone should be able to recognize materialism when it encroaches upon life.

The second thing we can do is reject materialism. It is one thing to recognize that life is being sucked into the mainstream of materialism, but it is another thing to decide it is wrong, for the reasons we mentioned earlier, and then to have the moral courage to reject the attitude and its attendant lifestyle.

The third and most difficult thing is to resist materialism. Everyone who would live rightly in our fallen world faces an ongoing battle. There are enticing vices to embrace, selfish attitudes to indulge, inappropriate relationships to pursue, and physical appetites to satiate. Let me make three suggestions that can be applied on an ongoing basis. We need to learn to trust God rather than the things he has made. An obvious example will suffice to show how difficult this can be. We live in an age of technology in which, given our assumption that we have the right always to be happy and healthy, we place great faith in our machines and regard our physicians with an almost religious devotion. It goes without saying that God made the physicians, the technology comes from his raw materials, and in the long run the best thing that technology, physicians, and medicine can do is postpone the inevitability of death, which is still in the Master's control. Therefore, we should always bear in mind that it is he who merits our trust rather than all the wonderful things he has so graciously given us. This deep sense of spiritual reality will safeguard us against untoward materialistic tendencies.

The next thing is to see yourself as belonging to God rather than belonging to yourself. The orthodox believer knows that he is not his own because he has been bought with a price, and he should therefore glorify God in his body (1 Cor. 6:19–20). But if we learn to recognize that, if we belong to God, we are his responsibility, and conversely, if we belong to ourselves, we are our own responsibility, then our fixation on material concerns will be considerably diminished. As Jesus said, "Do not worry about tomorrow, for tomorrow will worry about itself" (Matt. 6:34).

Finally, we can learn to handle our resources as stewards rather than as owners. As long as I hold on to my goods and chattels, I will have my hands too full to have room for anything else. God, knowing our natural acquisitiveness, devised a wonderful way of countering this tendency. He revealed a truth that would help us to hold lightly that which we have every tendency to cling to stubbornly. He told us that it is more blessed to give than to receive—one of the less-known and less-quoted maxims of the Master—and in so doing reminded us that materialism can be a blight to the soul, but resisting it can lead to blessing eternal.

John Wesley said, "Earn all you can, save all you can, and give all you can." J. Paul Getty said, "The best things in life are things." Ivan Boesky said, "My master is my purse." Which of the three was closest to the Master? That's easy! But here's a tough question. Which of these three is closest to you?

# 4

## Edmund P. Clowney

Edmund P. Clowney pastored three Orthodox Presbyterian churches before teaching practical theology at Westminster Theological Seminary. In 1966 he was appointed president of Westminster, a position he held until 1984, when he became associate pastor of Trinity Presbyterian Church, Charlottesville, Virginia.

Clowney has authored *Preaching and Biblical Theology, Called to the Ministry, The Message of First Peter,* and *The Story of Jesus in the Old Testament.* He earned a Th.B. degree from Westminster Theological Seminary and an S.T.M. degree from Yale Divinity School. He has also done graduate study at Union Theological Seminary (New York).

# Preaching Christ from Biblical Theology

We preachers delight to talk about preaching, even without the lure of adding an autobiographical touch. Hear us when we tell you what the Bible says about preaching, but take our practical hints with several grains of salt. The more personal we become, the less useful we are likely to be.

To be sure, a how-to hint may sometimes provide a habit for a lifetime. I suspect Jay Adams may have forgotten this, but at one time he suggested a "scattergram" method for collecting your thoughts. Take a piece of paper the size of a desk blotter. As you review your notes on a Scripture text, scatter jottings on the sheet. Loosen up. Write them anywhere, any which way. Then, armed with three or four colored markers, circle with the same color the jottings that have something in common. From this exercise in color coding, the divisions of a message may emerge. Well, they *may* emerge, especially if you have Jay Adams's fertile mind and share his zest for colored markers.

But now, of course, the same process of scattering and gathering can be done on a computer, with outlining software. If a computer monitor freezes your mind the way a white sheet of paper used to, by all means go for the markers. But if the whir of your discount clone booting up starts your juices flowing, then get the software.

Moreover, any aids to collecting your thoughts only serve the portable computer between your ears. Many users testify that their neurons boot up best while walking, driving, or, yes, talking. Still further, any thought-collecting process that is to start with the Bible and end with a congregation has got to be saturated with prayer all the way. Crayola markers or IBM computers have to be prayerfully used. Sitting at my old word-processor produced some back strain. To ease it I bought a chair that supports a kneeling posture. It was a good idea. Nothing beats kneeling in prayer to organize a message.

More important by far than the details of method that we use is our understanding of what preaching is. Most preachers can well remember the man who modeled the ministry of the gospel for them. From my earliest childhood to college years I heard the preaching of one man, Warren R. Ward, at Westminster Presbyterian Church in West Philadelphia. Tall, white-haired, dignified but passionate, Warren Ward preached the Bible with evangelistic zeal. His preaching exalted Jesus Christ and put the claims of Christ above every goal in life. At the summons of his preaching I looked up through tears to Christ crucified. It was his custom to kneel on one knee at his chair when he first ascended the platform. It was far more than a custom, I knew. Warren Ward understood that preaching was a savor of life unto life, or death unto death.

Taking a recommendation from my predecessor and teacher of homiletics, R. B. Kuiper, I began my teaching career at Westminster Theological Seminary with a Dutch dictionary and a copy of Hoekstra's *Gereformeerde Homiletick*. Both Kuiper and Hoekstra insisted that biblical revelation shows the unity of God's plan of salvation. The Old Testament points forward to Christ as surely as the New Testament proclaims the fulfillment of God's promises in him. A sermon that ignores the wider context misses the real point of any passage. The realization gradually dawned on me that Jesus Christ is the reason for the Bible. Because the Father had determined to send his Son into the world to save sinners, the world was preserved under the rainbow, Abraham was called out under the stars, Moses was charged at the burning bush, David was promised the eternal rule of his Son—everything that God did was preparing for Jesus.

To preach Christ from all the Scriptures requires careful interpretation, not wild flights of imagination. We need to ask, "What truth about God and his saving work is disclosed in this passage?" When we can answer that question, we are on firm ground to ask two others: "How is this particular truth carried forward in the history of revelation? How does it find fulfillment in Christ?" Because the Old Testament points beyond itself, it is rich in symbolism. We cannot miss the symbolism of the sacrifices commanded in the law, of the temple as God's dwelling place, of the sacred calendar with its day of atonement and year of jubilee. We must recognize, too, the symbolism implied in the calling of God's servants: prophets, priests, and kings. Even the events of the Old Testament may have a symbolic dimension: the exodus certainly does; so do the deliverances accomplished by those whom God raised up to be judges and kings of his people. Indeed, we come to see that the whole structure of God's dealings with his people is preparing us for the new covenant realities. This is how the New Testament writers constantly find types of Christ in the Scriptures. What is symbolical in the Old is found to be typical in the New; it points us to the fullness of Christ.

Jesus Christ and the Bible go together. The Scriptures bear witness to him; he bore witness to them in word and deed. He understood himself and his work in terms of the Scriptures. Indeed, the Spirit who inspired the Old Testament writers was the Spirit of Christ (1 Pet. 1:10–11).

To preach effectively we must know the Bible and know the Lord. The trials and defeats that we suffer remind us of how inadequate we are. We shrink from speaking the words that deal with the issues of eternal life and death. We cry with Paul, "Who is sufficient for such a task?" In our helplessness we learn that our sufficiency is of him. Through the valley the rod and staff of the Lord prepare us to preach.

Besides knowing the Word of the Lord and the Lord of the Word, we must know people. I made that observation in a seminar only to have D. Martyn Lloyd-Jones take issue with me. The good doctor was on leave from Westminster Chapel in London, lecturing on preaching at Westminster Seminary. He stoutly maintained that all the preacher needs to know about his people is what the Bible tells him about them. I think I understand the force of what he said. Yet Lloyd-Jones was called to the pulpit ministry from a medical practice in Wales. Without a physician's intimate knowledge of people, would he have probed with such skill into the hearts of his hearers?

The disciplines that best prepare us to preach are the disciplines that best prepare us to know the Bible, the Lord, and people. I have been reading and studying the Bible ever since my teacher in the junior department of Sunday school suggested that I should. I must confess to my shame, however, that only in the last nine years of my life have I made it a fixed practice to *write* my reflections on a Bible passage every single day. This habit is wonderfully addictive. Somehow the discipline of writing seems always to lead on to new understanding, new conviction, new fellowship with the Lord. It is well worth paying the price to be regular.

Meditation on Scripture is a fertile source of texts and themes for teaching. J. van Andel, an old Dutch preacher, wisely said that the pulpit should not drive us to the text, but the text to the pulpit.

The text should drive us to people even before we reach the pulpit. That happens in corporate Bible study; it also happens as we share with others what we have just discovered in our personal reading. If your daily reflections are kept in diary form, you may want to keep a separate file of sermon ideas. But it is even more important to *use* what you have learned. It is amazing how often an opportunity comes. The same applies to your sermon preparation. Don't wait till Sunday to share what you are discovering. It will be just the word you need in a counseling situation, a hospital call, a deacons' meeting. Can you tell your children in advance what the sermon will be about? The more your message is field-tested, the more you will grow into its truth—and how to communicate it.

As we know our people better, their questions and problems will drive us to the Bible. Some sermons are directly expository, explaining and applying what the text says. Other sermons may be more topical, but nonetheless biblical. Peter's sermon at Pentecost was topical. He drew from more than one Old Testament text to explain what was taking place. To answer people's questions, to draw together for them the range of biblical teaching, there are times when we may make more than one text the basis of our message.

In developing the exegesis of a passage, I have always used the original languages of Scripture, and have found word studies particularly fruitful. I know that focusing on separate words may cause us to miss the forest for the trees. We may also make the mistake of weighting down each use of a word with the whole range of its possible meanings. But theological dictionaries like Kittel's famous work supply rich lodes of information about word usage. Concordance study is also necessary. I regularly consult Greek and Hebrew concordances. Concordance work is being greatly facilitated by text retrieval computer programs. (See John J. Hughes, *Bits, Bytes and Biblical Studies* [Grand Rapids: Zondervan, 1987] and his *Bits and Bytes Review.*) Concordance work not only helps us to understand the variety of word usage, but also uncovers passages that are linked by the use of a number of words in common. God's revelation to Abram in Genesis 15:17 may seem mystifying until concordance work turns up the use of the same vocabulary in the description of God's appearing at Sinai (Exod. 19:18; 20:18) and at Zion (Isa. 31:9). (The word translated "lamp" or "torch" in Genesis is translated "lightning" when linked with the thunder of Sinai.) The passage in Jeremiah 34:18–20 shows the meaning of walking between divided pieces: it is the form for a self-maledictory oath. Put together the theophanic symbolism of the fire and that of oath-taking, and it is clear that God himself is swearing by his own life to keep his promise to Abram.

When I have studied the key words in a text, I examine the grammatical structure. Here I do not hesitate to use parsing guides and grammatical notes in commentaries. The next step is to get the flow of the passage as a whole in its setting. There are often subtle literary or thematic connections that run through a whole passage and context. For example, in Genesis 32 and 33 the theme of confrontation and of two companies runs through the narrative. It always helps to ask: "What is most like this in other parts of Scripture?" Then ask, "How does this differ from what it most resembles?" (The Lord's challenge to Jacob as he enters the land is similar to his challenge to Moses as he went down to Egypt, and to Joshua as he stood before Jericho.)

Literary form helps us to catch significant repetitions and emphases. Since most Old Testament stories are told through dialogue between two persons, it is helpful to notice where the story moves on more quickly by shifting to the third person, and where it returns to the concreteness of dialogue. Robert Alter, in *The Art of Biblical Narrative* (New York: Basic, 1983), opens the world of literary form in Old Testament narrative, as does Tremper Longman III in *Literary Approaches to Biblical Interpretation* (Grand Rapids: Zondervan, 1987).

Sometimes the notes from my personal Bible reading help me to see connections beyond the immediate passage. In the Gospels, for example, it is always fruitful to look for a connection between a narrative and what precedes and follows it. The Gospel of Mark provides a classic instance. Mark's distinctive accounts of the healing of the deaf man and the blind man (7:32–37; 8:22–25) are found in a context where Jesus laments the spiritual deafness and blindness of his disciples (6:52; 7:18; 8:18, 21). They, too, may yet see men as trees walking, but Jesus will bring them to see all things clearly, to hear, and to speak plainly!

It pays to understand the geographical and historical settings of the text. For example, the town of Nain, where Jesus raised the widow's son, is only a few miles from Shunem, where Elisha restored a dead son to his mother. The connection was not lost on the people of Nain, as their reaction shows (Luke 7:16).

The whole force of Jacob's dream at Bethel is changed when we note that he saw a stone stairway, not a ladder, and that it is compared to the tower of Babel by the repeated phrase about the top reaching to heaven (Gen. 11:4; 28:12). Further, the clause, "The LORD stood above it" (Gen. 28:13 KJV) must be translated, "The LORD stood beside him," as we learn from the identical prepositional construction used to describe the Lord's "going up from beside" Jacob at Bethel the second time (Gen. 35:13). At Bethel God came down to Jacob. That is why Jacob called this place "the house of God" and said, "Surely the LORD is in this place, and I was not aware of it" (Gen. 28:16).

I have found *The Macmillan Bible Atlas,* by Yohanen Aharoni and Michael Avi-Yonah (rev. ed. [New York: Macmillan, 1977]); *The Illustrated Bible Dictionary* (3 vols. [Wheaton: Tyndale, 1980]); and Roland deVaux, *Ancient Israel* (2 vols. [New York: McGraw-Hill, 1965]) necessary tools in studying the situation of Old Testament texts. *The New International Dictionary of Biblical Archaeology* (Grand Rapids: Zondervan, 1983) summarizes research in that field.

To make your preaching more vivid, look for the information you would need to produce a television documentary of the text in its setting.

The significance of the text for your hearers flows from the meaning of the text as fulfilled in Christ. The application of a sermon needs research no less than the exposition. I well remember a time when I wrote adult Sunday school materials for an evangelical publisher. The format included a verse-by-verse commentary on the lesson text. I was prepared for that; I had the tools for exegesis and soon finished that section. Then I found that the format also included about the same number of words in illustrative applications. I sat staring at the typewriter. I'd like to tell you how I've since solved the problem. The trouble is, I haven't. I tear out illustrations from news magazines only to lose them in unfiling folders. I desperately search through back periodicals for a dimly remembered story that exactly meets my needs. The only applicatory illustrations I haven't lost are those that I filed with the sermons in which they were used. I've done better with books. With highlighters and flyleaf jottings I can keep track of useful quotes and illustrations.

Do I have a word for you if you share my disorganized plight? Yes, don't despair. If you lack a good resource file, at least the illustrations you do find will be current. Keep abreast of the news, tear out juicy surveys, profiles, or statistics from *Time, U.S. News, Christianity Today,* or *World* (Asheville, N.C.). There is a real possibility that you will find good use for an article before it's hopelessly lost. Watch commercials on television; make note of your own experiences and other first-hand accounts before the details are forgotten. Keep reading. It is fair enough to describe a fictional situation in your sermon with a "just-suppose" introduction. The better you know the world of your hearers, the better you can illustrate and apply your messages.

Clear structure is needed for strong preaching. For years, the speed of the TGV train from Paris to Marseille was reduced by half at Avignon because the track wasn't level enough to carry a train at speeds well over two hundred miles an hour. Constructing a sermon outline is track work.

Begin with the theme of the text. The theme is a concise statement explaining what the text is about. Until you discern the theme you have not grasped the unity that makes the text a text. To be sure, the limits of a text are sometimes evident from its literary form—a psalm, a proverb, a distinct narrative. But you still must understand what the main thrust of the passage is. You do not impose a theme on the text, you discover it. In the accompanying sermon, I have taken as the theme of this parable, "Sharing the Father's Welcome." The divisions of the sermon must be logically subordinate to the theme, and they must be coordinate with one another. Sometimes divisions that follow the sequence of the text will repeat the same ideas. In the following outline, used for the accompanying sermon, notice that in both main divisions we see first the alienation of a son, then the welcome of the father. An alternate, more topical outline is therefore possible. The alienation of the two sons could first be considered, then the grace of the father toward each. Such an outline would not be best for this passage; it interrupts the story. But often it is wise to turn an outline "inside out" in this way.

## Sharing the Father's Welcome

    I. The Grace of the Father's Welcome
        A. Measured by the unworthiness of the sinner
           1. His rebellious alienation
           2. His penitent confession
        B. Measured by the welcome of the Father
           1. Total restoration
              a. Forgiveness (Buddhist parable)
              b. Readoption
           2. Total joy
              a. Triumph of joy
              b. Root of joy—Father's love
   II. The Demand of the Father's Welcome
        A. The alienation of the older brother
           1. Despising the Father's joy
           2. Rejecting the Father's grace
           3. Resenting the Father's love
        B. The invitation to the older brother
           1. Compassion—again down the path
           2. Promise of the inheritance
           3. Appeal—come in to the feast

C. The demand on the older brother
  1. The demand of love made
  2. The demand of love fulfilled
     a. What should an older brother do? (Donald Dawson's search)
     b. What the Firstborn of many brethren did
D. The joy of the true Elder Brother

# Sharing the Father's Welcome

Jesus continued: "There was a man who had two sons. The younger one said to his father, 'Father, give me my share of the estate.' So he divided his property between them.

"Not long after that, the younger son got together all he had, set off for a distant country and there squandered his wealth in wild living. After he had spent everything, there was a severe famine in that whole country, and he began to be in need. So he went and hired himself out to a citizen of that country, who sent him to his fields to feed pigs. He longed to fill his stomach with the pods that the pigs were eating, but no one gave him anything.

"When he came to his senses, he said 'How many of my father's hired men have food to spare, and here I am starving to death! I will set out and go back to my father and say to him: Father, I have sinned against heaven and against you. I am no longer worthy to be called your son; make me like one of your hired men.' So he got up and went to his father.

"But while he was still a long way off, his father saw him and was filled with compassion for him; he ran to his son, threw his arms around him and kissed him.

"The son said to him, 'Father, I have sinned against heaven and against you. I am no longer worthy to be called your son.'

"But the father said to his servants, 'Quick! Bring the best robe and put it on him. Put a ring on his finger and sandals on his feet. Bring the fattened calf and kill it. Let's have a feast and celebrate. For this son of mine was dead and is alive again; he was lost and is found.' So they began to celebrate.

"Meanwhile, the older son was in the field. When he came near the house, he heard music and dancing. So he called one of the servants and asked him what was going on. 'Your brother has come,' he replied, 'and your father has killed the fattened calf because he has him back safe and sound.'

> "The older brother became angry and refused to go in. So his father
> went out and pleaded with him. But he answered his father, 'Look!
> All these years I've been slaving for you and never disobeyed your
> orders. Yet you never gave me even a young goat so I could cele-
> brate with my friends. But when this son of yours who has squan-
> dered your property with prostitutes comes home, you kill the fat-
> tened calf for him!'
>
> "'My son,' the father said, 'you are always with me, and everything I
> have is yours. But we had to celebrate and be glad, because this
> brother of yours was dead and is alive again; he was lost and is
> found.'" [Luke 15:11–32 NIV]

Americans have taken to hanging up yellow ribbons along with the
red, white, and blue. It all began at the outset of Ronald Reagan's
presidency, when the hostages were released from Iran. They were welcomed with yellow ribbons fluttering from trees and utility poles in
Washington, D.C., and on Main Street, U.S.A. The image came from a
ballad about a girl signaling a welcome to an errant lover by tying yellow ribbons "'round the old oak tree." The song has mercifully faded,
but the symbol has caught on. A yellow ribbon has become our sign of a
joyful welcome home.

One of the stories Jesus told gives us the picture of a yellow ribbon
tied across the open gate of heaven. Jesus described the joy of heaven in
welcoming home a penitent sinner. The familiar story is often called the
parable of the prodigal son. Some have said it might better be called the
parable of the elder brother, since it ends with his reaction to his
brother's homecoming. But the central figure in the story is the father,
who would welcome both sons to his feast. Jesus tells the story so that
we can understand the welcome of his heavenly Father and join in its
joy.

In the first part of his story, Jesus shows the grace of the Father's welcome; in the second part he tells us about the demand of that welcome.

### The Grace of the Father's Welcome

The story begins with the younger of two brothers. This youth is living at home and hating every minute of it. Everything turns him off: the
household, the farming, the lifestyle of his father. There is only one
thing about his father that he does like: the old man's money. But the
prospects of cashing in on it are remote. His father shows no sign of an
early decease. At last the young man's patience runs out. "Father," he
says, "give me what's coming to me from your estate."

It would be a rude demand in any society; it was especially harsh in
view of the Old Testament laws of inheritance. Jewish wisdom, too,

advised fathers against dividing their holdings before the day of their death:

> For it is better that your children ask of you
> Than that you should look to the hand of your sons. [Eccles. 33:21 RSV]

But the father does what his younger son asks. He divides his estate. The young man finds himself holding title to at least a third, perhaps half, of his father's living. He gathered it all together. That is, he converted it into cash, so that he could put it in a bag and pull the string around it. Now he had what he had always wanted. He could go where he wanted and do what he wanted.

He did. He left home at once; every step was a step into freedom, so he kept on traveling. With a world of distance between him and his father's house he could live a little.

In his story Jesus does not give any details as to how the prodigal spent his money. Did months or years pass before his high living had to be scaled down? Did his funds evaporate in a rush, or did he ration sin on a budget? In any case, at last it was no more a question of the cheapest wine shops or the cheapest women. It was the question of a crust of bread. The prodigal became penniless just as a famine struck the country, inflating the price of food. His wasted inheritance had bought him no friends. He had to get a job if he was not to starve, and the only job he could get was as a swineherd, feeding pigs, The point is not that feeding pigs is a messy occupation. The point is that pigs are an unclean animal in the technical sense of Old Testament law. Every bond with his father's house was broken. The prodigal was an alien, far from home, estranged, lost, unclean.

His repentance is not glamorized in the story of Jesus. It began not in the depths of his heart but in the pit of his stomach. He watched the pigs crunch the dry carob pods that he fed them. His meager earnings could not provide him with daily bread at famine prices. Perhaps he could manage carob pods. They were, after all, edible. How hungry he was! What meals he used to enjoy! His mind went back, not to the luxurious banquets that had cost him his inheritance, but to the dinners in his father's house. His father's house! "How many of my father's hired men have food to spare, and here I am starving to death!" (v. 17).

Yes, he had said it aloud. It was true. He had been a fool, and a wicked fool at that. "He who keeps the law is a discerning son, but a companion of gluttons disgraces his father" (Prov. 28:7). He had to go home. He had to face his father again. What could he say? "Father, I have sinned against heaven and against you. I am no longer worthy to be called your son; make me like one of your hired men" (vv. 18–19).

His father would take him in and give him employment and food. He was sure of it. He had no right to claim the old relationship, but he could see again his father's face.

The prodigal's confession of his complete unworthiness prepares us to marvel at his father's mercy and the grace of his welcome.

We may gain fresh amazement if we compare the story Jesus told with a somewhat similar story in the literature of Mahayana Buddhism. In a famous Lotus Sutra the story is told of a young man who leaves his father's house and is gone for many years, "twenty or thirty or forty or fifty."[1] His father searches for him and moves to another country, where he becomes immensely wealthy. The son, on the other hand, continues his wanderings as a despised beggar. One day the son happens to come to the town where his father lives. He does not recognize his father, but curiously stares at the princely magnificence of this elderly man. The father, fanned by attendants, sits on a throne under a jeweled awning, his footstool decorated in gold and silver. He is concluding business deals in gold bullion, corn, and grain with a surrounding crowd of merchants and bankers. The beggar is thoroughly alarmed. "People like me don't belong here," he thinks. "Let me get out of here before I am seized to do forced labor."

But the father recognizes his son at first sight and sends his servants after him. They bring him back, kicking and screaming in terror. Sure that he will be put to death, he faints. The father sprinkles cold water on him, and tells the servants to free him, without identifying himself to his son, or his son to his servants. Instead, he sends servants to find him again in the slum section of the city and to bring him back with an offer of employment. The servants disguise themselves as street people, smearing dirt on themselves and wearing rags, so as to gain the trust of this beggar. Their mission succeeds, and the poor man is set to work at the lowliest of tasks. (The estate is not equipped with septic tanks.) Through a window the father watches his son as he is shoveling the waste. He, too, smears on dirt and puts on rags so as to go and talk to his son and encourage him on the job. The son works faithfully on the grounds, but continues to live in a shack nearby. Many years later, the father expresses great appreciation for the son's faithful work; he declares that he will treat him as a son and make him his heir. The son is indifferent to all the wealth that is now declared to be his; he continues to live in his shack and work on the estate.

After some twenty years, "the householder perceives that his son is able to save, mature and mentally developed; that in the consciousness of his nobility he feels abashed, ashamed, disgusted, when thinking of his former poverty." Aware of his approaching death, the householder

1. Chapter 4 of the *Saddharma-Pundarika,* in vol. 21 of *Sacred Books of the East,* ed. Max Müller, 98–117.

calls his relatives, officials, and neighbors and declares before them all, "This man is my natural son, the heir of all that I possess."

The moral at the end of the chapter is that "As we have always observed the moral precepts under the rule of the Knower of the world, we now receive the fruit of that morality which we have formerly practised."

What is the difference between these two stories? One word describes it: *grace*! Amazing grace! Watch the father in the story of Jesus. Far down the road he sees that familiar figure. He sweeps up the skirt of his robe, thrusts it into his belt, and runs down the road to meet his son. He flings his arms around him, hugs him to his chest, and kisses the dusty cheeks of that swineherd. "Father," the son begins, "I have sinned against heaven and against you. I am no longer worthy to be called your son."

The father will not hear more. Turning back to the house with his arm around his son, he calls to the servants, "Quick! Bring the best robe and put it on him. Put a ring on his finger and sandals on his feet. Bring the fattened calf and kill it. Let's have a feast and celebrate. For this son of mine was dead and is alive again; he was lost and is found" (vv. 22–24).

So full and free is the forgiveness of the father that he will have no delay in restoring to his son the symbols of his status. The best robe is a symbol of honor; the signet ring bears the father's seal; even sandals carry meaning—servants went barefoot. And then the feast! What a welcome!

Where is the father's prudence? Didn't the younger son disgrace his name? What has the man been doing? What of those rumors? What does he expect now? More money?

No, the father does not arraign his son with questions; he welcomes him in the triumph of joy. His son was dead and is alive, was lost and is found. The father's joy is kindled by the fire of his love. Scripture often pictures the love of a father: Abraham taking his beloved son, Isaac, up Mount Moriah. Must he, indeed, offer him up in sacrifice there?

Old Israel had been shown the bloodstained coat of Joseph, his favorite son, and had given him up for dead, the prey of some wild beast. Then he learned that Joseph, sold as a slave by his brothers, was a prince in Egypt. He went down to Egypt and was met on the way by Joseph. His son, whom in his grief he had counted to be dead, was alive in his arms.

King David was a poor father, by turns too strict and too indulgent, but he loved his rebellious son Absalom desperately. When the great battle was fought between the forces of David and Absalom, the king seemed less concerned about the outcome than about the safety of his son. When a messenger of victory confirmed that Absalom was dead,

David wept, "O my son Absalom! My son, my son Absalom! If only I had died instead of you—O Absalom, my son, my son!" (2 Sam. 18:33).

Yet the greatest cry of a father's love in the Old Testament comes not from David, but from his God. The Lord had owned the people of Israel as his son in Egypt. His demand to Pharaoh was, "Let my son go, so he may worship me" (Exod. 4:23). The Lord guided his firstborn son through the desert, as a father might teach an infant son to walk. When Israel became a rebellious son, God pronounced his judgments on his apostasy. Yet with a heart of love he cried out,

> "How can I give you up, Ephraim?
> How can I hand you over, Israel? . . .
> My heart is changed within me;
> all my compassion is aroused." [Hos. 11:8]

Jesus knows the God of the fathers, the God of the prophets; indeed, he knows the heart of his Father, the joy of his Father's grace.

### The Demand of the Father's Welcome

The scene shifts. We are out in the field as the furrows fall into shadow. The older brother is coming in from his work. As he nears the house, he listens and looks up. Yes, it's music, the music of a band playing. The house is blazing with light. There is singing, dancing; the whole hilltop is rocking. He calls to one of the hands. "What," he asks, "is going on up there?"

We have the feeling that he knows very well what is going on. There hasn't been a party like that since his brother left home! The servant answers, "Your brother has come, . . . and your father has killed the fattened calf because he has him back safe and sound" (v. 27).

The older brother flings down his staff, folds his arms, and begins a slow burn. A celebration, indeed! He's not too surprised that the prodigal has shown up, but what has he done to deserve this? He should be flogged rather than feted! He is disgusted at his father's behavior. At least he can't expect me to celebrate, he thinks. After all, the property has been divided, and what remains is mine: the best robe, the signet ring, and most particularly that sleek calf saved for a great feast.

He despises the father's joy, is made furious by his grace, and resents his love for the prodigal.

The servant takes the news to the father. His older son is stalking about in the field, furiously angry, and refuses to come in to the feast. The father quickly leaves the feast; he goes down the path the second time to call his older son home. Clearly the older brother in the story images the Pharisees, Jesus' self-righteous opponents. In the preceding chapter of Luke another parable issues a stern warning to them. They are like guests who refuse an invitation to a banquet. The offended host sends his servant to bring in other guests from the streets and alleys of the town and from the highways and byways of the country. Every seat will be filled with the poor, the crippled, the blind, and the lame. There will be no room any longer for the invited guests.

It is the Pharisees who despise the poor and who disdain Christ's call to the feast of the kingdom. They are warned that others will be seated at heaven's feast, and they will find themselves forever excluded. But in this parable, Jesus still holds the door open for the Pharisees. They are standing outside, furious because Jesus is celebrating with publicans and sinners. But Jesus says the Father still comes down the path to call to them. Let them consider what it means if they reject his call, if they refuse to come in to the feast of glory.

The father pleads with his older son to come in to the banquet. He receives a bitter response: "Look! All these years I've been slaving for you and never disobeyed your orders. Yet you never gave me even a young goat so I could celebrate with my friends. But when this son of yours who has squandered your property with prostitutes comes home, you kill the fattened calf for him!" (vv. 29–30).

That bitter son is farther from home there in the field than the prodigal was in the pigpen. He has no love for his father. Keeping his father's orders is drudgery; working for him is slavery. His real pleasure is not with his father. Like the prodigal at the beginning of the story, he would prefer celebrations with his own friends. He has no conception of his father's love—for his brother, or for him. He has no love for his brother, either. He will not call him "my brother" but only "this son of yours."

His father's rebuke is gentle: "My son, . . . you are always with me, and everything I have is yours. But we had to celebrate and be glad, because this brother of yours was dead and is alive again; he was lost and is found" (vv. 31–32).

The tenderness is there. Did it mean nothing to the older son that he was ever with the father? Was his relation with his father really that of a slave? Did he begrudge a fattened calf when the whole inheritance was his? Did he care nothing that his brother was not dead but alive?

Yes, the rebuke is tender, but the demand is clear. If he is indeed a true son of the father, he must come in to the feast. He cannot remain there in the outer darkness, burning with anger and jealous rage.

Suppose the older brother had indeed known his father's heart. What would he have done? Surely he would have come running into the house when he was told that his brother had returned. Might he have done more? Well, if he had really shared his father's feelings, he, too, would have been looking for his brother. Perhaps, being already out in the field, he might have seen him first and gone running to meet him. Could he have done more?

During the war in Vietnam, Army Lieutenant Daniel Dawson's reconnaissance plane went down over the Vietcong jungle. When his brother, Donald Dawson, heard the report, he sold everything he had, left his wife with twenty dollars, and bought passage to Vietnam. There he equipped himself with a soldier's gear and wandered through the guerilla-controlled jungle, looking for his brother. He carried leaflets picturing the plane and describing in Vietnamese the reward for news of the missing pilot. He became known as "Anh toi phi-cong"—the brother of the pilot. A *Life* magazine reporter described his perilous search.[2]

Yes, the older brother could have done more. If he had really cared, he could have done what Donald Dawson did. He could have gone to the far country, looking for his brother. Indeed, this is not an idle suggestion, for it is at the heart of the parable. This parable is one of three that Jesus told, all recorded in Luke 15, and all in response to the bitter criticism of Jesus by the Pharisees and teachers of the law. Jesus was surrounded by tax collectors and sinners, eager to hear his teaching. The Pharisees muttered, "This man welcomes sinners and eats with them" (v. 2).

Jesus replied with the parable of the lost sheep, the lost coin, and the lost son. Each story ends with a joyful feast to celebrate the finding of what had been lost. The shepherd calls his friends to a party because he has found his sheep; the woman invites her friends because she has found her lost coin. The father celebrates the recovery of his lost son, and calls the older brother to join in the joy. Jesus is teaching that there is joy in heaven over one sinner who repents. But he is also contrasting his ministry with the attitude of his critics. They complain because he associates with sinners. He replies that he seeks sinners because his Father does. Jesus is pictured in the shepherd who seeks the one sheep that is lost. He is prefigured, too, in the woman who sweeps her house to find the coin that was lost. Jesus does not appear, however, in the parable of the prodigal son. Instead, he steps out of the story and puts in his place the figure of the Pharisee. The older brother is doing just what they were doing: refusing to associate with sinners. Jesus is doing the opposite. He understands his Father's heart of mercy. He is not only willing to go in with sinners to heaven's feast; far more, he has come to look for sinners where they are. He has come to seek and to save that which is lost. He seeks out tax collectors, stops under the sycamore-fig tree to call Zacchaeus down, and invites himself to his house. He finds a fallen woman by a well in Samaria, and speaks forgiveness to a murderer crucified with him.

We do not understand this parable if we forget who told it, and why. Jesus Christ is our older Brother, the Firstborn of the Father. He is the

2. "A Haunted Man's Perilous Search," *Life*, vol. 58, no. 10, March 12, 1965.

seeking Shepherd who goes out to find the lost; he is the Resurrection and the Life who can give life to the dead; he is the Heir of the Father's house. To him the Father can truly say, "Son, all that I have is yours." He who is the son became a servant that we might be made the sons and daughters of God. This parable is incomplete if we forget that our older brother is not a Pharisee but Jesus. He does not merely welcome us home as the brother did not; he comes to find us in the pigpen, puts his arms around us, and says, "Come home!"

Indeed, if we forget Jesus, we do not grasp the full measure of the Father's love. The heavenly Father is not permissive toward sin. He is a holy God; the penalty of sin must be paid. The glory of amazing grace is that Jesus can welcome sinners because he died for them. Jesus not only comes to the feast eating with redeemed publicans and sinners; he spreads the feast, for he calls us to the table of his broken body and shed blood.

The author of Hebrews reminds us that Jesus sings God's praise in the midst of his brethren.[3] The joy of heaven's feast is already anticipated in the fellowship of the singing Savior. Jesus knows his Father's heart and rejoices with him. Full of joy through the Holy Spirit, Jesus said, "I praise you, Father, Lord of heaven and earth, because you have hidden these things from the wise and learned, and revealed them to little children. Yes, Father, for this was your good pleasure" (Luke 10:21).

Come home to the Father's love, to the joy of Jesus' feast. Are you a prodigal, far from the gate of heaven? It is Jesus who now comes to lift you up. Are you a smug Pharisee, flaunting the filthy rags of your self-righteousness outside the Father's house? Hear the words of Jesus: his Father calls you to repent and come home as a little child. Or are you somehow both at once: prodigal and proud, debased but despising? No matter; cast all away and hold fast to Jesus.

Or are you a believer? Has Jesus found you like the lost sheep and borne you home on his shoulder? Then consider the demand this parable puts on you. You have tasted of heaven's grace. You know the embrace of your Father's love. You know that he rejoices over you with singing. What does heaven's joy, his joy, over lost sinners mean to you?

You say, "It means that I, too, must welcome sinners, be ready to eat with them, even as I have been brought to his table." Is that enough? The true Son, who knows his Father's heart, did not simply share with sinners his robe, his ring, his sandals. He went to find them to bring them home. Where will you look today?

"Whoever does not love does not know God, because God is love" (1 John 4:8).

---

3. Hebrews 2:12. Not only is the cry of abandonment at the beginning of Psalm 22 fulfilled by Jesus; the cry of victory in verse 22 of that psalm is also his. The author of Hebrews ascribes it to him in this passage.

# 5

## Sinclair B. Ferguson

Ordained in the Church of Scotland, Sinclair B. Ferguson enjoyed successful pastoral and teaching ministries in Scotland before joining the faculty of Westminster Theological Seminary as professor of systematic theology in 1982. He has written *A Heart for God, John Owen on the Christian Life, Kingdom Life in a Fallen World,* and *Know Your Christian Life,* and has edited the *New Dictionary of Theology* and *Pulpit and People.* He earned his Ph.D. degree from the University of Aberdeen.

# Communion with God through Preaching

It is one of my convictions that the less a preacher says about himself, the better! I would be grieved, therefore, if these pages were read as anything more than the reflections and method of one who is more anxious to learn from his fellow preachers than to teach them. I write out of the general context of the Scottish Presbyterian tradition, and the emergence in it in recent decades of a return to biblical and expository, frequently systematic, preaching.[1]

1. For an analysis of some of the characteristics of this school, by Professor Douglas Kelly of Reformed Theological Seminary, see "The Recovery of Christian Realism in the Scottish Expository Ministry Movement," in *Pulpit and People,* ed. Nigel Cameron and Sinclair B. Ferguson (Edinburgh: Rutherford House, 1986), 17–28.

One's philosophy of preaching will inevitably be influenced by one's view of Scripture in general, and in particular by one's understanding of the biblical doctrine of preaching. In relation to the latter, my own thinking has been molded by two leading principles.

The first principle is the inspiration of the *whole* of Scripture. If "all Scripture is God-breathed and is useful . . ." (2 Tim. 3:16), it follows that all Scripture is relevant to preaching and, indeed, preachable. No pastor can dodge his responsibility to ransack the whole of Scripture and expound it in its entirety.

My own experience is that some form of systematic treatment of the books of Scripture, in a balanced diet of books and themes, instruction and application, is beneficial to both pastor and people. It certainly has the merit of exposing both preacher and people to the whole of biblical teaching, as well as imposing disciplines of study and of instruction. I am not convinced that lengthy series are necessary or helpful. But flexibility is important—especially flexibility to the work of the Spirit!

The second principle concerns the practical impact of preaching. It is striking that Paul's statements about the usefulness of Scripture for equipping the man of God for service (teaching, rebuking, correcting [2 Tim. 3:16]) lead him immediately to speak about the work of the ministry in terms that indicate the connection between what Scripture is for and what preaching does ("Preach the Word; . . . correct, rebuke . . . careful instruction" [2 Tim. 4:2]). The Spirit's Word has a gracious, sanctifying purpose—to cleanse the mind, touch the conscience, purify the heart, sharpen our consecration, cleanse and heal the wounded spirit, and conform us to the image of Christ. In preaching especially, the Word of God is the Spirit's sword. It reaches the heart.

For this reason, preaching must be thought of as more than instruction. The preacher is not acting as a lecturer who sees his task as the impartation of information to the mind. He is a pastor, who is personally engaged in his hearers' lives; he sees his task as feeding, nourishing, strengthening, warning, and in every way seeking their hearts.

In my own experience as a hearer, there is nothing more mysterious or wonderful than the fact that in preaching, Christ himself speaks (cf. Rom. 10:14; John 10:4, 14). Nothing can compare with knowing that Christ has reached your heart and by the pressure of his word on your spirit is dealing with you. The goal of preaching, then, is nothing less than communion with God.

Even if one is committed to some form of systematic preaching from Scripture, choices must be made about each book, and within each book about each segment. This itself involves answering the question central to the preaching itself: How best can I bring God's Word and these people together? The contents and balance of Scripture will need to be related to the situation and needs of a given congregation.

I have elsewhere outlined what I see to be the essential elements involved in the preparation of sermons.[2] Here I would like to develop them in a more personal way.

*Selecting.* The major principle for selecting the preaching segment is conformity with the unity of thought in Scripture itself. The segment chosen should not be so long that properly expounding it will contravene this principle so that virtually two or more different thrusts are involved. Nor should the segment be so short that expounding it contravenes the meaning of the text in its context.

*Understanding.* I cannot expound what I do not understand. At its lowest level, the sermon must explain what Scripture says—not merely repeat it, or develop a word association from it, or respond emotionally to it, or even immediately apply it. The Levites of Nehemiah's day provide us with a great biblical example: "They read from the Book of the Law of God, making it clear *and giving the meaning so that the people could understand what was being read"* (Neh. 8:8, emphasis added).

Why is this so important? Because the Word of God misunderstood is not the Word of God but the word of man. Proper hermeneutical principles are vital for another reason also: most Christians read their Bible in the same way that their pastors preach from it. Our people take their hermeneutics instruction from us every time we preach. Instinctively and intuitively they imbibe the approach to which they are exposed week after week. If people sit regularly under a ministry where the Scriptures are mishandled, they will have great obstacles to overcome in order rightly to handle it themselves.

At this point one will reach for one's basic exegetical tools. Here, I think, we must allow for variation of intellectual ability, training, and even personal disposition. My own preference is *not* to reach for my commentaries immediately, unless I find my mental processes in need of the exegetical equivalent of electric shock treatment. I have often found great stimulus in doing the basic spadework myself, using my linguistic abilities and tools (however limited), working with my lexical aids, doing a little concordance work. If we are amateurs rather than professional linguists, we need to beware of the temptation to mishandle language and of the "concordance mentality."[3]

My own practice is to fill a blank page with random jottings of the information I glean from my study. To employ a culinary metaphor, these are the ingredients in the recipe, but they are not set down in the order in which they are to be used; nor are they the cake!

---

2. In *The Preacher and Preaching,* ed. Samuel T. Logan, Jr. (Phillipsburg, N.J.: Presbyterian and Reformed, 1986), 192–211.

3. I commend as a healthy antidote to common homiletical diseases in this area, Moises Silva, *Biblical Words and Their Meaning: An Introduction to Lexical Semantics* (Grand Rapids: Zondervan, 1986).

At this stage, my question is *theoretical* only: What do these words signify? Why is this passage in this context? What is the flow of thought? Is there a nuance of meaning here? What is the function of this section? Having tossed these questions around as I have worked with the text, I will sometimes reach for the commentaries for correction of my own exegetical work, if necessary; for further exegetical information; and for stimulation to further thought. Here a good commentary can act on one's mind like seasoning in food—drawing out and enriching the preparatory work one has already done. I find that some commentaries are helpful only linguistically, while others (not necessarily those with whose authors I am in greatest doctrinal sympathy) stimulate the juices of my own mind. It is always good to have at least one of each kind!

*Crystalizing.* I mentioned that in the second element of preparation, my aim is "*theoretical* only," understanding the text. But I do not think of these elements as necessarily chronologically distinct. Since the entire exercise of preparation has the preparation of a message in view, inevitably while working with exegetical material on one blank sheet, I will also be jotting down strands of thought (often isolated in a circle, and "arrowed" to the exegetical material). These materials will eventually provide structure, illustration, and application.

What I mean by crystalizing is that during and after my exegetical work, I am searching (or better, listening) for the big idea, or burden, or thrust of the passage—the principle that will give the entire message unity and coherence, as well as energy. Here a picture sometimes comes into my mind: of a dog with a bone chewing and sucking the nourishment out of it.

When I have ministered in an extended way to a congregation, I have found it valuable to read over my next preaching segment(s) at the end of the previous Sunday. I have found it helpful in the process of crystalizing the message to live with the passage during the week, in the hope that it will become more and more a part of me as I deliver it. Here another picture is more appropriate—that of placing a peppermint under one's tongue and enjoying the flavor over an extended period of time!

*Structuralizing.* While working on the thrust of the message, I am also working in a preliminary way on the presentation or structure. But now this must be focused: How will the message from the passage be most effectively (clearly, grippingly) communicated (explained, illustrated, applied) to this congregation? Each of these factors (message, passage, congregation) is relevant to structuring the message effectively with a view to its communication. The context in which the sermon is preached does not determine the meaning of the passage, but it does influence the manner of its communication. Here, again, on yet another sheet of paper, I work on various outlines.

Another metaphor describes my psychological process—that of the potter and the clay. I want to allow the material to "take shape" in my hands in a way that is appropriate to this particular "raw material," but also in a way that is appropriate to the consumer. In this context the preacher also works as the image of the God who created a world-mass that was without form and void, and then in a further stage of activity (the six days) gave it both order and beauty. Sometimes it is at this point that I realize that there are really two or more messages in the work already done. (It is also my experience that further development of thought sometimes emerges only during or after the preaching of the message!) At this stage, what has been provisional in my mind is now becoming more like the final form of the sermon itself.

Our Lord seems to have employed different kinds of structures in his preaching. The Sermon on the Mount, the parables, the Olivet Discourse, the Farewell Discourse all have different structures. Perhaps we should learn from this that we should ourselves avoid getting into a certain rut in the way we structure our messages. The structure should present a unified theme, because this is what gives the content of the sermon its energy and impact. Each element in the structure (whether we make separate points or headings, or build up the sermon like a pyramid) should be consistent with the theme and a development of it. And, of course, the message should move inexorably towards a climax, the equivalent of our Lord's pithy conclusions at the end of the parables or the Sermon on the Mount.

People used to speak of Alexander Maclaren's "golden hammer" with which he would "tap" his text and watch it fall into appropriate divisions. I have no such golden hammer. But the picture is a helpful one. For at this stage I often take a fresh sheet of paper and, almost doodle-like, cover it in possible divisions for the message until I am satisfied that the one that fits has emerged. By this stage, of course, I have already tried to do some hard work, and if the raw materials do not throw up an outline despite all my efforts, I usually gather my worksheets together and turn my attention to some other activity, returning briefly to the sermon at the end of the morning, or perhaps in some spare moments later in the day. Often I find that living with the material a little longer is more productive than staring any longer at the unformed mass. Indeed, quite often a great deal of my preparation will be done in short bursts like this. Here is another area of the preacher's work where I think there are no universal rules, and we need to learn individually how we best function.

*Concretizing.* This final element of preliminary preparation involves bringing together the horizon of the text with the horizon of our situation; it is a matter of bringing the Word of God to bear here (rather than there), now (rather than then). The crystalized message, now given structure, is like a skeleton. It must be given the flesh and bones of the context in which it is to be delivered. This means shaping and coloring the material so that it may be a weighty hammer, or a sharp sword, or a refreshing drink, or an attractive and desirable present to those who will hear.

At this stage I focus on three questions. (1) How can I best put on display the central message of the passage or text? (2) Are there illustrations that will help me to do this? (3) In what ways is the teaching of this passage to be applied to our lives today?

Here again 2 Timothy 3:15–4:5 helps us. All Scripture is useful for teaching, rebuking, correcting, and equipping God's people. In the seasoned preacher I imagine there is an instinctive use of these categories. But a good exercise for beginning preachers (in which category I cheerfully include myself!) is to take a fresh worksheet, line it off into four squares headed doctrine; rebuke; correction, or restoration; and equipping. Then simply fill in the blanks under each heading from the preaching segment. The great virtue of such an exercise is that it becomes immediately obvious that the passage itself contains an abundance of material.

The exercise can also bear some surprising fruit. Assume, for example, that we are preaching through Colossians and have reached chapter 3. We have dealt with the great theme of union with Christ (vv. 1–4), and its implications in the putting off of the old man with his deeds and the putting on of the new (vv. 5–9, vv. 10–11). We have come to the exhortation in verse 12: "Therefore, as God's chosen people, holy and dearly loved, clothe yourselves with compassion, kindness, humility, gentleness and patience . . ." Under "equipping," we have material here describing the quality of Christian life that bears fruit. Under "rebuke," we recognize how little these qualities are evident in the church. Under "correction," we see that these are the marks of the life of the new man in Christ; these are the marks of family likeness that we find illustrated in Jesus. His Spirit is given to us to produce these effects.

But what about "doctrine"? Here, perhaps, is our biggest surprise. For Paul sees these things as the fruit of God's election. We are to live this way specifically because we are "God's chosen people." Immediately, further expository riches are available to us. Why does this doctrine produce this effect? Again, doesn't the fact that election is the root of such a lifestyle put a new complexion on the doctrine of election? Again, the rebuke of this passage is deepened: have I used the idea of election only in controversial discussions, and not recognized that it is meant to humble me, make me patient and gentle? Again, as this text breaks open, I see that in the last analysis it is simply urging me to be like Christ. He was the elect of God, holy and dearly loved. Because of that he was compassionate, kind, humble, gentle, patient. Holiness in him was not harshness, but graciousness. There is doctrine, rebuke, correction, and equipping all in one!

Of course, this material needs to be organized and locally applied. Often we need to show how general principles of application are to be particularized in our lives. But the point is that in applying the biblical principle (2 Tim. 3:15ff.) of using Scripture, we discover an almost embarrassing richness of material.

Only in this context do I normally contemplate extrabiblical material in the form of illustrations, brief quotations, and the like. There is an abundance of such material in Scripture, and I think a good case can be made out for the importance of using it. All preachers can do this. Not all preachers are themselves gifted illustrators, but God has provided us with a thesaurus of sermon illustrations in his Word! Nevertheless, a judicious use of an illustration or a striking quotation can do a great deal to put into the memory of our hearers a velcro strip, on which the substance of the sermon will stick!

I use personal illustrations sparingly, and I think we should shun illustrating biblical truth in such a way that we ourselves ever become the focus of attention. The same applies to illustrations of personal Christian experience. What is done in secret should be kept secret, said Jesus (Matt. 6:1–8). Behind a number of pulpits in my native Scotland, the words of James Denney are inscribed alongside the biblical text "Sir, we would see Jesus" (John 12:21 KJV): "No man can at one and the same time show that he himself is wise and that Christ is mighty to save." We should inscribe these words on our hearts.

In theory, I leave the conclusion and the introduction (in that order) to the final stage of preparing the material. But these elements, too, may have been clarified for me much earlier in the preliminary study. At this stage, however, I will want to make sure that the introduction really does introduce what is going to be said, and that the conclusion really does arise from the heart of the message and forms a fitting climax to it, in the way it displays the Lord himself and/or in the way it strikes home to the heart.

My own practice is not to write out my sermons. If I did, this would be the stage at which to do it. Again, individuals differ here, and at times I have worked through a sermon in verbal detail. But at the end of my preparation I do produce a careful synopsis of the message—written or typed in such a way that there is still room for further annotations. Depending partly on my own frame of mind, I will produce a final outline the night before, or immediately before, preaching—or alternatively, preach without visual use of the outline. If the structure of my message is logical and coherent, the difference in preparation is simply that of an extra stage in which I mentally review the headings, subpoints, introduction, and conclusion of the message. I do that either on my feet, walking, or on my knees, but rarely at my desk! My own experience is that preaching without notes of any kind can be an exceedingly liberating experience. That does not make it any more spiritual to preach without notes than with them; nor does it make our preaching better than anyone else's. It may, however, make our preaching fresher and more personal.

I have said nothing so far about prayer. We know that prayer is vital, although, like so many others, I am deeply aware that here I fail so badly. In a striking phrase, Luke tells us that the apostles gave themselves "to prayer and the ministry of the word" (Acts 6:4—how significant is the order?).

From another point of view, however, everything I have said is simply a description of the external form and activity of a prayerful spirit. For me, it is of primary importance that all my preparation be done in the context of a praying spirit, in a more or less conscious sense of looking to the Lord and depending on the grace of his illuminating and enlivening Spirit. This is punctuated by specific ejaculations and periods of petition for both exposition and application of the Word. It is not my constant practice, but I have on occasion prayed through the sermon virtually line by line, seeking special grace for elements in the message that may be difficult to understand, or for applications that may be painful. Sometimes one rejoices, or is pained, because of the specific application a message may have to particular people, and will pray for application in their case.

When I think of what happens during preaching, my mental picture is of Christ calling his sheep by name and of them recognizing his voice as he speaks to them individually and focuses his attention on their specific needs. Or, to use a picture from John Owen, I think of the Spirit moving among the people, giving to each a parcel of identical shape, size, and wrapping (the sermon); but as each opens it, the gift inside is specially appropriate to each hearer. My prayer, therefore, is that my material may be in harmony with his purpose and my spirit sensitive to his gracious character, so that I may not distort him in my words or by my spirit.

Some of the most treasured moments I have experienced as a listener have been when God's Word has penetrated so deeply into the inner recesses of my heart that unconfessed and sometimes unrecognized sin has been brought to the surface, confessed, and forgiven; or when Christ the divine physician and diagnostician has put his finger on some inner hurt or twist and cleansed, straightened, and cured it. This is what always accompanies being brought into the presence of God by his Word. This is what I want for my hearers more than anything else. God's Word reaches and nourishes the whole man, not merely the mind. But, because it reaches the whole man through the mind, prayer (before and during preaching) for unction, and diligent mental preparation must not be thought of as alternatives. Together they form the heart of the apostolic pattern for the preaching ministry.

Having already extended these personal reflections, I must conclude them with a final observation. It took me a little while as a preacher to appreciate the significance of the fact that God's Word is a two-edged sword. It wounds the listener, in order to heal him; but it also wounds the preacher. I believe this is the ultimate explanation for many of the mysterious experiences we have in preaching. At times we are elated, yet the people seem not to share that elation. At other times, even while we speak we are inwardly weeping over our failures, and confessing "I am a man of unclean lips." Yet so often we discover that on such occasions God spoke with great grace and power. No one else knew what we were going through (except perhaps a fellow preacher who recognized some of the telltale signs!). Or, more accurately, no one beside the Lord. He knew, because he was speaking to us through his Word, as well as through us to others. In this intimate way, the Lord teaches us that while ours is the responsibility rightly to handle the Word of God in preparation and exposition, yet it remains the Spirit's sword, and not ours.

The Spirit works sovereignly, like the blowing of the wind. At the end of the day, for our own blessing as well as that of others, we must place all our preparation in his hands, for the fulfilling of his purposes in us, as well as through us. In this sense, too, those who preach the gospel live (spiritually) by the gospel they preach.

# The Death of Sin—The Way to Life

Therefore, there is now no condemnation for those who are in Christ Jesus, because through Christ Jesus the law of the Spirit of life set me free from the law of sin and death. For what the law was powerless to do in that it was weakened by the sinful nature, God did by sending his own Son in the likeness of sinful man to be a sin offering. And so he condemned sin in sinful man, in order that the righteous requirements of the law might be fully met in us, who do not live according to the sinful nature but according to the Spirit.

Those who live according to the sinful nature have their minds set on what that nature desires; but those who live in accordance with the Spirit have their minds set on what the Spirit desires. The mind of sinful man is death, but the mind controlled by the Spirit is life and peace; the sinful mind is hostile to God. It does not submit to God's law, nor can it do so. Those controlled by the sinful nature cannot please God.

You, however, are controlled not by the sinful nature but by the Spirit, if the Spirit of God lives in you. And if anyone does not have the Spirit of Christ, he does not belong to Christ. But if Christ is in you, your body is dead because of sin, yet your spirit is alive because of righteousness. And if the Spirit of him who raised Jesus from the dead is living in you, he who raised Christ from the dead will also give life to your mortal bodies through his Spirit, who lives in you.

Therefore, brothers, we have an obligation—but it is not to the sinful nature, to live according to it. For if you live according to the sinful nature, you will die; but if by the Spirit you put to death the misdeeds of the body, you will live, because those who are led by the Spirit of God are sons of God. For you did not receive a spirit that makes you a slave again to fear, but you received the Spirit of sonship. And by him we cry, "*Abba,* Father." The Spirit himself testifies with our spirit that we are God's children. Now if we are children then we are heirs—heirs of God and co-heirs with Christ, if indeed

we share in his sufferings in order that we may also share in his
glory. [Rom. 8:1–17 NIV]

Have you ever heard people speaking about "getting out of Romans 7
and into Romans 8"? They usually mean something like this: Romans
chapter 7 depicts a Christian who is struggling with sin and failure;
Romans chapter 8 describes the Christian who is filled with the Spirit
and no longer experiences that old conflict. When we are filled with the
Spirit, it is claimed, we no longer live "in Romans 7," but victoriously
"in Romans 8." All of us, naturally, are attracted to a life of that kind of
victory!

Sometimes the same thing is described in the language of Romans
chapter 6, which speaks about Christians being "set free from sin":

> Buried with Christ and raised with him too,
> What is there left for me to do?
> Simply to cease from struggling and strife;
> Simply to walk in newness of life.
> Glory be to God!*

There is one major problem with this description of victorious
Christian living. It does not take account of what Paul actually says in
Romans 8. He speaks about Christians "groaning" because of their deep
longing to be set free once and for all from the struggle and battles of
their present experience (v. 23). And these are the very people who are
both led by and filled with the Spirit!

The truth is that struggle and strife in the Christian's life have not yet
ended. Until they do, Paul provides a rule, or principle, that needs to be
engraved on all of our memories and written on all of our hearts.

What is it? "If you live according to the sinful nature [flesh], you will
die; *but if by the Spirit you put to death the misdeeds of the body, you will live,*
because those who are led by the Spirit of God are sons of God" (Rom.
8:13–14, emphasis added). Essential to truly successful Christian living,
to what Scripture calls "holiness," is what our forefathers called "the
mortification of sin," putting to death the misdeeds of the flesh.

If we are honest, there are two things we should probably admit
immediately. First, our failure to deal with our own sin; and second,
how poorly equipped we feel we are to do so. Many of us have heard
thousands of sermons, gone faithfully to Sunday school, and read
Christian literature throughout our lives. Yet how little serious thought
most of us have given to this fundamental issue in our Christian lives:
"What steps can I take to overcome my sin?" Too frequently we have

---

*T. Ryder, "Buried with Christ," in *Favorite Hymns of Praise* (Chicago: Tabernacle, 1967),
318.

neglected the theme of the mortification of sin and have harvested the inevitable crop—a life in which the fruit of Christian character is choked by the weeds of too-easily-tolerated sin.

Yet, our Lord Jesus Christ repeatedly emphasized the importance of learning to handle and overcome our sinful tendencies. The commands to "Pluck out!" "Cut off!" "Deny!" were regularly on his lips as an essential part of his teaching. For Jesus, positive thinking about the Christian life was impossible unless there was also negative thinking about sin.

In this passage, Paul echoes both the balance and the content of Christ's teaching when he says, "If you are to live in the Spirit, you must put sin to death by the Spirit." Notice the three central elements in what he says.

## The Mindset

There are certain things Paul assumes in issuing this exhortation.

The first is that we need to deal with sin—"If . . . *you* put to death. . . ." He has already said that the Christian is free from sin (Rom. 6:17). We are no longer its slave; its dominion has been overthrown. But its presence has not yet been abolished. There is still sin in our hearts and minds. As Christians we are the battleground for the conflict between the flesh and the Spirit. Consequently, only those who sense the continuing influence of sin will ever see why mortifying it is so essential.

Sin will not go away of its own accord; we are responsible to put it to death. When we first become Christians the sinful tendencies in our hearts suffer a powerful grace-blow. We may feel as though the reign of sin has not only been overthrown in us, but its very presence completely destroyed.

True, sin is no longer our master (Rom. 6:14). But if we think that its influence has been destroyed, we are self-deceived. "If we claim to be without sin, we deceive ourselves and the truth is not in us" (1 John 1:8). Sinful tendencies remain, insidiously hidden in our minds, our wills, and our emotions. If we do not deal with them, they will dominate us. "Kill sin," said one of the Puritans wisely, "or sin will kill you."

Paul's second assumption is that we are able to deal with sin. He has already said in Romans 6 that because we are in Christ, and under his lordship, we are no longer slaves of sin. Christ's death to sin paid all our obligations to it and brought sin's dominion to an end; righteousness is now our master. We are no longer controlled by the flesh (Rom. 8:9), nor are we under obligation to live in subservience to the desires of the flesh (Rom. 8:12). Instead, we are indwelt by the Spirit of the holy Savior. He has the power to make us holy, too. In dependence on him we can turn away from sin. He points us to Christ and can help us to live in an increasingly Christ-like way. The great body blow has already been dealt to our sin. The great act of mortification took place when we were united to Christ and died to sin's dominion. Only the mopping-up operations are now left. But they can be both prolonged and painful. Dealing with sin is a lifelong battle. It is crucial that we continue it.

These, then, are two things you need to know as you set out on the struggle against sin. You must deal with it (nobody else will handle your struggle against sin for you). Further, you can deal with sin. Christ provides all the strength you need.

But notice that Paul's words contain a third assumption—that you want to deal with your sin. Otherwise there will never be any success.

In the spiritual life we invariably get what we really want. If we want holiness, we will get it; if we want compromise, we already have it in large measure. The issue is: Do you want to bargain with sin? Or do you want to overcome it? Do you want to embrace your sin? Or do you want to strangle it?

Do you have the biblical mindset?

The commands and exhortations in Scripture never stand on their own, as though we were expected to grow in sanctification under our own steam. God is our Father, and like any true caring father, he provides his children with reasons and motives. Sometimes, of course, he says, "It should be motive enough for you to do this simply because I tell you to do it." Then, trusting his loving wisdom and grace, we learn to obey him. So we discover that his word is always wisest and best. But at other times, Scripture provides us with more detailed motives for obedience. That is true here in Romans 8:1–17.

## The Motives

Why, then, should I join in the struggle to overcome indwelling sin? Paul gives us three motives.

Motive number 1: In the Christian life you reap what you sow. If you live in the style of the flesh, you will die; if you live in the style of the Spirit you will live (v. 13). Paul is echoing what he has already said: "The mind of sinful man is death, but the mind controlled by the Spirit is life and peace" (v. 6). There are only two possible character crops: if we sow sinful seed we will reap the fruit of spiritual death; if we sow holy seed, we will reap a harvest of spiritual vitality.

Do you see how marvelously helpful Paul's whole perspective here is? When we experience temptation to sin we invariably find ourselves attracted to a short-term view of things. One of temptation's great weapons is its ability to blind us to the long-term effects of yielding to the sinful desires of the flesh.

Put a small coin near enough to your eye and it can obliterate from sight a check for a million dollars—with your name on it! The cheap coin will become the most valuable thing you can see, and you will be blinded to the fortune that is within your grasp. That is how the sinful tendencies of the flesh deceive and overcome us. We grasp what we desire now; we are blinded to the eventual outcome. We do not see where sin will lead us—into more sin, and eventually into spiritual decay. Nor do we see where obedience and holiness would lead us—into spiritual strength, joy, victory, and peace. We forget that there will always be a harvest.

In the physical realm we reap what we sow; sow calories to our appetite and we reap fat; sow overindulgence in alcohol and we reap both an external and an internal harvest. Exactly the same is true in the spiritual realm:

> Sow a thought, reap an act
> Sow an act, reap a character
> Sow a character, reap a destiny.

Never ask only: Do I want to? Always ask: What will be the ultimate harvest? What will I reap from this? And learn to take the long-term view of holiness.

Motive number 2: Because you belong to God's family. Don't you understand that you have a family obligation? "Those who are led by the Spirit of God [i.e., led to put to death the misdeeds of the body, v. 13] are sons of God" (Rom. 8:14). The implication is obvious: holiness, turning away from sin, denying the lusts of the flesh are all part of the ethos of the family of God. We are God's adopted children. It is no longer appropriate for us to live in the style of the old family, in which self-pleasing and sin were part of the atmosphere.

Paul develops this even further. Not only is there the objective fact that we are children of God, but we have also received the Spirit of sonship (v. 15). The Holy Spirit indwells us. He creates in us a new instinct to be holy because our Father is holy. Turn our backs on this and we are guilty of grieving the Spirit who has sealed us for the day of redemption.

> Think what Spirit dwells within thee,
> What a Father's smile is thine;
> What thy Saviour died to win thee,
> Child of heaven, should'st thou repine?

Of course not!

Motive number 3: Christ died to put away your sin. Perhaps this is the strongest motive of all. It is certainly one that Christians have always found helps them tremendously in their battles with their own particular sins.

The basis for what Paul says in Romans 8 is his teaching in verses 3 and 4. God has done what the law could not do because of our sinful flesh. He sent Christ to condemn sin in the flesh. Why? "In order that the righteous requirements of the law might be fully met in us, who do not live according to the sinful nature but according to the Spirit" (v. 4). Christ died for sin so that you would no longer go on living in sin.

When we experience external temptation to sin, or feel the power of sinful desires from within, we are to resort to the cross of Christ, where that sin was condemned in Christ. We are to say to ourselves, "How can I possibly live to this sin, sow to this flesh, when my Savior died for the specific purpose of delivering me from sin? To do so would be to trample under my feet the blood of the covenant he shed for me."

Do you ever do that? You cannot say that you lack the motives to deal with sin. But perhaps you do lack the motivation—and that indicates you have never caught a glimpse of the harvests of shame and grief, or joy and triumph, which the seeds of sin or of sanctification produce. Your heart must be hard and cold, your need desperate, if these things do not motivate you to deal with your sin.

Even if this were all Paul had said, he would have given us half the equipment we need for the battle. But, in fact, he says more, and this leads us, thirdly, to consider

## The Method

Paul's teaching in Romans 8 is full of important hints to help us answer the questions, "How, then, do I actually go about overcoming my sinful thoughts and tendencies? What are the basic steps I need to take?"

Let us notice, briefly, some of them.

First, *commit yourself to comprehensive holiness.* In the United Kingdom there are two kinds of automobile insurance policies. One is called "third party." It covers damage and injury done only to the third party in an accident—it is insurance that operates to protect the policyholder from liability only for what he may do to others. By contrast, "comprehensive" insurance covers all parties involved.

The mistake some of us are liable to make in dealing with sin is to do so on a "third-party" basis. We try to restrain its effects on other people. So long as we are covered there, we are indifferent to any other effect sin may have. But we can never handle sin that way. We must engage in all-or-nothing opposition to it. This is why Paul says, "Put to death the misdeeds of the flesh" *without exception or reservation.* Not "misdeeds affecting others," or "your most obvious misdeeds" or "at least some of your misdeeds." He means all of the misdeeds of the flesh.

If you have ever gone on a diet, "putting to death" your appetite for food in order to deal with its physical consequences, you will probably understand why Paul's exhortation is so comprehensive! You thought that all you needed to do was to cut down on your intake. But then you discovered that the reasons you overate or nibbled between meals were much more complex. Perhaps your overeating was a compensation for loneliness, or perhaps you were over-tired and it helped you to feel you could keep going—and so on. Soon you realized that it was not merely your calorie intake that needed to be transformed, it was the way you were handling your whole life. You thought you needed a diet; you discovered that what you really needed was a change of lifestyle. This is exactly what we discover when we begin to starve one of our sinful passions. It cannot be isolated; it is simply one expression of the basic perversity of our hearts. If we are to deal successfully with one manifestation of sin, we need to seek grace to deal with every manifestation of sin.

Second, *guard your mind from the things of the flesh and fill it with the things of the Spirit.* I remember as a teenager coming across a striking statement in one of John R. W. Stott's books, "The secret of holiness is in the mind." I have more and more come to appreciate how true this is. What we "mind," or set our minds on, largely determines the purity of our lives. The central battle we fight is the "battle for the mind."

Paul emphasizes this in Romans 8. Living according to the flesh is the product of thinking according to the flesh. Living according to the Spirit is the consequence of thinking in line with the Spirit (v. 5). What you set your mind on determines whether your life is full of peace or full of death.

What then are we to do, in practical terms, to starve sin and to develop a sanctified mind? We must rein in our minds when we find them being drawn to sinful desires, as if by a magnetic field. Positively, we must seek the Spirit's help to focus our minds on Christ, and develop a pattern of thinking in which we refer everything back to our fellowship with him in his death to sin and his new resurrection life to God (Rom. 6:10–11). That is what setting the mind on the Spirit means. Remember the words that had such a transforming effect on Saint Augustine: "Clothe yourselves with the Lord Jesus Christ [a positive mindset], and do not think about how to gratify the desires of the sinful nature [a mortificationary mindset!]" (Rom. 13:14).

Third, *recognize that mortification of sin is not an isolated activity.*

One reason evangelical Christians often have instinctive reservations about "mortification" is that it conjures up pictures of a lonely (and miserable!) monk, sitting in his small cell, beating himself with a whip. But that is far removed from the biblical teaching.

For one thing, such "harsh treatment of the body . . . lack[s] any value in restraining sensual indulgence" (Col. 2:23). It hurts the body, but it cannot heal the mind.

For another, we are not called to deal with sin in isolation. Paul says, "You [plural] are to put to death the misdeeds of the flesh." Obviously, each one of us is to do it. But Paul's words also imply that we should strengthen one another to do it.

What does this mean in practical terms? Simply that our fellowship with other Christians is one of the chief instruments God has given us to overcome sin. Worship, with its sanctifying influence on our spirits, the enlivening of our aspirations, the setting of our mind on things that are above, does this. The preaching of God's Word, feeding us with God's truth, searching our consciences, giving us fresh appreciation of Christ's holiness and grace, promotes it. So, too, do prayer, informal fellowship, and times of mutual encouragement. Presumably this is one reason why James says that in certain contexts we should confess our sins to one another and pray for one another to be healed. Sharing the way in which we have been overcome by sin is often a vital step to overcoming it and reasserting the power of Christ in our lives.

The great masters (evangelical and Reformed) in the teaching of mortification also mention a further principle: Sometimes you will not make much headway in dealing with some sin that seems to have you in its grip until you share your sense of defeat with someone else. But when you do so, you will immediately deal a death blow to it.

Why should that be? Because sin, and the person of Satan behind it, have all the marks of a blackmailer. You know what I mean. You are ashamed of your sin. What would people say if they knew what was in your heart? Where would your Christian standing be if others knew what you were struggling with? And so you not only struggle alone with your sin, but you are driven to despair. You are shamed into breaking openhearted and honest fellowship with others. Secretly you resign yourself to condemnation and defeat. You are really being blackmailed, and you end up doing "secret deals" in order to escape detection. You are held to ransom by your own failures!

Now, clearly it would be a mistake to begin to wash your dirty linen in public. Public confession of that kind should take place only when scandalous public offense has been caused by our sin and the name of Christ and his people have been publicly besmirched and should be publicly cleansed. But can you not find some Christian brother or sister you believe may understand your need, privately share your failure, and ask him or her for prayer?

Confession of sin will have two immediate effects. It will break the spell that has brought you into such spiritual bondage; it will bring release. And, beyond that, it will open the channel to the encouragement, counsel, and accountability of others—from which you have dangerously isolated yourself.

Never forget: there is no temptation you alone experience. We have been brought into fellowship in order to help one another grow in holiness.

Fourth, *deal immediately and radically with your sin.* Perhaps the most obvious of all the things Paul says here is that when it comes to handling sin, compromise is fatal. Since sin enfolds itself in our very being—our mind, will, emotions—our only hope is definite, immediate, and radical rejection. That is why this exhortation is short and sharp: "Put to death the misdeeds of the flesh! Kill them!" As soon as we are conscious of thoughts and desires that are unholy, we must reject them, starve them to death, and seek to replace them with holy thoughts and desires.

Of course, this is neither pleasant nor easy. But what has become of our view of the Christian life if we regard this teaching as extreme or medieval? It was *Jesus* who said, "Deny yourself, take up the cross, pluck out the offending eye, cut off the offending hand!" If we really love him, we will do what he commands. Mortification is for lovers of Christ! Those who are Christ's have crucified the flesh with its passions and desires (Gal. 5:24).This is what it means to live by the Spirit and keep in step with the Spirit (Gal. 5:25)!

These, then, are the principles of Paul's teaching: the mindset we are to have, the motives Scripture provides, the method that God has given us for dealing with sin. Of course, these are only the general principles. They need to be worked out individually and applied in detail, if we are to deal with the "sins that so easily prevail."

Perhaps in your case there is some specific sin with which you need to deal. You have struggled with it off and on; you have made little real progress; you may have begun to despair, or what in some ways is worse, you may have a level of toleration of it. Let these words be rewritten by the Holy Spirit on your mind, memory, and conscience—as though engraved with a pen of steel: If you live to the flesh, you will die spiritually; but if you live in the Spirit, putting to death the misdeeds of the flesh, you will live, now and eternally.

Never take the short-term view. Think about the implications; consider the harvest. Remember that mortification is for lovers of Christ! Live for him, and through the Spirit's help put sin to death.

> One thing I of the Lord desire—
> For all my way hath miry been—
> Be it by water or by fire,
> O make me clean!
>
> I watch to shun the miry way,
> And stanch the spring of guilty thought;

But watch and wrestle as I may,
Pure I am not.

So wash Thou me without, within,
Or purge with fire, if that must be,—
No matter how, if only sin
Die out in me.*

*Walter Chalmers Smith, "One Thing I of the Lord Desire," in *The Church Hymnary*, rev. ed. (London: Oxford University Press, 1927), 461.

# 6

## Leighton Frederick Sandys Ford

After earning his M.Div. from Columbia Theological Seminary, Leighton Frederick Sandys Ford became the associate evangelist and vice president of the Billy Graham Evangelistic Association, a position he held for more than thirty years. In 1986 he founded the Leighton Ford Ministries.

Ford has authored six books, including *The Christian Persuader, One Way to Change the World, New Man . . . New World,* and *Good News Is for Sharing. Time* magazine identified Ford as "among the most influential preachers of an 'active gospel.'" He received his LL.D. from Gordon College and his D.D. from Houghton College.

# Jotting, to Outlining, to Preaching

Preaching has had a deep impact on my life from boyhood. When I was very small my adopted mother took me to hear great preachers. As a boy at the Canadian Keswick Bible Conference, I was deeply impressed with the preaching of J. Sidlow Baxter, a contributor to this volume. Through my involvement in the early days of Youth for Christ, I first heard the preaching that riveted my imagination and set my life's course.

Billy Graham has had the greatest impact on my life and preaching. His dramatic, urgent, fiery sermons to the youth at Winona Lake, Indiana, and other Youth for Christ rallies and his obvious gift from God in extending an invitation riveted me.

Bob Pierce, the founder of World Vision, also made a deep impression on me in the late 1940s by the pathos of his description of the suffering orphans of Korea. During seminary days I was deeply impressed with the craftsmanship of James Stewart of Edinburgh, and the way he could take Scripture and make it burst with great imagination in the minds of his hearers. Joe Blinco, an English Methodist, who joined the Graham team the same year I did, deeply influenced me through his use of humorous stories which provided the backbone of his messages, and by the sheer reality of his presentation. The clarity of John Stott in opening up a topic or a Scripture until one felt it was the only way to do so, and the fullness and logic of Harold John Ockenga's content, impressed me. I can remember hearing Canon Bryan Green, the Anglican evangelist, speak to overflow crowds at the cathedral in Montreal, and noting his conversational style, his popular apologetics, and his appeal for a verdict at after-meetings in which inquirers remained behind.

Later, I learned from outstanding black preachers like E. V. Hill and Harold Carter that three or four neat, logical points are not the only way to preach—or perhaps even the best way today. Through these and others I have learned that God communicates his truth through many different styles of preaching.

As I wrote this essay I was in Australia holding an evangelistic celebration. I decided to use a new message prepared and preached there as a sample of my preaching, and to guide you on a step-by-step walk-through of my preparation of this sermon.

On the way to Australia I was reading a book by Warren Bennis on *Leaders*. Bennis tells of Frank Dale, who took over as publisher of the *Los Angeles Herald Examiner* at the end of a violent ten-year strike. Because of the strike, the front part of the building had been barricaded and closed for eight years.

On his first day at work Dale recalls: "I had to walk through the back door, have my fingerprints and my picture taken. . . . I called the people on duty at the time around the desk and in an informal setting—I had no one to introduce me . . . I did it myself so I would be right there and without any formality at all I said, 'Maybe the first thing we ought to do is open up the front door and let the sun in.' Everybody stood up and cheered. Grown men and women cried. That was a symbol, you see, that barricade was a symbol."[1]

That story got hold of my imagination. I could see that crowd standing up and cheering. I could imagine them taking down the barricades and throwing open the front door.

I recalled that I had announced I could preach one night at our com-

---

1. Warren Bennis and Burt Nanus, *Leaders: The Strategies for Taking Charge* (New York: Harper and Row, 1985) 37, 38.

ing evangelistic celebration on "Hope for Beginning Again." I thought, "There it is. There is the idea."

Preaching is bridge-building from the world of the Bible to the world of today. Or to put it another way, it is showing how the Story with a big S—Jesus' Story—relates to the story with a small s—our story.

So I thought, "Let's open up the front door—open the door—What does the Scripture have to say about opening the door?"

I took a piece of yellow lined paper and wrote across the top, "Let's open the front door"—with the following notes:

From W. Bennis

*Scriptures on opening the door*

I am the door (John 10)

near the door (Luke 13:24)

open the door (Rev. 3:20)

*Walls, closed doors*

"the doors being shut from fear" (John 20)

door of the heart opened, Lydia (Acts 16:14)

God opened the door of faith (Acts 14:27)

"I see heaven open," Stephen (Acts 7:56)

walls of prejudice (Eph. 2)

*Berlin Wall*

*Our walls*

Sin—Hebrews—"new and living way"

held prisoner (Gal. 3:23)

*Unbelief*

fear—Patsy (John 20)

*Bitterness/broken relations*

death (1 Pet. 3:18–19)

Moody, led a little boy into his meeting by the hand

Here I was on the plane, simply capturing the central idea and flipping through my New Testament to everything I could think of, without a concordance, about doors—opening doors—and jotting down related incidents that came to mind. This was all I could do at the time, so I put the piece of paper away and went on to other work.

A couple of days later I came back to those notes and looked at them again. As I read over the various Scriptures my mind was drawn to John 20. I read through the story of the disciples who huddled inside a little upper room with the doors locked because of their fear of the Jews. Jesus in his risen body appeared to them. He didn't go through the front door. In effect, he, too, went through the back door. (He didn't even need a door because of his resurrection body!) What he said led them to "open up the door." Here was a new beginning—the Story of Jesus illuminated by the story of Frank Dale. Wasn't that a picture of what Jesus wants to do in our lives?

If I had been at home I would likely have taken my concordance and gotten more Scriptures about the door. I would have taken my commentaries on the Gospel of John and sermons on that particular passage and read them carefully. On the road I don't have many tools; I have to rely on previous study and careful observation. So I read and reread, thought and rethought about, John 20.

Consciously or unconsciously, as I read the Scripture I was asking myself three questions.

*The Observation Question*—"What happened at that time?"—Jesus says, "Peace"—the common greeting of "Shalom"—He reinforces it by "showing them his hands and his side"—His wounds show the price at which he brought that peace—the "doors are shut"—Why? What were they afraid of? He "breathed on them"—Imagine Jesus doing that—"wind equals spirit"—He was acting out the parable of the Holy Spirit coming upon them.

*The Reflection Question*—"What does it mean for all time?"—What truths are there in this passage that are always true?—the truth of Jesus' death—He really died—His wounds could be seen—the truth of his resurrection—He was the same though his body had different qualities—the truth of mission—Jesus calls us not only for salvation, but to be sent—the truth of the gift of the Holy Spirit.

*The Application Question*—"What does this mean at this time, for me, for those to whom I am preaching in Australia?"

The first rough jottings were now replaced by a rudimentary outline. On another sheet of paper I wrote:

LET'S OPEN THE FRONT DOOR
John 20
*What are the doors?*
new start
showed his hands
new task, so send I you
new power
breathed the Holy Spirit
*FEAR OF FAILURE* (self)
What would you do if you knew you could not fail?

*FEAR OF RELATIONSHIPS*

hurt from the past

Janie

*FEAR OF DEATH*

"Why do men chase women?"—question from a movie

answer—they are afraid of death

Sandy's death

*FEAR OF GOD*

A student and prayer for his migraines

I put these notes aside for another day or two, but on the back burner of my mind the pot was boiling. When I read I looked for something that was applicable. If I heard someone say something that had to do with a dead end or a closed door, I noted that. While talking to two young Australian associate evangelists, I picked their brains and asked them, "What other Scriptures bear on this?"—and noted

Psalm 24, "Lift up your heads, O you gates; . . . that the King of glory may come in"

John 10:9, "I am the door"—went out to find pasture

Hebrews 9:7, The priest went to the Most Holy Place once a year, never without blood

Hebrews 10:19–20, "We have confidence to enter . . . by the blood of Jesus, by a new and living way"

Matthew 7:7, "Knock, [and] the door will be opened"

Not all of these Scriptures became part of my message but some did.

Thursday morning came. We had opened our celebration the night before. Tonight was the night for the topic, "Hope for a New Beginning." I decided to preach on opening up the front door.

Once again I took my lined yellow pad, this time to develop a full message. Let me describe what was on that sheet.

At the very top was the title, "Let's Open the Front Door!" In the center was the text, "With the doors locked for fear" (John 20:19). Below that were the three major points I would make:

*NEW PEACE*—a new beginning

"He showed his hands and side"

emphasis: forgiveness

*NEW PURPOSE*—a new task

"I am sending you"

emphasis: relationship

*NEW POWER*—new power

"He breathed on them and said receive the Holy Spirit"

emphasis: failure, self

At the bottom was the story that came to me which pulled it all together, so I wrote, "Charlotte, the door is locked, closed, and double-bolted." On the margins to the left and to the right I put in other material.

How would all this apply to the Australians who would be listening? At the top right corner I wrote in capital letters—HOW MANY CLOSED DOORS ARE REPRESENTED HERE TONIGHT? and underneath that I wrote:

unemployment

broken relationships

no communication

inner doors of hopes and dreams

self-doubts

doors to God

fear, guilt, and bitterness

Down the right-hand side of the same piece of paper I wrote—across from each major point—thoughts, Scriptures, notations of stories, key words or names that would remind me of instances.

For example, the *Advertiser* had carried a story about how suicide—especially teenage suicide—increased in the first three months of the year, and I noted that.

In my earlier notes I had down "Janie," referring to a woman I know who was sexually abused by her brother when she was a teenager and only recently has been able to talk about that and to forgive her brother.

The structure was becoming clear; the whole effect was still cluttered—but the theme was ringing in my mind, "Doors are locked in our world—doors are locked in your life—Jesus Christ has the keys—given to him by the Father—He can take those keys and unlock the door and let the sunlight of God into your life."

If I had been at home I probably would have sat down with my wife, Jeanie, and gone through the whole idea with her. I think more in terms of ideas; she thinks more in terms of people. She might have suggested applications that would not have occurred to me. Since she wasn't with me, I kept thinking during the course of that busy day. And I kept praying, "God, what do you want me to say?"

At one point, I sat down with my long-time associate, Irv Chambers, and told him what I was planning to preach on that night. I related to him the story of Frank Dale of the *Los Angeles Herald Examiner.* Irv listened and said, "I don't quite get it. Why couldn't he go in the front door?" I realized that in retelling the story I hadn't clearly explained that the front door of the building had been barricaded for eight years. I made a mental note that when I preached I needed to make that plain.

That afternoon when I had a free hour, I did the final organizing and sculpting.

Again, I sat down and took sheets of yellow paper—this time four sheets instead of one.

On the left two-thirds of each sheet I put the title, the opening illustration, the Scripture, and the question, "How many locked doors are represented here?"

Under that I put the different doors that are closed.

Then in bold letters: "JESUS CHRIST BRINGS THE KEYS TO UNLOCK THE FRONT DOOR."

After that came the outline.

*New Peace*—the key to unlock the doors closed by sin, failure, guilt

*New Purpose*—the key to unlock the doors closed by broken relationships

*New Power*—the key to unlock the doors closed by failure and selfdoubt

Under each heading I listed the Scripture references, key points in the story, brief explanations, assertions to make, questions to ask.

At the end of each point I wrote in bold letters—"OPEN UP THE FRONT DOOR."

On the right one-third of each page I put other material which I might or might not use—several illustrations, humorous stories with just two or three key words to bring each to mind. The key to effectiveness, I knew, was deciding what to leave out and what to include.

It was now four o'clock. Since I had other things to do, I stopped work on the sermon.

By six o'clock, I was back in my room. Now I was ready for the final preparation. I took the four sheets of the outline.

With a red pen I underlined key headings. I put a box symbol before the illustrations and quotations. With a darker pen I underlined the subpoints.

I reread the Scripture. I reread the outline and let it soak into my mind. I sat and thought about it quietly and prayerfully, asking God if there was any fresh insight that should come to mind now. Sometimes I read through the outline aloud to fix it in my mind. Other times I read it quietly (as I did this time).

Now it was seven o'clock, time to go. I paused at the door of my room for a final prayer. Then I was off to the meeting, my notes now slipped into a notebook.

<u>During a meeting I sometimes quickly go through my notes again. I may even take a small piece of paper and, without referring to the full notes, write down the outline and some of the key words, just to make sure that it is fixed in my mind.</u>

At 8:10 P.M. it was almost time to get up and preach. I breathed a brief prayer. Then, confident that God had given me his Word for that night, I stood up to preach.

During the message, repeatedly—especially at the end of each major point—I asked the question: What door is closed in your life? I made the assertion—Jesus Christ has the key to open up that door. I reminded the people several times of the invitation to come to Christ, to ask him to turn that key and open the door.

Thus, the closing invitation did not stand by itself. All along I prepared the people for it. It was, therefore, a fitting climax to the sermon. That night thirty-nine came forward. Some of them had kept the front doors of their lives barricaded to God for as long as the *Los Angeles Herald Examiner* was closed. But that night Jesus Christ turned a key and they opened up the front door to him.

# Let's Open Up the Front Door

> On the evening of that first day of the week, when the disciples were together, with the doors locked for fear of the Jews, Jesus came and stood among them and said, "Peace be with you!" After he said this, he showed them his hands and side. The disciples were overjoyed when they saw the Lord.
>
> Again Jesus said, "Peace be with you! As the Father has sent me, I am sending you." And with that he breathed on them and said, "Receive the Holy Spirit. If you forgive anyone his sins, they are forgiven; if you do not forgive them, they are not forgiven." [John 20:19–23 NIV]

A few years ago one of America's great newspapers, the *Los Angeles Herald Examiner,* went through a violent ten-year strike. People were hurt, some even killed, and the doors of the building were barricaded for eight years.

Finally, some of the employees got together on a peace platform, and said, "We've got to stop killing each other. Let's end this thing." A new agreement was made and a new publisher, Frank Dale, was hired.

The first day Dale went to work he had to go in the back door because the front doors were locked. There was no one to welcome him.

He went to the newsroom and gathered the people who were there around the desk. Without any planning he said what came to his mind, "Maybe the first thing we ought to do is open up the front door."

There was a silence. Then everyone stood up and cheered. Grown men and women cried, tears running down their cheeks.

As Frank Dale later said, those closed front doors had been a symbol of defeat, of siege. And what he was saying was, "Let's let the sun in."

That story is a parable—a modern parable—of what happened when Jesus came to the disciples after his resurrection.

According to John 20, on the evening of the day that Jesus arose, his disciples were together in a room with the doors locked for fear of their enemies.

Then Jesus came and stood among them. He didn't go in the front door—that was locked! Actually he didn't even need a door because his risen body had the property of being able to pass through barriers. But he went, so to speak, in the back door—and opened up the front doors of their lives.

They were gathered in fear because of enemies on the outside. Inside was a sense of failure because they had let Jesus down. But Jesus brought the keys that opened up the front doors.

He brought *new peace* as he said to them, "Peace be with you!"

He brought *new purpose* as he said, "As the Father has sent me, I am sending you."

He brought *new power* as he breathed on them and said, "Receive the Holy Spirit."

Have you ever walked down a street and looked at the closed front doors of houses and wondered what lay behind them?

I wonder that as I look at you who are here in this crowd tonight. How many locked doors are represented here? How many doors of opportunity are closed because of unemployment? How many doors of broken relationships are closed? How many doors of hurts that have made us withdraw are here? How many doors of broken communication are here?

How many doors of failure and defeat are here? The slogan of your area is "The Golden Opportunity," yet your newspaper tells of increasing suicide—even among teenagers.

How many inner doors are locked—locking in the dreams and hopes and abilities and creativity that you feel you can't use?

How many doors are locked to God—by barriers of fear, doubt, guilt?

Billy Graham says that when he was growing up, there was a man who ran a liquor store in his hometown of Charlotte, North Carolina. A drunk called him about one o'clock one morning and asked what time he opened up. The owner sleepily replied that he opened at 9 A.M. The man hung up. An hour and a half later he called again and asked the same question. Again, the store owner replied more irritably that he did not open until nine. At 3 A.M. the phone rang again. An even more drunken voice asked the same question. So the owner lost his temper and said, "Look, if you promise not to call again and let me get a good night's sleep, I will come down there at 8 A.M. and let you in."

There was a pause. Then a befuddled voice said, "I don't want *in*—I want out!"

Tonight there are many of you who are saying, "I want out." The Good News is that Jesus Christ brings the keys to unlock the front doors of our lives.

## The Key of New Peace

The door of your life may be closed by sin and failure and guilt, but *Jesus brings the key of new peace* to unlock that door.

When he walked into that room on the first Easter, he said, "Peace be with you!" "Peace" was a common greeting, very much as we in America might say, "Hi," or you in Australia might say, "G'day, mate."

"Shalom"—peace—was the common greeting of one Jew to another, or as Arabs would say, "Salaam."

Yet there was a deeper meaning. We would all like a peaceful life without disturbance. But Jesus was bringing peace with God.

True peace is not the absence of problems. It is the presence of the rightful King at the center of your life. God made this world. He made you. He is your rightful King. But you and I don't want him to be King. We have chosen to try to be king ourselves. That is what sin is. It is not just stealing or killing or sleeping with someone other than your spouse. I like to spell sin—"s-I-n." The big I. Me first. I want to build my kingdom. And when we do that we are at war with God, with others, and with ourselves. We need peace.

When Jesus walked into that upper room, he not only said, "Peace," but he showed them his hands and side. Why did he do that? In his hands were the marks of the nails that had held him to the cross. In his side was the wound from the spear driven in. Jesus was saying, "Peace is costly. It cost me my life on the cross. It will cost you your sin."

"Who are you to be calling me a sinner?" you may ask. "I haven't hurt anybody. I get along fine with God. God's my mate. God's my friend."

But the Bible tells us that "all have sinned and fall short of the glory of God." Compared to someone else you may be pretty good. But how are you compared with God? We are all infected with the disease of sin. But the symptoms are different.

Just before I left home my wife, Jeanie, had a severe case of the flu. She was aching and had a 104-degree fever. I had the same flu, but I had a very mild case and didn't have any of those symptoms, just a little chill. But we both had the same disease. The whole human race has the disease of sin: the symptoms may be different but each of us needs the peace of forgiveness that only Christ can bring.

That's why 1 Peter 3:18 tells us that Jesus Christ "died for sins once for all, the righteous for the unrighteous, to bring you to God." It took the death of the perfect Son of God to open up the front door.

Back in the days of the Old Testament, the Jewish people had a tabernacle, a large tentlike place in which they worshiped God. At the very center of that tent was what was called "the Most Holy Place"—a place that represented the very presence of God himself. But only one person—the high priest—could go into that holy place. He could go only once a year. And he had to bring a sacrifice of blood.

According to Hebrews 9:7, "Only the high priest entered the inner room, and that only once a year, and never without blood, which he offered for himself and for the sins the people had committed in ignorance." Without the shedding of blood there was no forgiveness (Heb. 9;22), yet it was impossible for the blood of animals to bring complete forgiveness. That is why the high priest could only go in once a year.

Now Jesus Christ is the great High Priest, the bridge between a holy God and sinful people. He came not to enter a manmade sanctuary but heaven itself. He came not to offer the sacrifice of animals, but to sacrifice himself. He came not to enter into God's presence once a year but to open the door so that anyone could come to God at any time.

"Now he has appeared once for all at the end of the ages to do away with sin by the sacrifice of himself" (Heb. 9:26). So, says the Scripture, we may have "confidence to enter the Most Holy Place by the blood of Jesus, by a new and living way opened for us . . . , and since we have a great priest . . . , let us draw near to God with a sincere heart in full assurance of faith, having our hearts sprinkled to cleanse us from a guilty conscience . . ." (Heb. 10:19–22).

An old hymn says:

> There was no other good enough
> To pay the price of sin;
> He *only* could unlock the gate
> Of heaven, and let us in.

Jesus came to bring you the key of new peace. And he is saying to you tonight, *"Open up the front door—and enter into salvation and heaven* through the peace that I have made for you."

Will you take that peace as a gift right now?

### The Key of New Purpose

Then there are some of you tonight who have doors closed by broken relationships. Just as sin and guilt make us hide from God, so fear and hurts make us hide from others. Those disciples on that first Easter were hiding in fear from those on the outside.

Jesus brought to them the key to unlock the front door—the key of new purpose. And he brings that same key to you tonight.

He said to his fearful followers, "As the Father has sent me, I am sending you." That is what he is saying to you tonight. I bring you a new purpose. *You* are going to become a little *Me*.

Why did the Father send the Son into the world? According to John 3:17, he came not to condemn the world but to save it.

In Mark 10:45 Jesus said, "The Son of man came not to be ministered unto, but to minister [to serve], and to give his life a ransom for many" (KJV).

Just as Jesus came to save and to serve, he brings that purpose to us. He unlocks not only the door of heaven, but also the door of service and of caring for those who have been hurt by life's broken relationships.

I know a woman who lived with a deep hurt locked inside for many years. When she was young she was abused sexually by her brother. She never told anybody. For many years she carried that hurt deep inside her, and all of those years she was seeking God.

Finally, she was led to a Bible class. She went faithfully week after week. After several years, she came to faith in Christ and was able to open her life to a friend she met in that class. She told of the abuse in the past and they prayed about it. In her heart she released that hurt to God.

But she also had to go to her brother. "I want you to know," she said, "that I forgive you for what you did to me. I have never talked to you about it, but Christ has come into my life as my Savior and Lord. I know he wants me to forgive you." Once she did that, she, too, was released and set free.

In John 10, Jesus gave one of his great "I am"s: "I am the door; whoever enters through me will be saved. You will come in and go out, and find pasture" (John 10:9).

See how Jesus defines salvation—it is to go in and to go out. We go in to find fulfillment, a new and abundant life in Christ. But then he leads us out into new relationships in our communities.

What purpose do you have? Do you know why God has put you here? You don't have to go to the other side of the world to find God's purpose. He can make that clear to you right where you are, just as he sent those first followers right into Jerusalem to be his ambassadors, little Christs in the very city that had crucified him.

Stanly Grenz tells of a young East German named Richard. Richard's parents are communists and his father has been a government leader. For many years Richard dreamed of a new life in the freedom and prosperity of the West. As a teenager he walked up and down the Berlin Wall trying to find a way through, but finally realized there was none and gave up. He thought of taking a flight to Cuba and getting off the plane in Canada, but realized it might be many years before he could save enough money to make that flight. Then he began to think that even if he got to the West, it might not be all he wanted.

Richard was drafted into the East German army. In despair he decided that he would take his life. So he took an overdose of pills. Almost miraculously he was discovered and taken to the hospital before any permanent damage to his body or his brain occurred.

After he recovered he was invited to a little Baptist church in East Berlin. There he heard the gospel clearly and logically presented. Counselors spent hours talking with him and finally Richard opened the door of his life to Christ.

He still lives at home. It has taken a long time, but his parents have slowly come to tolerate his new faith. His father even brought back from a trip to the West a small Bible that Richard wanted. Now he is thinking of the possibility of serving in the ministry.

Richard would not go to the West now. God has given him contentment and he believes that the Lord has given him a new purpose—to serve his people as an ambassador of Christ.

What is your purpose? Are your goals too narrow, too short-term?

Then open up the front door and go out in service and love, in faith and hope.

## The Key of New Power

Others of us today have doors locked by failure and by self-doubt. For that Jesus brings the key of new power.

Just as sin makes us hide from God, and fears make us hide from others, so failure makes us hide from life.

How many here tonight have turned to alcohol, or to drugs, or to thinking about suicide because of that sense of failure?

Think of those to whom Jesus appeared and said, "I am sending you—to be little 'Me's."

How could *they* go out to be "little Christs"?

There was Peter who had denied him three times. How could *he* be a little Christ?

There were James and John, two of Jesus' closest followers. They'd been bickering about which of them was going to be greatest among Jesus' followers. They had a major ego problem. How could they be little Christs?

There was Thomas, who so often has been dubbed "doubting Thomas," because of his skepticism. How could he be a little Christ?

There were the women, who in the ancient world were nonentities, zeros with no worth. How could they be little Christs?

But Jesus came to them and breathed on them. He said, "Receive the Holy Spirit."

In Jesus' language, "breath" was the same word as "spirit" and "wind." So Jesus' breathing was an acted parable to show that the Holy Spirit is the breath of God, the wind of God, the real person of God breathed into our lives.

When Jesus breathed on those doubting men and women, it was a forecast of what would happen. He was going to go back to his Father. When he left, he would send his Holy Spirit to live in them and empower them to be what he called them to be.

Here was the key—of new power—for them and for you.

Is the fear of failure holding you back from life?

Someone has called this the "Wallenda factor." Do you remember the Great Wallenda? Karl Wallenda was the famous tightrope aerialist who once said, "Being on the tightrope is living; everything else is waiting." He fascinated crowds by walking his tightropes, always without a safety net.

In 1978, Wallenda fell to his death trying to cross a seventy-foot high wire in downtown San Juan, Puerto Rico. His wife later said that was his most dangerous walk. She recalled, "All Karl thought about for three straight months prior to it was *falling*. It was the first time he had ever thought about that, and it seemed to me that he put all his energies into *not falling* rather than walking the tightrope."

Before the fatal walk Wallenda even personally supervised installing the tightrope and checking the guy wires. "Something he had never even thought of doing before."[2]

This was the Wallenda factor. When Karl Wallenda put all his thought into *not falling* instead of *walking* the tightrope, his fall was almost certain.

Is the fear of failing the locked door in your life?

There is a positive way to look at failure. Failure doesn't have to be negative. It can be part of learning. In fact, in some things if you are not falling down, you are not learning.

My friend Eloise Orr has taught hundreds and hundreds of young people to water ski. She herself learned to ski when she was in her early sixties and it took her ten months! She says, "I am the best water ski teacher there is—because I know every way not to do it."

Eloise Orr knows that failure is not final—that it can be the springboard of hope.

So it is when Jesus Christ comes with the key of new power to unlock the door, when he breathes on us his Spirit and says, "Trust me, obey my call, and my Spirit will be with you and in you" (rsv).

Isn't that what Paul meant when he said to his young friend Timothy, "God did not give us a spirit of timidity, but a spirit of power, of love and of self-discipline" (2 Tim. 1:7)?

Was this not what Jesus meant when he said, "Knock and the door will be opened to you. . . . How much more will your Father in heaven give the Holy Spirit to those who ask him!" (Luke 11:9, 13)?

Are you holding back on a commitment of your life to Christ because of that fear of failure from the past?

2. Ibid., 69, 70.

When God calls you to Christ, he doesn't say there will not be failures. But he does promise that through his forgiveness and the power of his Spirit failure need never be final.

*So open up the front door.* Surrender yourself to the Spirit of God, and let him come in to control your personality.

What is the locked door in your life? Is it sin and guilt? Fear? Failure?

Look at the keys that Jesus is offering: new peace, new purpose, new power.

Will you dare to let him turn that key and open that front door?

A close friend of ours came to Christ during an illness. His wife resisted the call of Christ for a long time, not wanting anybody but herself to control her husband! She came very unwillingly to a couples' conference, and made it very plain that she didn't want to be there. In fact she told my wife the first day, "I'm here, but I want you to know that the door is locked, closed, and double-bolted."

It turned out to be a wonderful weekend of laughter and fun, of fellowship and openness, of sharing and teaching, and God touched Charlotte's life very deeply.

On the final morning after communion, Jeanie said, "Charlotte, is that door still locked, closed, and double-bolted?"

Holding up her fingers an inch apart she said, "No, it is cracked open that much."

It was another year before the keys were really turned in Charlotte's heart. But then she said, "Now the door is wide open." In a testing time that followed she said she could never have made it, if it hadn't been for the Christ who walked into her life and opened the door.

When Jesus Christ died and rose, God opened the front door to heaven and salvation. Now is he opening the door of faith for you?

If so, will you say now, "Lord Jesus, I have heard you knocking at the door. It has been locked and bolted by my sin, fear, and failure. But I am asking you now to turn the key and open the door. Wash away my sin. Take me out of myself and give me a new purpose to live for you and your kingdom. Breathe upon me your Spirit that I may have new power to do your will."

Open up those front doors—today!

# 7

## H. Beecher Hicks, Jr.

After pastoring Baptist churches in Pennsylvania and Texas,
H. Beecher Hicks, Jr., became senior pastor of the Metropolitan
Baptist Church, Washington, D.C., in 1977. He has also served as
visiting professor at the School of Divinity, Howard University. He
has written *Preaching Through a Storm* and *Images of a Black Preacher*
and has coauthored *Kindling Wood: A Collection of Sermons.* He
attended Colgate Rochester Divinity School, where he earned his
M.Div. and D.Min. degrees.

# Bones, Sinew, Flesh and Blood
# Coming to Life

There is no way to avoid it. I confess: I am one of those proverbial
Saturday-night preachers. I would much rather tell you that by
Thursday I am fully prepared and am simply reviewing my notes and
digesting thoughts and concepts. Unfortunately, that is not the case. On
any given Saturday night you can usually find me seriously at
work—Bible in one hand, concordance in the other, computer warmed
and ready with a thesaurus propped up on the side. I do not recommend
Saturday-night sermonizing. It is an unhappy practice that is physically
demanding, emotionally frustrating, and rarely produces power either in
the sermon or in the preacher.

This preaching business is tedious and treacherous stuff. It is increasingly so for those of us who are engaged in the week-by-week, Sunday-by-Sunday adventure of proclaiming the gospel. Most of us want to be disciplined homiletic practitioners. Realistically, however, most of us have discovered that those neat principles and procedures which we learned in seminary either do not fit or are irrelevant when we are faced with the prospect of preaching a sermon within the next twelve hours.

## The Bones

"How do you choose your sermons?" members of my congregation frequently ask. The question is not easily answered. I spend my waking moments always in search of a sermon in the hope that, sooner or later, a sermon will find me. Sermons are usually all around us, if we are sensitive and open to the leading of the Spirit to reveal his message to us. Having said that, however, it is still necessary to point out that sermon selection and sermon preparation are an ongoing process which requires disciplined prayer and planning.

In recent years I have discovered the value of series preaching. Series preaching removes the weekly *angst* of sermon selection and provides a diet of disciplined study for both preacher and listener. Currently, I am engaged in preaching through the entire Book of Romans. The church is participating enthusiastically in study and preparation along with me. This preacher-parishioner partnership has brought a new level of excitement and participation in worship. As a result of individual and corporate Bible study the congregation has a common knowledge base that makes it receptive to new and fresh interpretations of the Word.

It is also helpful, when preparing to choose a subject or theme, to listen to sermons by others, to read church bulletin boards as you drive through the city, and to read the listing of local services in the Saturday paper. Their sermon subjects reveal something of the thought patterns of your colleagues. I read everything in print I can find about preaching, including the sermons of others. I also subscribe to many religious periodicals and preaching publications. It is a poor preacher who drinks only from his own well.

I make it a practice to read thoroughly the commentaries on my chosen text. In fact, I read every commentary available to me, in order to be certain of the historical data and to be sure that my interpretation is not far afield from the interpretations of others. I do not rely on the commentaries for outlines or points, but I do use them as valuable resources for the thinking and viewpoint of others. Some of the newer commentaries—such as Warren Wiersbe's *BE* series, and William Barclay's *Daily Bible Study* series—can be read quickly and easily. More important than all of this is that quiet moment when the preacher's soul stands before the Savior—that quiet moment when the preacher's "empty pitcher" is presented before the "full fountain" in the sure and certain confidence that the One who visited Cana will visit him, changing his tasteless water to enriching wine and filling his pitcher to overflowing.

## Sinew

Once the subject and the text of the sermon have been determined, an important key to preaching is to be able to ask the right question of the text. I tell my Bible students constantly, "If you ask the wrong question, you get the wrong answer!" For me, every sermon is pinned to a question or to a recurring thematic phrase. The essence of the sermon is to work through the possible answers to that question, to approach the question or theme from as many angles as possible (what some preachers refer to as "milking the text"), and then, by sheer force of logic, to come to the response which seems appropriate in light of the biblical meaning of the text and its contemporary relevance.

This is often easier said than done. At times I find it most difficult to determine the question or thematic phrase that will provide the focus and frame for the sermon. That question or phrase will determine the content of the first sentence of the sermon. In many ways it is the first step of a journey, a spiritual odyssey which pulpit and pew take together. It is a journey from concern to celebration. As with most writing, I find the first sentence of the sermon the most critical. Sometimes I have spent hours composing that first sentence, simply because I am convinced that it is so pivotal to the integrity of the rest of the sermon. Usually, the first sentence is my theme sentence. It may be an interrogative or a declarative sentence. In most instances, however, it is a refrain to be heard again and again within the body of the sermon. Every preacher knows that it is always important to be able to state, in one simple sentence, the aim, purpose, and theme of the sermon. Once this is achieved, that aim, purpose, and theme remain ever before me, and before the congregation, until the sermon's end.

While I develop a simple outline for writing the manuscript, I use it wholly as a suggestive guide. Sometimes I slavishly follow the outline from introduction to conclusion. At other times I abandon the outline early on, preferring the leading of another Power.

My sermons are basically a blending of the topical and the textual types. Even when my sermon is essentially topical, it will be sustained by a textual undergirding. I am convinced that there is a thirst today among our people for exegetical, Bible-based preaching. To the extent that my sermons remain organically connected to the text of Scripture, they are also expository in nature. This is to say that the sermon is designed to expound the truth of God as revealed in his Word and through his Son. Our people no longer wish to be entertained with some unbelievable, nonsensical, archaic story. They prefer to be taught and trained with the Word of God at the base and at the apex, so that they may grow in knowledge and spiritual grace.

No matter what the approach, it is sometimes hard to find the sinew that will hold the bones together. In a word, moments come when nothing works. Much like a baseball batter, the preacher goes through spiritual preaching slumps. Similarly, the only way to come out of the slump is to keep on preaching!

When a preacher is in a slump, or when preaching has no power, this is the time one becomes acquainted with Dr. Flunk. Dr. Flunk, in my cultural tradition, is one with whom all preachers are intimately acquainted. Dr. Flunk visits all of us, usually on Sunday mornings, but sometimes he comes even when we are studying or writing our sermons. His presence can be recognized when everything we say falls on deaf ears, no one says "amen," no one even nods silent approval, and everyone from the choir loft to the door becomes comatose. Dr. Flunk disregards our degrees and ignores every one of our academic achievements. He sees to it that the sermon over which we have worked long and hard comes out sounding like theological drivel and biblical nonsense. There is no way to avoid him. He comes when he will. He is designed to keep the preacher humble, to help the preacher keep his preaching in perspective, and above all, to help the preacher refrain from taking himself too seriously. He is a master at his work. Yet we are called to preach in spite of the presence of Dr. Flunk!

## Flesh and Blood

My method of preaching, then, includes planning the preaching, consulting available resources, taking time for spiritual reflection and discipline, preparing an outline, and writing a clear and precise first sentence.

When all this is done, however, it is still necessary to give the sermon flesh and blood. In my sermon preparation I am always aware of what commentators, other biblical scholars, and various preachers have said on the chosen subject, but I am also aware of the events reported on the front page of the newspaper. I always feel an underlying sense of urgency to bring contemporary relevance to my sermon by speaking freely and honestly to those current issues which affect the lives of the people and their community. Contemporaneity is not a sideline in sermon preparation. To speak to contemporary people in their contemporary situation, to make the hermeneutical leap, goes hand in hand with faithful declaration of the Word. The preacher must never be afraid to speak boldly to the times. This is not only sound preaching, it is the very essence of prophecy.

In addition to the newspaper and the commentaries, one must always have an ear to the ground to hear human groaning and to feel human hurt. One must never forget that the persons who fill our pews come with needs and desires, pain and perplexities, tears and sorrows, anxieties and burdens. There is a common posture of pain that has stooped the shoulders of even the strongest in our midst. In our pews there is always a Jacob struggling with Esau, a Samson in jeopardy with Delilah, an Elijah struggling with Ahab and Jezebel, and a Gadarene who is unsure of his identity and in conflict with his own personality. As the gospel speaks to human need and human hurt, so must our preaching. Preaching is not authentic until it does so.

I am fundamentally a manuscript preacher. From time to time, however, I employ the extemporaneous or outline method as well. I find great benefit in preaching from a manuscript, primarily because it permits verbal precision and the marshaling of data and facts which might be lost in the use of less formal methods of presentation. Nevertheless, I am convinced that one method is not necessarily preferable to another. I do confess a kind of holy envy of those preachers who are able to preach flat-footed and without script or notes. But I content myself with the reminder that we are all given gifts, as the Scripture says, "differing according to the Spirit."

I now use a word processor in my sermon preparation. The word processor is perhaps the device a preacher needs most at his disposal for the creative shaping and reshaping of the sermon. With its ability to store, retrieve, and edit at a moment's notice, it is a tool no preacher should be without.

On to the sermon! Now I am writing—with my trusty word processor—and several things should be noted. First, as I indicated earlier, I usually have a theme sentence which is often stated at least twice in the first or second paragraph. Second, I use the interrogative method, asking one question over and over until the importance of that question and its answer becomes apparent. Third, when asking a question which serves as the basis of the sermon, I come to a clearly defined answer. Every sermon must come to a logical conclusion. Whatever we do, we must get Job off the ash pile, Lazarus out of the grave, and Ezekiel out of the valley! It is our duty not to leave the congregation sore, buried, or bewildered! Fourth, there is usually an unmistakable beat or rhythm to preaching. Often my wife will come upon me in the process of writing my sermon and will hear me humming as I write. I hum because there is music in words. Words have sound, tone, meter, and feeling. It is important to me, as it may be to others, to hear the melody that accompanies the words. Fifth, my sermon manuscript is printed out or typewritten on 8 1/2-by-11 paper in either double- or triple-spaced lines.

## Can These Bones Live?

The longest walk that any preacher takes is the one from his study to the steps of his pulpit. Arrogance is no longer present. There will be no thought of any personal achievement which may have brought him to this hour. The authentic preacher comes to the pulpit unsure if the bones can live. He can only respond to the question by saying, "Lord God, thou knowest!"

The authentic preacher comes to the pulpit not knowing how to preach, not knowing what to preach, not even knowing why he is so engaged. Yet, the preacher knows Who! Who it is that must be preached. Who it is that has laid claim upon his life. Who it is that requires not his ability but his availability to be used in this manner. Who it is that becomes the preacher's preacher. The bones can live. The bones can take on sinew and flesh and blood. But only when the wind of the Spirit of God blows upon them afresh and anew. After all, this preaching business is not ours. It is his and his alone.

Years ago, I am told, an old organist sat at his bench playing the instrument for the final time. He was a good organist and had served the church faithfully and well. Now a new organist was to come and the old organist wanted to step aside with dignity and grace. He struck the last chord, closed the instrument, locked it, and placed the key in his pocket. He then made his way to the rear of the church. There, eagerness flashing in his eyes, the young organist was waiting for him. He asked for the key and, after a moment's pause, he fairly raced to the organ, opened it, and began to play. The old organist had played with precision the notes before him, but this new organist played with a depth of soul and feeling that brought tears even to the eyes of the retiring organist. Reports of his artistry spread by word of mouth, and soon people came from miles around to hear him strike the keys of the console. This new organist was a master at his craft; to that, the ear and the soul would abidingly attest. He was, in fact, none other than Johann Sebastian Bach. As the old organist left the church he though to himself: "Just suppose I had not given the master the key!"

We do not know what spiritual music these sermons of ours have in them, but we do know that they shall be what he wants them to be, if we simply give the Master the key.

# When Religion Fails

Then I said, I will not make mention of him, nor speak anymore in his name. But his word was in mine heart as a burning fire shut up in my bones, and I was weary with forbearing, and I could not stay. [Jer. 20:9 KJV]

Jeremiah is my favorite prophet. Of the seers and sages who pass along the scenes of Old Testament times, it is the prophet Jeremiah who, more than others, captures my soul and engages my spirit. To be honest, I do not know why Jeremiah is my choice among the prophetic spokesmen. Of his life and times one can say only that his were humble beginnings. From his birth in Anathoth, sometime around the year 640 B.C. until the time of his death somewhere in Egypt, Jeremiah lived the life of prophetic loneliness and priestly despair.

Not only was Jeremiah plagued with the disease of loneliness, but the very word he preached condemned him to a life of unpopularity and branded him a traitor to his nation and to his people. So despondent and depressed were his prophetic profession and predicament that Jeremiah cursed the day he was born and cursed as well the man who brought the news of his birth.

Jeremiah had no self-confidence. He was known to stutter when he attempted to preach, and all of history has proclaimed him to be a "weeping prophet." Jeremiah did not possess the oratory of Isaiah or the pathos of Hosea. Jeremiah's soul did not contain the compelling compassion of Amos, the proclivity for preaching of Ezekiel, nor did he possess the charismatic ecstasy of Elijah or Elisha. And yet, for all that Jeremiah was and for all that Jeremiah was not, to this very day he remains my favorite prophet.

The fact that Jeremiah is my favorite prophet may be of little consequence to you, yet you may be interested to know that Jeremiah was one of those prophets for whom the religious enterprise failed—this despite the fact that he was an integral part of the structure of religion, expounded the value of religion, and wore the robes of the priest and prophet. In the ministry of the Reverend Doctor Rabbi Jeremiah there was a marriage of helplessness and hopelessness so that he said of himself that his head was like waters and his eyes flowed with a fountain of tears. When no relief appeared in sight, this preacher stood on the platform of mental confusion and spiritual bewilderment and asked, "Is there no balm in Gilead? Is there no physician there?" In a very real sense, Jeremiah was one for whom religion had failed.

And so, I thought I ought to bring this matter before you today, not to depress you, but simply to call attention to the fact that in some instances religion does fail.

Religion is designed to shed light in dark places, provide answers for plaguing questions, provide a way out for those who are trapped in life's dungeons, and show a way out for those who are lost or languishing in defeat and despair.

But when religion fails, questions go unanswered.

When religion fails, the sunlight of God is in spiritual eclipse.

When religion fails, those who ought to preach are strangely silent and still.

When religion fails, an illicit relationship exists between a pathetic pulpit and an ungodly pew.

When religion fails, theology won't sustain you, and philosophy won't support you, and hermeneutics can't hold you, and kerygma and koinonia and diakonos and didache all seem remote and divorced from the real world in which you live.

When religion fails, the choir sings in confusion and the organ strikes a discordant note in misery's minor key.

When religion fails, folk come to church hungry and when they leave, they still have found no bread.

When religion fails, the fellowship is fractured and there is no sweet communion of the saints.

When religion fails, church time is nap time and careless souls can be at rest.

When religion fails, people look for the church in the structure of the church, but the building can't bless you, the pews can't protect you, the windows can't wash you, and the preacher can't redeem you.

And, in case you have never given the matter serious thought, there really is a time when religion fails. There are many among us for whom religion has failed. As I move about my day-to-day ministry, I encounter time and again those for whom religion is not a priority.

Some young men and women will tell you that religion has failed them intellectually. They say that there are some principles, some concepts, some ideas in the realm of religion that have no basis in verifiable fact and, in terms of sheer common sense, are intellectual nonsense. For them religion has failed to convince the mind.

I have come upon others who will tell you, "When I was a child I was made to go to church morning, noon, and night. I vowed that when I grew up I would never go to church again." For them religion has failed to provide a satisfying lifestyle.

It will come as no surprise to you to be told that the church is in trouble. The authority of the church is being questioned as never before. The authenticity of the claims of the church is being examined as never before. The integrity of the church is being held under the light of ethical scrutiny as never before. And often the church is found to have failed.

Many parents spend much time trying to put their children in church, but very little time trying to put the church into their children. As a result, when the world offers an alternative lifestyle, when the world offers "bright lights and big cities," and all the church offers are "straight paths and narrow gates"—when the world says what you need is self-assertion and self-reliance, and all that the church says is, "Blessed are the meek, for they shall inherit the earth"—religion has failed.

Every day I come across people who have concerns and questions about institutional religion and the institutional church. For them, it is not Jesus who has failed, but the institution that claims to represent Jesus that has failed. Many complain that the church is in danger of giving religion a bad name. Young and old, rich and poor—they all have questions about the church.

What do you say when people tell you that there's no difference between the folk "in here" and the folk "out there"? What do you say when people tell you that radio preachers and electronic pulpiteers use the media to steal from the needy in order to line the pockets of the greedy? What do you say when people ask you why must a prayer tower become a perch for a mercenary prophet? What do you say when the world sees preachers slandering preachers, and when those who preach against sin fall victim to sin themselves? What do you say when the "moral majority" is exposed to the world as an immoral minority? What do you say when "Praise the Lord" gives the world nothing to praise, leaves the culture nothing but questions about the Lord, and when People That Love suddenly become people that lust? I'd like to know. What do you say? That's what happens when religion fails.

Examining this matter at closer range, I want you to see that, whether you recognize it or not, religion sometimes fails you in your own circumstances. Have you ever known a time when your prayers appeared to go unanswered? Have you known the experience of asking the Lord day after day and night after night for some blessing, for some need to be met, for some burden to be lifted? Yet, the Lord would not answer your prayer. He wouldn't say, "Yes"; he wouldn't say, "No." He wouldn't say, "Maybe," or "Wait a while longer," or "We'll see," or "Sometime soon." No matter what you did your prayer was not answered. Personally speaking, whenever one's prayers go unanswered, religion has failed.

Have you ever experienced how hard life can be? Have you ever known trials and tribulations in your life? Have you ever known what it is to be lonesome and to be forced to walk down through the "valley of the shadow of death" alone? You've tried to live right, but it looks as though life still turns its back on you. You've tried to love everybody, but it still seems you've got enemies on every hand. You bring your tithes and offerings to the Lord, but your bills keep on climbing higher and higher. You "wonder why the test when [you've] tried to do your best." The Bible says that "all things work together for good," but things don't seem to be working at all for you. Has that been your experience? Is that your experience now? If you've come to know how hard life can be, then perhaps you understand what I mean when I say that religion sometimes fails.

Have you ever experienced how religion sometimes fails even when you are at worship? Because of our diversity we don't all have the same experience in worship. Sometimes you come to worship and no matter how fervent the prayer, it does not speak to the inner depths of your spirit. No matter how moving the anthem, somehow it leaves you cold. And no matter how powerful the sermon, it just doesn't speak to your need. Folk can be saying "amen" all around you, but you're sitting there with your lips tighter than Fort Knox. Folk can be clapping their hands and getting up on their feet, but you're just sitting there with your hands folded and legs crossed. Some folk go out of church on fire for the Lord, but you go out still fighting off the cold with that fur you came in with. Excuse me, but I need to tell you right here that if you come to church and you don't ever feel *anything,* if you come to church and you don't ever hear anything that makes you say "amen," if you come to church and you're so sophisticated that you can't clap your hands, or tap your feet, or nod your head, or move *something,* your religion has failed.

If your religion has failed—if it has failed to satisfy you intellectually, or if it does not offer you an acceptable lifestyle, or if you have become disenchanted with the institutional church, you may be interested to learn what is really at work when your religion fails.

Whenever religion fails *it is always good to discover what kind of religion you have.* Deacon George Jones used to go down the aisle of the Mount Ararat Church in Pittsburgh, Pennsylvania, with a communion tray in his faltering hand, and I'd hear him line out the hymn, "Have You Got

Good Religion?" And back across the congregation would come the response, "Certainly, Lord!" But not everybody has good religion. I realize we are in a "church growth" era today, but if I read my Bible properly authentic religion has never been quantitative. It has always been qualitative. Jesus was discussing this matter of good religion with his disciples one day. He said, "Not every one that saith unto me, Lord, Lord, shall enter into the kingdom of heaven; but he that doeth the will of my Father which is in heaven" (Matt. 7:21).

If there is such a thing as "good religion," there must by force of logic be such a thing as "bad religion."

Bad religion says there's a cloud on every horizon, but good religion says there's a bright side somewhere.

Bad religion says that man is hopelessly lost, but good religion says that God will look beyond his fault and see his need.

Bad religion says that seeing is believing, but good religion says we walk by faith and not by sight.

Bad religion says that prayer is a waste of time, but good religion says that prayer changes things.

Bad religion says that a day's work is never done, but good religion says, "God knows how much you can bear."

Bad religion sings a song of skepticism and doubt, but good religion sings, "My hope is built on nothing less than Jesus' blood and righteousness."

Bad religion says I have to look out for number one, but good religion says, "Seek ye first the kingdom of God, and his righteousness; and all these things shall be added unto you" (Matt. 6:33).

Bad religion says the world is against me and enemies are on every hand, but good religion says, "Thou preparest a table before me in the presence of mine enemies . . ." (Ps. 23:5).

Bad religion says there are questions that can't be answered, but good religion says, "We'll understand it better by and by."

If your religion fails, it may be that you have the wrong kind of religion in the first place. If your religion fails, it may be that your religion is homocentric rather than theocentric. That is to say, your religion will fail if it is centered on man rather than on God. I don't care who the man is: preacher or teacher, apostle or prophet, bishop, archbishop, or pope. If he is a son of Adam, if he's made out of flesh and blood, if he's made out of tissue that's bound for corruption, if he's made out of matter that is measured by its own mortality, if he's riding a funeral train with graveyard sons and daughters, man will fail.

My hope is not homocentric; it's theocentric.

I don't want man in charge of my world; he might forget to keep the world whirling in its orbit.

I don't want man in charge of my sunshine; he might keep me living in the shadows.

I don't want man in charge of my water; he might forget to let the rain fall on me.

I don't want man in charge of justice; he might not know anything about mercy.

I don't want man in charge of the Holy Ghost; he might make out a program and not give the Holy Ghost time to come in.

I don't want man to be in charge of the music; he might make me sing what's on the paper and refuse to let me sing what's in my soul.

I don't want man in charge of my religion, because if man fails—and he will—my religion fails.

I need to leave you now, but I wanted to tell you that Jeremiah is my favorite prophet even though he had some experiences in his life that caused him to believe that his religion had failed. Of all the prophets Jeremiah had perhaps the most sensitive spirit, and sometimes people did not understand the shifts in his moods.

But you must have sympathy for Jeremiah, primarily because Jeremiah believed that his religion had failed. He believed that his religion had failed because his prophecy went unfulfilled. It's a terrible thing when folk listen to the prophet and what the prophet says does not come true. Jeremiah believed that his religion had failed because his family turned their backs on him. It's a terrible thing when a man has to walk through hell and those who are closest to him don't even feel the heat. Jeremiah believed that his religion had failed because nobody paid attention to the sermons he preached. He told people that the harvest was past. He told them that the summer was ended. He told them to amend their ways and their doings. But nobody heeded him. He preached his heart out, but nobody came forward. He took them down to Gilead where physicians were to be found and discovered that the doctors had all gone on strike and that there was not a pharmacist anywhere in town. Jeremiah believed that his religion had failed because his friends made fun of him. In fact, Jeremiah said that because he preached he "was made a reproach and a derision" all day long.

When your religion fails, something has to be done. So I ask Reverend Jeremiah, "What are you going to do?"

"I'm not going to mention him any more."

"I'm not going to speak any more in his name."

"And I'm not going to church any more."

But I also hear Jeremiah saying, "There is a fire shut up in my bones!"

I know religion fails sometimes but I, too, have a fire shut up in my bones.

I know religion fails me intellectually sometimes, but then his ways are not my ways and his thoughts are not my thoughts.

I know that religion often fails to provide the lifestyle that you're seeking, but I came to tell you today,

> There's not a friend like the lowly Jesus.
> No, not one!
> No, not one!

I know religion fails and your prayers are not answered sometimes, but I tell you just to keep on praying and keep on believing, and after a while he will answer your prayers.

> In seasons of distress and grief,
> My soul has often found relief,
> And oft escaped the tempter's snare,
> By thy return, sweet hour of prayer.

Do you want to know why I have a fire shut up in my bones? Do you want to know why I keep on struggling? Do you want to know why I keep on preaching? Do you want to know why I keep on going, sometimes up and sometimes down? Because even when my religion fails, God never fails.

He never fails! He never fails!

I've failed him. But he has never failed me.

Religion may fail, all others may fail, but God never fails!

# 8

## Herschel H. Hobbs

For twenty-five fruitful years Herschel H. Hobbs pastored the First Baptist Church in Oklahoma City, Oklahoma. He preached on the International Baptist Radio Hour from 1968 to 1976. He served as president of the Southern Baptist Convention, Baptist Convention of Oklahoma, Baptist World Alliance, and Southern Baptist Pastor's Conference.

Hobbs has more than one hundred books to his credit. Among them are *The Crucial Words from Calvary, Messages on the Resurrection, The Epistles to the Corinthians, An Exposition of the Gospel of Matthew,* and *The Cosmic Drama: An Exposition of Revelation.*

He attended the Southern Baptist Theological Seminary, where he earned the Th.M. and Ph.D. degrees.

# Aiming for a Verdict

There is no greater calling than the call to preach the gospel of Christ. If I had ten thousand lives to live I would want to spend every one of them as a pastor and preacher. Not because it is an easy life; it is a demanding one. Neither because of monetary reward. If a person's goal is to make money, the gospel ministry is not the vocation in which to do it.

God calls all Christians to serve him. But in a special way he calls some into distinctively Christian vocations. A preacher should not choose the ministry but should be chosen for it. Yet so deeply personal and spiritual is this call that no preacher can explain his call to another. But a preacher knows he is called. Otherwise he should not try to fill this role. I have known some who rejected God's call. But I have never known any of them to be happy doing anything else.

There are many definitions of preaching. Of course the classic one is that of Phillips Brooks: "Preaching is the communication of truth by man to men." My favorite is that of Dr. James Randolph Hobbs (no relation), author of *The Pastor's Manual.* "Preaching is incandescent personality radiating the Light of the world."

In a class in homiletics the professor raised the question as to the difference between teaching and preaching. He concluded that both are necessary in a sermon. Teaching that does not preach is not teaching; preaching that does not teach is not preaching. Teaching informs the mind; preaching motivates the will.

## Influences on Preaching

So often a young preacher faces the temptation to try to imitate the methods and preaching style of an older, successful preacher. To do so is to become an imitation of the real thing. In one of his books the late Dr. Roy McLain, while pastor of First Baptist Church, Atlanta, Georgia, expressed his reaction to this temptation. "I decided to become the 'best me' I could be." Years prior to this I had made the same decision.

However, I must acknowledge my special indebtedness to four men, two of my seminary New Testament teachers and two pastors. From Dr. A. T. Robertson I learned the historical-grammatical method of Scripture interpretation. I can best express Dr. W. Hersey Davis's influence in his own words: "So many preachers have harrowed over [scratched the surface of] favorite passages of Scripture until when you announce your text most people already know what you will say. Set your plow to go down deep and turn up some fresh soil." Whether or not I have succeeded, I have tried.

Due to his prominence as a preacher, Dr. George W. Truett was the model selected by many in my generation. The only thing about his preaching that I set myself to follow was his clear enunciation. This proved to be of inestimable value, especially in eighteen years as preacher on the Southern Baptist international radio program "The Baptist Hour," where the only listener contact was the voice. From Dr. Hobbs I learned to preach without written notes or a written outline. True, it involves added work in that one must rethink every sermon before repeating it. But it enables one to maintain a degree of freshness and the all-important eye contact with the audience.

## General Considerations

Early in my ministry I determined to major on expository preaching. To me this means to draw out of the Scriptures their original meaning and then apply it to present needs. Expository preaching does not depend so much upon the length of the passage but upon how it is treated. It is possible to do this even with one word. Of course, I allow myself the freedom of using other types of sermons when it seems advisable. But for the most part I adhere to exposition.

A few times I preach on one word or verse. More often I use a short or long passage of Scripture, a book, a character, or a doctrine. I never start with a topic and then select the Scripture to fit it. I do it the other way around.

Ideas for sermons may come from reading a book, a conversation, recognition of a need, or current events. There are ideas everywhere if one is alert to grasp them. But most of my ideas come from devotional reading and exegetical studying of the Scriptures. During these times, sermon ideas jump from the Scriptures like trout in a lake.

I cannot say that I have had dry seasons when sermon ideas were scarce. My problem is time to preach the sermons I want to preach, or else deciding when to preach a given sermon.

One way to avoid such seasons is advance planning. When I was a pastor I usually planned for a six-month period. In the process, set days and seasons (e.g., Mother's Day, Holy Week, Easter) were automatic. At least two Sundays were given to preparation for the spring revival. In the fall I dedicated one month to preaching on stewardship, leading up to the pledging of the church budget. December was set apart for a short series of sermons dealing with the incarnation. When these were put in place, I used the remaining Sundays to deal with themes related to needs within the church family.

For fourteen years beginning in 1951, I preached through the Bible. It proved to be one of the most helpful things I ever did—for both myself and my congregation. I did not preach on every verse or chapter, of course. In the process I treated such themes as the creation, fall, flood, and a series of biographical sermons on Old Testament patriarchs. These are just samples, but they suggest the general procedure. One sermon each was given to books like Ruth, Ecclesiastes, and the Song of Solomon. Selected psalms and proverbs were included. In the prophets I dealt with great themes such as the Suffering Servant in Isaiah. Throughout the Bible I sought to provide historical continuity briefly in each sermon. Someone asked if this program did not keep me out of the New Testament a long time. I replied that I ended up in the New Testament in every sermon. For the New is the fulfillment of the Old.

The effectiveness of this program is seen in the following incident.

When I retired from the pastorate a prominent businessman said to a friend, "I have learned more Bible under his preaching than in all the rest of my life put together." I attribute that comment to this extended program, plus a steady pattern of expository preaching.

Preaching through the Bible calls for in-depth study whereby the preacher learns more of the Bible than ever before. It provides variety, gives continuity, leads to preaching on otherwise neglected themes, and avoids hobbies. Facetiously, I have told pastors it makes for long pastorates. If on a given Sunday the pastor says, "I am starting to preach through the entire Bible. My text today is Genesis 1:1," it is a nice way of saying, "Don't try to get rid of me. I plan to be here a long time."

A brief word needs to be said about illustrations. When properly used, they become aids in transmitting truth. Long ago I put my books of illustrations on the shelf. I glean illustrations from current life—something I read, hear, or observe. I do not write them out and file them for future use. Instead I file them in my subconscious mind. Psychologists say that we use only a small percentage of our mental capacity. We can train our minds to do what we want them to do. Through long practice I find that in sermon preparation the very illustration I need floats up into my conscious mind. At times this is true even as I deliver the sermon. To me, at least, such illustrations *live*. The method may not work for everyone, but it seems to work for me.

A seminary student wrote his master's thesis on my "Baptist Hour" preaching. During an interview I told him of this method. Later he wrote, "To some this may seem like a haphazard method. But in more than one hundred sermons I studied, he did not repeat a single illustration."

Anything that throws light upon a sermon is an illustration. Hence some of the most effective illustrations are found in the Bible itself. I do not hesitate to explain the meaning of Hebrew and Greek words. This is especially true with reference to the Greek papyri, the everyday writings generally from the same period in the first century A.D. as the New Testament itself. What did these words say to people when they first heard them in a Christian context? Some years ago I wrote *Preaching Values from the Papyri,* in which I used anglicized Greek words, so that even those not versed in Greek could use the book.

## Preparation of the Sermon

In baseball there are certain basic rules for hitting a ball. The batter must have a bat in his hand. He must stand at the plate. He must keep his eye on the ball. And he must swing the bat. Yet I have never seen two batters use the same stance at the plate.

Likewise, there are certain basic rules in homiletics. But this does not mean that every preacher follows exactly the same pattern in sermon preparation. Each one develops a method most appropriate for him. I suspect that to most people my method of sermon preparation will seem most unorthodox.

For instance, I preach out of the *overflow*. In college a lady who taught English said, "Any time a student can finish a written exam in the allotted time, the exam is not a test of his or her knowledge of the subject." Adapting this statement to sermonizing I say, "Any time a preacher exhausts his knowledge of his subject in one sermon, he is not properly prepared."

This principle has governed my study habits through the years. By the time you read these lines I will have written more than 120 books—most of them on Bible exposition. When asked how I have been able to do this, I say that it is the way I study. My mind will be as lazy as I let it be. So if I am simply preparing a sermon for next Sunday I will get just enough material for it. But if I am writing something I expect will be published, I will try to write something worthy of publication— whether or not I succeed. I am therefore motivated to study the Scriptures more carefully. Following Dr. Davis's suggestion, I try to set my plow so as to turn up some fresh soil.

As for specific preparation of a sermon, I employ the following procedure. First, I select the passage of Scripture. Using commentaries and the Hebrew or Greek text, I exegete the passage. In presenting the sermon I do not start out with exegesis. I treat this as I move through the passage in the sermon.

Next I decide on the title of the sermon. It must be short, designed to attract attention, and easily remembered. After deciding on the introduction and proposition, I choose the major points for development. The Scriptures are logical; for the most part they outline themselves. But I state the points in keeping with the purpose inherent in the sermon. Then I choose illustrations to be used at given points in the sermon. Finally, I work out the conclusion, designed both to summarize the message and to lead into the invitation.

As previously stated, I do not use written notes. But I definitely have notes in my mind. This method gives me what preachers used to call liberty in delivery. In delivery I seek to use simple language. I try to start at the emotional level of the audience and lead them to the level I hope to reach. My delivery is animated, but controlled. If the preacher does not get excited in the pulpit, the people will not get excited in the pew. For emphasis, however, the voice should be varied in tone. Often a whisper is more emphatic than a shout. Certainly one should not be a *little-Johnny-one-note preacher.*

## Purpose in Preaching

The most important thing in preaching is the listener's verdict. In presenting a legal case from start to finish a lawyer seeks a favorable verdict from the jury.

A story is told about a French surgeon who was describing to an English surgeon a new and very delicate operation he had performed. The Englishman asked how the patient was doing. The Frenchman replied, "Oh, he died. But it was a beautiful operation!" True or not, the story makes a point. Regardless of the beauty of the sermon, it is all for naught if it does not accomplish its purpose.

In seeking a favorable verdict I endeavor to apply each point to the needs of the listeners. But the climax comes in the final application and invitation.

No sermon should end without an invitation. I read the following comment by a sales manager to his pastor following a worship service. "Pastor, you preached a great sermon! But if you were one of my salesmen, I would fire you! You *sold* us on your product. We were ready to *buy* it. But you did not let us sign on the dotted line."

My invitations are very simple: for lost people to receive Christ as Savior; for Christians to unite with the local fellowship; for Christians to register whatever decision the Holy Spirit has laid on their hearts. As long as people are responding, the invitation continues. But I do not prolong it unduly.

Someone asked Dr. Truett if he had any rule for deciding how long to extend an invitation. He replied, "Yes. And it is very simple. If the Holy Spirit is working, we dare not quit. If not, we dare not presume." Amen!

# Salvation Simply Stated

> For it is by grace you have been saved, through faith—and this not from yourselves, it is the gift of God—not by works, so that no one can boast. For we are God's workmanship, created in Christ Jesus to do good works, which God prepared in advance for us to do.
> [Eph. 2:8–10 NIV]

Karl Barth was one of the greatest theologians of modern times. Someone asked him late in life, "What is the greatest theological truth you ever discovered?" He replied,

> Jesus loves me, this I know,
> For the Bible tells me so.

If the questioner expected an extended discourse on some profound doctrine he was disappointed. But never did Dr. Barth demonstrate more clearly his true greatness as a theologian than in this simple answer.

God simplifies; man complicates. Nowhere is this better demonstrated than in Ephesians 2:8–10. In my judgment this is the greatest and plainest single statement on the plan of salvation found in the Bible. Yet men have complicated it by adding to it such things as church membership (some in a specific church), observance of the ordinances, legalism, good works *ad infinitum,* so that multitudes throw up their hands in exasperation over what God expects of them. The result is that they live in either despair or indifference.

It is important, therefore, that we examine this simple, yet profound, statement by the apostle Paul. He had one of the greatest of minds. But under the inspiration of the Holy Spirit he has stated God's plan of salvation in the simplest terms. Volumes could be written about these verses. But we may reduce them to three simple statements.

## The Basis of Salvation

The basis of salvation is the grace of God. "For by grace you have been saved." A friend of mine once said, "Grace means that God gives us what we need, not what we deserve."

Originally, the Greek verb related to the word *grace* (*charis*) meant to make a gift, then to forgive a debt, then to forgive a wrong, and, finally, to forgive sin. So basically grace denotes a gift. Theologians speak of it as "unmerited favor." If someone sold you a piece of land valued at ten thousand dollars for "one dollar and other considerations," it would be a bargain but not a gift.

Paul emphasizes this fact in the phrases "and that not from yourselves . . . not by works, so that no one can boast." In the Greek text the word *that* is neuter in gender. Both "grace" and "faith" (*pistis*) are feminine in gender. The word *that* cannot, therefore, refer to either grace or faith. It denotes instead the act of being saved. In the expressions *not from yourselves* and *not by works*, "by" (*ex*) means out of and points to the source of salvation. In both of these cases "not" (*ouk*) is the strong negative. Most emphatically, then, the source of your salvation is not yourself or your good works. Salvation is God's gift to you.

"Workmanship" (*poiéma*) is the noun related to the verb *to do* or *to make*. It denotes the product of one's work. So you are the product of God's work, not yours. The word *created* refers to God's work. You may build or fashion created materials into a product. But only God creates, whether it is something material or something spiritual. And this spiritually creative work is "in Christ Jesus" or "in the sphere of (*en*) Christ Jesus." "Therefore, if anyone is in Christ, he is a new creation; the old has gone, the new has come" (2 Cor. 5:17).

Your salvation does not depend upon what you do, but upon what God in Christ has already done for you. Note carefully that Paul says, "You have been saved." "Been" denotes the passive voice. "I hit the ball" (active voice). "I hit myself" (reflexive voice). "I have been hit by the ball" (passive voice). The passive voice expresses something done to you by another person or thing. Here the person is God in Christ.

As a seminary student, I heard George W. Truett preach a sermon on grace. He said, "I would not trust my salvation to the best second I ever lived." Not the best day, hour, or minute, but the best second! I thought, "If he has to say that, what must I say?"

## The Channel of Salvation

"By grace you have been saved, *through faith*." "Through" renders the Greek word *dia*, which expresses intermediate agency. So the salvation provided by God in Christ flows from the inexhaustible spring of God's grace. The channel through which it flows into your life is faith. There is no one English word that can translate adequately the Greek verb for faith (*pisteuō*). It means "to believe, to trust, and to commit." You must believe the biblical record about Christ, trust your soul to him alone for salvation (Acts 4:12), and commit yourself to his will and way.

It is not enough to believe about Christ. "Even the demons believe that—and shudder" (James 2:19; see also Mark 1:23–24). They know who he is. But they do not trust in him or commit themselves to him. You can walk through the gates of hell intellectually believing every word the Bible says about Jesus Christ, if you stop short of trusting in him as Savior and committing yourself to him as Lord!

You can read a bank's statement and believe that it is a safe bank. That is believing about it. You believe in it when you trust your money to it by committing—that is, depositing—your money to the bank for safekeeping. It is likewise with your soul.

This is what Paul meant in 2 Timothy 1:12: "I know whom I have believed, and am convinced that he is able to guard what I have entrusted to him for that Day." Unfortunately, the translation *I know whom* is incorrect. The Greek text says, "I know *in* whom." Here we have the difference between believing about and believing in Christ. Paul actually wrote in banking terminology. The phrase *what I have entrusted* translates three Greek words meaning "the deposit of me," or "my deposit." The verbs *believed* and *convinced* are both in the perfect tense indicating completeness.

Literally, then, Paul wrote, "I know in whom I have fully believed, and am fully persuaded that he is powerful to guard my deposit, looking toward that Day." The Greek text reads "that the Day," an expression which denotes a particular day—the day of final judgment. Paul had deposited his soul in the bank of God's mercy and grace in full assurance that Jesus Christ would keep it saved and safe.

Furthermore this must be a personal faith. The New Testament knows nothing about proxy faith. It is not a passive "sit and wait" faith. It is an active "I will arise and go to Jesus" faith.

There are some things others can do for you. But the most vital things you must do for yourself. You must eat, drink, and breathe for yourself. And to obtain salvation you must believe in Jesus for yourself.

John D. Rockefeller, Sr., in his late years was reported to be the richest man in the world. He was a member of the Euclid Avenue Baptist Church in Cleveland, Ohio. One Sunday a guest preacher delivered the sermon. After the service Mr. Rockefeller thanked him for his sermon. To express his appreciation he gave the minister a personal check for one hundred dollars. The minister was pleased, not simply because of the money, but because he had received a personal check from the world's wealthiest man.

The next day the minister sought to cash the check at the bank on which it was drawn. After looking it over, the teller returned the check to him. Thinking something was wrong, the minister asked, "What is the problem? This is the right bank! The check is made out to me! Mr. Rockefeller himself gave it to me! The signature is genuine! Surely it is good for one hundred dollars!"

The teller replied, "Yes, friend, this is the right bank. I do not doubt your identity. The signature is genuine; I have seen it many times. And it would be good for one hundred million dollars. There is nothing wrong with the check. You simply forgot to endorse it."

By endorsing the check the man demonstrated his faith in the bank and the signature, and he appropriated the check personally so that he would receive the money Mr. Rockefeller wanted to give him.

God has made out a check in your name, payable in the currency of salvation. It is drawn upon the bank of his infinite mercy and grace and is signed in the indelible blood of his Son. But in order to receive this salvation you must endorse the check. Your endorsement is your personal faith in Jesus Christ as your Savior and Lord.

## The Permanence of Salvation

"For it is by grace you have been saved." Note also the permanence of salvation. Like "believed" and "persuaded," the verb *saved* is in the perfect tense. This, as I commented earlier, is the tense of completeness. It expresses the idea that you were saved in the past and you are saved at the present moment, and carries the implication that you will continue to be saved in the future.

Just as in the beginning your salvation does not depend upon what you do but upon what God in Christ has done for you, so the permanence of your salvation does not depend upon what you do from day to day but upon what God in Christ has already done for you. Paul says that you are not saved by your good works but "to do good works, which God prepared in advance for us to do." Good works are the fruit, not the root, of salvation. "Walk" refers to the manner of one's life. It should be a life rich in deeds that are pleasing to God.

In the New Testament the verb rendered "save" may mean to heal, to rescue from danger, or even to solve a problem (Phil. 2:12). In the spiritual sense it has a threefold usage, depending upon the context. It is used for regeneration (John 3:3, 17), sanctification (2 Cor. 2:15), and glorification (Heb. 9:28).

Regeneration refers to the saving of the believer's soul. Sanctification, or being set apart for God's service, refers to the believer's new life in Christ. Glorification refers to the believer's glory and reward in heaven. Thus it is correct to say, "I am saved," "I am being saved," and "I will be saved." At the moment of regeneration you are sanctified or set apart for God's service. You do not grow into sanctification; you are to grow and serve in the state of sanctification. All who are regenerated will be in heaven. But the degree of your growth and service in the state of sanctification will determine the degree of your glory and reward in heaven. This is why "God prepared beforehand that we should walk" in the sphere of good works. Salvation, however, is all by God's grace and through your faith in him.

A man who did not believe in the permanence of salvation said to one who did, "I wish I believed as you do. If so, I would get saved and then have the time of my life doing what I want to do." "Yes," replied the other, "but if you really are saved, what you will want to do is quite different from what you are thinking of now."

God's plan of salvation is simple to understand, but demanding to fulfill. To paraphrase another, it has not been found complex and ignored. It has been found demanding and not tried.

> My hope is built on nothing less
> Than Jesus' blood and righteousness;
> I dare not trust the sweetest frame,
> But wholly lean on Jesus' name.
> On Christ, the solid Rock, I stand:
> All other ground is sinking sand.

# 9

## John A. Huffman, Jr.

Since 1978 John A. Huffman, Jr., has pastored Saint Andrew's Presbyterian Church, Newport Beach, California. Before going there, he pastored churches in Florida and Pennsylvania.

Huffman has written eight books, including *Becoming a Whole Family, Wholly Living: A Study of Philippians, Liberating Limits: A Fresh Look at the Ten Commandments,* and an exposition of the Book of Joshua in the Communicator's Commentary. He received two degrees—an M.Div. and D.Min.—from Princeton Theological Seminary.

# Balancing Biblical and Relational Truth

Phillips Brooks, in his classic *Lectures on Preaching* (1877), defined preaching as the "communication of truth by man to men. . . ." Another way of stating this is that authentic preaching is that process in which God's revealed truth is conveyed through a person to other persons. The preacher must not neglect the two essential elements of eternal truth and human personality.

As a young man I planned to go into politics. I was a Christian. I wanted to serve Jesus Christ. However, I had been somewhat frustrated by some of the models of ministry which I had observed. This caused me to shy away from a career in the ministry.

On the one hand, I had seen preachers who were superbly gifted

communicators who dealt with the real earthy problems of human existence. It appeared to me that the more practical they were the more
they tended to wander away from biblical revelation, speaking about
those everyday matters which evoke such enormous human interest. I
respected them for their personal qualities and genuine desire to help
people. But I wondered about the dependability of their theological
utterance, for often it was based more on psychology, sociology, and politics than on divinely revealed, biblical truth.

On the other hand, I was exposed to some pastors who prided themselves on being expository preachers, presenting verse-by-verse exegesis
of Scripture but failing to apply it in practical ways. It appeared to me
that there was a broad gap between the tedious but faithful articulation
of biblical truth in the pulpit and the application of that truth not only
to the lives of the hearers but to their own daily experiences as well.

When God finally caught my attention with a specific call into the
pastorate, I vowed that to the best of my ability I would try to bring into
cognitive and relational truth creative tension. I would do my best to
exegete and communicate the doctrinal truths of Scripture faithfully in a
way which related them to my own personal experiences and the everyday struggles of those with whom I was privileged to share God's Word
in the challenging task of preaching. Not only would I put a high priority on biblical study, I would also do my best to flesh out what Phillips
Brooks was talking about when he described what it meant to have the
truth "come really through the person, not merely over his lips, not
merely into his understanding and out through his pen. It must come
through his character, his affections, his whole intellectual and moral
being. It must come genuinely through him."

I began preaching in the early 1960s, an era in which professors of
homiletics tended to frown on the use of the personal pronouns *I* and
*you*. The classic rules of rhetoric were taught. However, we were dis-
couraged from becoming too personal in our pulpit expressions. As I
observed a parade of preachers at college and seminary daily chapel services, summer conferences, and Sunday church services, occasional persons stood out as true communicators. These persons usually were men
or women who had done their homework in biblical study and had fil-
tered the truth they proclaimed through their own experience to the
point that it came across with credibility. They were not afraid to use the
pronoun *I*. They did it not to promote themselves but to help relate to
their listeners. They impressed me as being authentic, whole persons
who did not just convey concepts of truth in essay form but gave them a
practical articulation that spoke to me as a human being, where I lived,
in a language I could understand.

About this time I became profoundly impressed with the brief
account Luke gives of the first thirty years in the life of Jesus. "And

Jesus increased in wisdom and in stature, and in favor with God and man" (Luke 2:52). This was a dynamic call to balanced living. If our Lord thought it was important to live on the growing edge of continual intellectual, physical, spiritual, and social discipline, how much more essential it is for us who are called to be his disciples to be men and women whose lives are dedicated to balanced growth. I determined early in my ministry to spend as much time in the daily newspaper and *Time* magazine as I spent in the Bible and vice versa. Since I couldn't find the perfect embodiment of my aspirations as a preacher in any one person, I came up with a composite of several preachers who had impressed me. I prayed that God would give me the evangelical fervor of Billy Graham, the intellectual credibility of Harold Ockenga, the down-to-earthness of Norman Vincent Peale, and a touch of the Holy Spirit emphasis of Alan Redpath. This combination I took as my ideal, knowing that to be a carbon copy of any one of these four men would be to become too specialized for the generalist's calling that was mine. To neglect the emphasis of any one of these four would be to impoverish my week-in-and-week-out pulpit ministry.

Early in my ministry I was profoundly influenced by two men. One was Richard C. Halverson, then pastor of the Fourth Presbyterian Church in Washington, D.C. He stressed a radical approach to priorities which put Jesus Christ first, spouse second, children third, and work fourth. I was aware of my own rationalization in putting work first. After all, wasn't my work as a preacher identical to my commitment to Jesus Christ? I constantly remind myself that my calling is no more important than the calling of any layperson in my congregation and that I have the same need to see life in its proper perspective as do those to whom I preach.

The second person who profoundly influenced me was David H. C. Read of the Madison Avenue Presbyterian Church in New York City. I took his continuing education course in preaching at Princeton Theological Seminary. He emphasized that every sermon falls into one of three categories. It is primarily either a declaration of the gospel, calling men and women to personal faith in Jesus Christ; or it is a form of teaching, expounding some doctrine from Scripture as that doctrine is applied to daily experience; or it is ethical in its imperative, calling people to holy and righteous living. Read maintained that every sermon should have a wooing element in it, but its primary emphasis should fall into one of these three categories.

Halverson's emphasis on priorities, coupled with Read's stress on a holistic understanding of preaching, supplemented by the biography of Jesus Christ and the contribution of an occasional preaching model, have served me well since my call to preach at age twenty-two in 1962.

I think of myself as a biblical/life-situational preacher. Preaching demands everything I have as a verbal communicator, nonverbal communicator, theologian, Bible student, observer of all of life, psychologist, family man—in all, a man of God who allows the biblical witness and the experiences of daily life with all its ambiguity fully to saturate my human personality.

My preaching may best be called textual, since my sermons always derive their natural growth from a biblical passage. Occasionally I preach topically from a specific text, and sometimes I do a series on personal relationships that draws from various texts in the Bible principles or insights that can be practically applied. My most common fare is series preaching in which I take as few as three or as many as thirty weeks to work through a passage or even an entire book of the Bible.

Most of my topical preaching springs out of passages that come to my attention during my devotional reading or out of particular felt needs in the congregation or in the community at large. I try to stay about three months ahead in planning the specific direction of my preaching. I am always thinking a year to a year and a half in the future in terms of basic themes which need to be addressed and a book or portion of Scripture that will receive concentrated exposition. Over the past five years, I have inaugurated a series each September that ties in directly with the biblical book our small, in-home covenant groups will be studying during the autumn season.

Although I usually have done enough basic exegesis to determine the texts and topics for the next several weeks, I begin my tough, laborious work on Tuesday morning, having taken Monday as my day off. I sit down with the Bible and carefully read the text in several English translations, then sketch a brief outline of the text, breaking it into its component parts.

After this initial hour of study I take a blank sheet of paper and put myself under the intense pressure of pretending that I have one-half hour to prepare a message for a youth group. I force myself to put down in one sentence what seems to me to be the central thrust of the passage and outline its main points, filling in under them any practical, biblical, or life-situational illustrations that come to mind. I put these notes in a file folder cataloged according to the text, and then move on to devote the rest of my Tuesday to administrative and pastoral matters.

Wednesday morning I try to spend two or three hours taking notes on ten to fifteen commentaries, such as *The Interpreter's Bible, The Expositor's Bible,* William Barclay's *Daily Bible Study* series, *The Communicator's Commentary, The New Bible Commentary,* and the best single commentaries on the book of the Bible from which my text is taken. I always try to end up checking to see what Spurgeon, Calvin, Wesley, Luther, and Maclaren had to say on that particular text. Once again, I put my research into the folder and take up other duties for the rest of the day.

Thursday is my day for more leisurely general reading in history, fiction, and politics. I try to stay on top of *Christianity Today, Leadership, The Christian Century, Time,* and *Psychology Today,* skimming several other periodicals as well. Thursday afternoon is sometimes punctuated by a round of golf, and I usually babysit that evening.

Friday is sermon preparation day. I try not to schedule lunch, opting for a sandwich in the office. First thing in the morning I go through all my notes, endeavoring to boil everything down to one focus sentence which capsulizes the central thrust of the passage. One to five major points usually emerge. During the week I have written down on individual slips of paper any illustrations that come to mind, either from life experience or from general reading. I have drawer after drawer of files which contain everything of interest I've seen through the years, all arranged alphabetically under whatever words have suggested themselves to my mind as the best labels. Occasionally I go to these files for additional illustrative help. By 2:00 P.M., if all goes well, a writing outline has begun to emerge. I record on a dictation machine equipped with a backup erase/edit mechanism the seventeen-to-twenty-page double-spaced manuscript which my secretary will place in finished form on my desk late that afternoon or early in the evening. Occasionally something goes wrong and I am forced to return to my office early Saturday morning. But my goal is to have a finished manuscript by six o'clock on Friday evening.

I spend Saturday tending to family and church matters, often performing several weddings on that day. Saturday evening is a quiet night at home for dinner with the family and general reading. Finally, by mid-evening, I read my sermon manuscript over once and write a preaching outline on a folded 8 1/2-by-11-inch sheet of paper. Then I read the sermon over once again. By 11:00 P.M., I try to go over it in my mind from memory.

Sunday morning I get up at five o'clock. I try to reproduce the sermon outline mentally from memory, read the manuscript through once, speed-read the entire *Los Angeles Times,* have my devotions, eat the most solid breakfast of the week, do my sitting-up exercises, shave, shower, and head off to church, prepared to preach at both services without notes, telling the Lord I've done my best and now the rest is up to him. I am not gifted with a good memory for word sequence, but I am fairly good at memorizing an outline with illuminating illustrations. I prefer the spontaneity of preaching without notes for the eye contact it allows and the freedom it gives me to read the body language of the congregation. Some of the verbal precision of the written manuscript is sacrificed, but the trade-off is valuable. Sunday afternoon I collapse at home with my family, take a nap, and later in the day edit the written manuscript so it is ready for the printer first thing on Monday morning.

This is the typical, ideal week. There are many interruptions which threaten this symmetry, and adjustments must often be made.

I also have my dry seasons. In the driest times, however, the Bible does speak. If I'm keeping alive in my reading and in my counseling, some truth from God's Word will inevitably emerge and will apply itself to the needs of my own life and the lives of those to whom I preach.

I have a strong commitment to continuing education. In addition to earning several graduate degrees, I regularly attend professional seminars and engage in periodic sabbatical study. I disappear alone for at least two weeks a year with a box full of books covering a wide range of topics. I sometimes set Thursday aside to catch up on the pile of unread periodicals. I occasionally listen to the preaching of others on the *Preaching Today* tapes produced by Christianity Today, or to a series by Charles Swindoll, Steve Brown, or Lloyd Ogilvie on a particular book on which I am currently preaching.

I conclude by saying that I have never found sermon preparation to be easy. It is the toughest work I ever do. It demands everything I have to offer, intellectually, physically, spiritually, and emotionally. I do not please everyone in my congregation. When I am especially expositional, some want me to be more relational and practical. When I present a relational series, some complain that I am not biblical enough. But for every one who complains there are many more who, in their own quiet and gracious ways, communicate their gratitude for the ways God has spoken to them through these efforts.

At times I get very tired and wonder whether I can go on another month, much less another quarter century. But those moments usually occur when I have failed to observe my own sabbath or attend to my own daily quiet time, or when I have allowed the tyranny of the urgent to rob me of the sacred hours of reading and reflection in the study, or equally sacred hours of pastoral care among my people, or the serendipitous moments at home with Anne and my daughters. When my own personal life is in balance, preaching becomes a joyful experience in which I know that God is speaking from his Word through my personality to other persons in a way that changes lives. That knowledge excites me with anticipation for the years ahead.

# You Can Live beyond Yourself!

Not that I have already obtained this or am already perfect; but I press on to make it my own, because Christ Jesus has made me his own. Brethren, I do not consider that I have made it my own; but one thing I do, forgetting what lies behind and straining forward to what lies ahead, I press on toward the goal for the prize of the upward call of God in Christ Jesus. [Phil. 3:12–14 RSV]

Do you ever feel boxed in? Do you ever have the feeling that life is passing you by? That the action is elsewhere? I've discovered a strange phenomenon. The people who complain about being boxed in, when pointed to a source of spiritual help, make a contradictory comment: "I can handle my own life."

The Bible speaks to you if you are boxed in. The Bible speaks to you if you think you have arrived. Paul, a prisoner at Rome, wrote to fellow Christians in Philippi, a community in northern Greece. This man communicated with deep, human dynamic. He said, in effect, "I'm still growing in my understanding of who I am, who God is, and what God wants me to be. I'm living beyond myself. It's the only way to live."

Can you say this? Do you have a forward thrust in all of your activities? Are you being stretched beyond yourself to an exhilarating lifestyle? Or have you settled into a comfortable routine which you can handle? Are you finding yourself confined by a box of your own making?

You can live beyond yourself! Paul outlines four steps for this kind of creative living.

## Respect Your Limitations

Step 1: Face up to the fact you are not perfect.

Humility is one of the toughest commodities to obtain. Paul was no mealy-mouthed, introverted individual. He suffered from no lack of self-confidence. Yet he did have a healthy respect for his own human limitations. He wrote, "Not that I have already obtained this or am already perfect; but I press on to make it my own, because Christ Jesus has made me his own. Brethren, I do not consider that I have made it my own. . . ."

Some of us lean continually on glass crutches made out of our own achievements. The Bible warns you against putting confidence in what you have been able to attain on your own. Many of us suffer from the Horatio Alger mentality. It's the self-made-man syndrome. It's commendable in many respects. It has particularly caught hold of some of us who are committed to the basics of capitalistic philosophy. We have applied ourselves with all diligence to our chosen professions. We have proved ourselves to be achievers. Perhaps you've earned a prominent position. Or a lot of money. Or you found a good marriage partner. You pride yourself on your achievements. Granted, they are many.

But you have forgotten that "every good and perfect gift comes from above." You've forgotten that it's impossible for you to make it on your own. Somewhere there's a father and a mother who invested themselves in you. Somewhere there's a friend who gave you some good counsel or loaned you some money. Somewhere there's a teacher who invested some time in you, believing that you showed promise. No one has made it on his own.

Even though there are some worthy candidates for the rags-to-riches award, Paul, the achiever, says, "I do not consider that I have made it my own." There's a big difference between Saul of Tarsus, the Pharisee, and Paul, the apostle, writing years later from prison. The same individual, yes. Early in life, he was the self-made man. He had risen to the top in his chosen religious profession. He relates how he felt about himself. A few verses before in this letter to Philippian fellow Christians, he describes how he had reason for confidence in the flesh—self-confidence, that is—if anyone ever had reason for it. He tells how he was circumcised on the eighth day, of the people of Israel, of the tribe of Benjamin. He describes himself as a Hebrew born of Hebrews. As to the law, a Pharisee. He talks about being one who had zeal as a persecutor of the church. As to righteousness under the law, he was blameless. Then he says, "But whatever gain I had, I counted as loss for the sake of Christ. Indeed I count everything as loss because of the surpassing worth of knowing Christ Jesus my Lord. For his sake I have suffered the loss of all things, and count them as refuse, in order that I may gain Christ and be found in him, not having a righteousness of my own, based on law, but that which is through faith in Christ, the righteousness from God that depends on faith."

Do you catch the turnaround in Paul's life? Jesus confronted him on the road to Damascus, turned his life around, and offered him an authentic sense of humility.

It's encouraging to be humble. Granted, it hurts at first. The initial awareness comes hard. The encouraging thing is that you're not so surprised by your own failures. The self-made individual constantly has to defend himself at the point of weakness. Paul Tournier, the famous psychiatrist, notes that there is a tendency to divide people into two categories—those who are strong and those who are weak. Society rewards the strong and tramples underfoot the weak. Somehow we view the strong as healthy. The weak we see as unhealthy. Tournier emphasizes that the reactions of both the strong and the weak are neurotic. I urge you to get a copy of his book *The Strong and the Weak*. He writes, "If weakness leads to a sense of failure, strength too has its vicious circle: one must go on being stronger and stronger for fear of suffering an even more crushing defeat, and this race in strength leads humanity inevitably to general collapse. . . ."

I believe that there is a great illusion underlying both the despair of the weak and the unease of the strong—and the misfortune of both. This illusion is the notion that there are two kinds of human beings—the strong and the weak.

The truth is that we human beings are much more alike than we think. What is different is the external mask, sparkling or disagreeable—the outward reaction, strong or weak. These appearances, however, hide an identical inner personality. The external mask—the outward reaction—deceives everybody, the strong as well as the weak. All of us in fact are weak. All of us are weak because all of us are afraid. We are all afraid of being trampled underfoot. We are all afraid that our inner weakness will be discovered. We all have secret faults. We all have a bad conscience on account of certain acts which we would like to keep covered up. We are all afraid of other people and of God, of ourselves, of life and of death.

There is something in each of us that wants to prove that we are strong. There is something in each one of us that wants to cover up our imperfections. The mature believer in Jesus Christ, however, understands who he is. He faces up to the fact of his own imperfection. Indeed, the most spiritual Christian is the one who thinks least of self, placing greater confidence in the Lord. The result is genuine self-esteem, coming from a realistic self-understanding. Reflecting on the fact that he is not perfect, Paul declares that in both his strengths and his weaknesses, he is understood, because, as he is, "Christ Jesus has made me his own."

Living beyond yourself involves facing up to your limitations, acknowledging that you're not perfect. Tournier talks not only about the neuroses of the weak and the strong. He also talks about wholeness which comes from acknowledging both our strengths and our weaknesses as distortions which can destroy us, unless we touch God's gift of grace to us in Jesus Christ. Grace is God's unmerited favor. It accepts you and me as we are and enables us to live beyond ourselves.

## Put Away Damaging Members

Step 2: Live with your back to the past.

Paul writes, "But one thing I do, forgetting what lies behind. . . ." You've just got to forget. How good is your forgetter? Expansive living involves putting away damaging memories.

This doesn't mean forgetting everything. You have to remember before you can begin to forget. You have to be selective in those things which you forget. You have to remember the pattern of your past successes. The mature believer in Jesus Christ is one who learns. He becomes educated by his victories. At the same time, he learns from his defeats. You have to remember the pattern of your defeats. You need to remember certain facts that happened in history and which then enable you to forget those things that are unhealthy. Christianity is a historical religion. It is based on certain facts that happened. God became a man in the person of Jesus Christ. He went to the cross. He died for your sins. He rose from the dead. It is on the basis of these facts which you need to remember that you now are set free to forget.

Do you carry the garbage out in Hefty bags? Some of us carry Hefty bags over our shoulders all through life. Every day we put them down and we put in a bit more garbage. Then we lift them up over our shoulders again. That's not living beyond yourself. That's living caught up in yourself. You simply do not expose yourself to God's grace. You are not living in the reality of what he's done for you. Once you put your trust in Jesus Christ you can lay that Hefty bag down at the cross. Leave it there. And those miscellaneous pieces of garbage you pick up each day—throw them down each day. Don't let them build up.

True education is remembering what you need to remember and then forgetting everything else. I have a friend by the name of L. H. Surbeck, who retired as a senior partner in the Wall Street legal firm of Hughes, Hubbard, and Reed. Back in 1963, when I was working in the travel business, we went around the world together. Our initial stops were in Japan, Taiwan, Hong Kong, the Philippines, and Singapore. In each of these places governmental and business leaders met with our group and gave us briefings. After each of these briefings, Mr. Surbeck would get me aside and ask me the most elementary questions about that part of the world. One day, in frustration, I said, "Homer, you've got to know more than you're pretending." He grinned and said, "You know, you'll never believe it, but back in the Second World War, I was loaned by my law firm to the Pentagon. I was in charge of intelligence for one whole area of Southeast Asia. When the war was over I simply erased everything from my mind and went back to the law firm. I didn't need to have my brain cluttered up with all those useless details. I figured that if I ever needed them again I could always ask someone some questions or read some books."

I asked him how he learned to erase things from his mind like that. He said, "My mother taught me how to do it. When I came home from school the first day, she sat me down saying, 'Homer, what did you learn today?' I tried to tell her everything I'd learned all day. 'But, Homer, I'm not interested in everything you learned all day,' she said. 'I want to know the most important fact, the most important thing.'" Mr. Surbeck went on to describe how night after night his mother drilled into him the concept that he was to prioritize and remember what was absolutely important, that all the rest was detail that could be forgotten. What my friend didn't say was that his mother had a pretty good pedagogical method. She knew that in setting up priorities we have to review the material to decide what we're going to cast away.

The Christian who is living beyond himself has learned to forget those things which are nonproductive for future creative living. There are two kinds of things which you need to forget.

First, you should forget the bad. Forgetting implies forgiveness. As a believer in Jesus Christ you have been cleansed of the garbage which cluttered your past life. All of us need an authentic catharsis, a real cleansing. We all need to have our lives ventilated and refreshed by the Spirit of God. If you've not received Christ's forgiveness, you cannot truly forget. You are just repressing guilt in your deep inner life, only to find it cropping out in unfortunate neurosis. God's grace is essential to understand that you are forgiven. You're still not a perfect person. But you are a new person in Jesus Christ. The German poet Goethe emphasized the possibilities of forgetting the bad, saying, "The one great truth is not that the past is dirty, but that the future is clean." Do you catch the upbeat of that statement? An outstanding editor once said, "The true secret of editing is to know what you should put in the wastebasket." Forgetting means clearing your mind of those things which could only destroy your creativity.

Second, you need to forget certain positive achievements. This is difficult. You and I love to pull out our old scrapbooks and read the clippings. We luxuriate in achievements of yesteryear. We should be able to indulge ourselves in a few whimsical moments reminiscing. But watch out. Sad is the individual who has only the clippings of the past. We label him a has-been. Don't rest on past laurels. If Paul is saying anything with regard to forgetting, he is warning the believer to forget all of the spiritual achievements of the past. To remember them is to backslide. That's the best way to dull your cutting edge. Live with your back to the past.

## Aspire to a Worthy Goal

Step 3: Keep your eyes on the right goal.

If you really want to live beyond yourself, you have to aspire to a worthy goal. Paul writes, "Brethren, I do not consider that I have made it my own; but one thing I do, forgetting what lies behind and straining forward to what lies ahead, I press on toward the goal for the prize of the upward call of God in Christ Jesus."

Do you have a goal for your life? Have you focused in on anything specific to aspire to? Have you put any goals for your life in writing? I suggest that you take out a piece of paper. Jot down in one sentence your whole basic purpose for living. A lot of us have momentary goals. We set them and immediately forget them. The achiever is the person who puts them down in writing, seeing them in their proper perspective. He puts first things first. He prioritizes.

Make sure your goal is worthwhile. Some goals get us nowhere. Some goals make little sense. Some are so distorted. Some never expand. Do you remember the little book *Jonathan Livingston Seagull*? The story is about a seagull who aspires to reach heights never previously reached by seagulls. His goal is to fly with precision, speed, and endurance at extremely high elevation. His father cuts him down to size by saying, "Jonathan, don't you forget that the reason you fly is to eat." How easy it is to choose for our goals things of lesser significance. How easy it is for us to opt for a style of life in which we fly to eat instead of eat to fly. How quickly our physical passions, good as they are, can take over, eliminating the tremendous heights of a high calling.

Don't get caught up in cultural religion. Don't come to church to placate (somehow) the fury of the gods. Don't be content with a one-dimensional life marked by a little bit of religious game-playing. Live beyond yourself to the glory of God. Don't allow yourself to die as a person. Allow yourself to expand.

One-dimensional living has so little to offer. Sometime ago Brigitte Bardot explained her view of getting old. She said that for her it would be "the day I could no longer have the man I'd like." The interviewer from *Vogue* magazine seemed a bit shocked. What was Brigitte Bardot looking for in a man? "That he attract me physically." Then she went on to describe herself as the "most important sex symbol of all time." But these were not the remarks which caught my attention. Her final observation was so precise, so deeply theological. She stated, "Time will destroy me one day, as it destroys everything. But no one else will ever be Bardot. I am the only Bardot, and my species is unique."

Here's a sad individual who sees herself as a commodity which will decline in value with age. She has everything, yet nothing. She can reach for a few more thrills, but her value is temporary.

Are you a commodity whose price goes up and down? Silver that sold for five dollars an ounce, a few months later went up to fifty dollars an ounce. Now it's back down to thirteen dollars an ounce. Your life can be a yo-yo if you're living one-dimensionally.

My predecessor at First Presbyterian Church in Pittsburgh, Robert Lamont, was in his study one day. A gentleman walked in and said to the secretary, "May I see Dr. Lamont? I'm an old classmate of his. I've been on the mission field, and I'm just passing through town and would like to say hello." A moment later Dr. Lamont came bursting out of the door of his office, the two men embraced, and the missionary said, "Bob, what's new?" As they pulled back from each other, Dr. Lamont said, "I'm just trying to discover the will of God and do it."

How about that for a goal? Could you ask for a better one? Make this the highest goal of all for yourself. Find the strength of the Holy Spirit to reach it. Don't allow yourself to become a commodity of declining value, vulnerable in the marketplace of life. Live in this additional dimension of the upward call of God in Christ Jesus, discovering his will and doing it. Keep your eyes on a worthwhile goal.

## Do Your Best

Step 4: Go for broke.

Paul says, "I press on." He uses the expression *straining forward to what lies ahead.* Can you think of a more creative lifestyle?

But don't take step 4 before you've taken steps 1, 2, and 3. I know people who go for broke, but they haven't admitted that they're not perfect. They're not living with their backs to the past. They don't have a worthwhile goal. They remind me of the chicken with its head cut off, fluttering all over the place, going all directions at the same time.

Make it your constant practice to give life everything you've got. Do your very best. There's nothing wrong with a Christian being an achiever, as long as your success is kept in proper balance with your humility. Strain every effort toward being the person God wants you to be, empowered by his Holy Spirit.

There's no room for amateurs in this business of serving Jesus Christ. A good Christian is one who blends talent with perspiration. God's gift of grace is yours through faith. A spin-off of his gift is your effort to be the person he wants you to be. There will be pain and defeats along the way. There will be times when your struggle to reach your goal will be frustrated. There will be times when your energies run low.

I'm challenged by the ethical writings of Reinhold Niebuhr, who talked about "the impossible ethical ideal." Grappling realistically with the basic sinful nature of mankind, Niebuhr explained that we need not be caught up in a pessimism which refuses to take responsible ethical action. Instead, we should strive toward what is an impossible ethical ideal, doing our very best to bring about the kingdom of God here on earth. Yes, we'll fall short. Our efforts will fail. But in the process, we shall make contributions far beyond those we would have made if we had compromised our goals and energies by a defeatist attitude.

The artist Sir Joshua Reynolds could not look at a picture in his studio without wishing to retouch it here and there. Forms on canvas seldom are as fair as the visions in a painter's mind. The spiritual outlook is ominous where there is no self-dissatisfaction, no sense of striving toward ideals which at times are unreachable.

I get excited about the Christian life and this business of living beyond myself. The reason is that my ultimate perfection is secure in the person of Jesus Christ.

On my desk are two symbols. One is a roughhewn, olive-wood cross, symbolic of a life crucified with Jesus. The other is a marble statue of the Greek discus thrower.

The cross calls me to self-denial, to the losing of myself in the service of my Lord and my fellow man. It reminds me of my own expendability. It highlights the sacrifice which Jesus made on the cross. It shows me that I could not save myself. All human effort falls short.

The discus thrower alerts me to my responsibility for self-mastery. Every muscle is geared to the moment. There's no sense of looking back. There's no wasted energy. All is devoted to immediate excellence in which one reaches the peak of his ability, with goals still beyond that lead to the prize which lies ahead.

God help you and me to live in the strength of the One whose resurrection set us free and whose Spirit empowers us. You can live beyond yourself!

# 10

## S. Lewis Johnson, Jr.

S. Lewis Johnson, Jr., has ministered at the Believers Chapel in Dallas, Texas, for more than twenty-five years. From 1950 to 1977, he taught New Testament and systematic theology at Dallas Theological Seminary. He also served as professor of biblical and systematic theology at Trinity Evangelical Divinity School from 1980 to 1985.

Johnson has authored *The Old Testament in the New* and contributed to *The Wycliffe Bible Commentary* and to *New Dimensions in New Testament Study.* He received his Th.D. degree from Dallas and did postgraduate study at Southern Methodist University, the University of Basel, and the University of Edinburgh.

# Expounding Individual Books

Among the influences that have moved me in the ministry of the Word of God are modern Bible teachers such as Donald Grey Barnhouse of Tenth Presbyterian Church, Philadelphia, whose ministry was vital in my conversion; H. A. Ironside of the Moody Church, Chicago, whose simple and clear Bible exposition exalted the Lord Jesus Christ; and from an earlier time, Charles Haddon Spurgeon, whose penetrating elucidation of individual texts and of the doctrine of sovereign grace has excited me for decades.

The greatest influence upon my preaching, however, arose from what I would call providential necessity. While teaching and studying in the graduate school of Dallas Seminary, from which I had graduated, Dr. Everett F. Harrison, one of my revered teachers, was called to become New Testament professor at Fuller Theological Seminary in Pasadena, California. He had resigned late in the school year and, due to the difficulty of finding a suitable replacement for him, I was asked to teach—in addition to the Hebrew that I was teaching—New Testament Greek exegesis. That led to an association of thirty years, spent preponderantly in lecturing on the New Testament Greek text exegetically and on related disciplines. Since the school was small at the time and the faculty few, my responsibilities required me to lecture on almost all of the New Testament text over a two-year cycle. While the toll was great in terms of time and effort, the rewards have continued to the present day. My present preaching ministry still follows basically a methodology of preaching systematically through the books of the Bible. That is the staple of the Sunday morning Ministry of the Word Service in Believers Chapel.

In form the ministry has followed that of John Calvin, who preached through whole books of the bible Sunday after Sunday. And in one other sense there is a resemblance to the ministry of the Reformers. T. H. L. Parker has said, "The reason for the great weight that the Reformers laid on preaching was not educational or social but theological."[1] The ministry that I have attempted to give has been given with an avowedly theological purpose of expounding the biblical teaching concerning the redemption of God in Christ and the believer's life of obedience in response. Beyond that there is no claim in the slightest that the ministry can be compared with the incomparable expositor from Geneva.

I conceive the task of the minister of the Word to be the exposition of the Scriptures, or the Word of God. Strictly speaking, the terms *exegesis* and *exposition* mean the same thing. For example, Webster defines exegesis as "exposition, explanation; esp: an explanation or critical interpretation of a text." In common religious usage, however, it is generally accepted that exposition denotes a more extended development and illustration of a passage, or text, with the use of other passages in comparison and contrast. It is in this sense that I think of the term *exposition.*

My task, then, as I see it is to explain the Scriptures, believing also that illustration and application of the sense given is a proper extension of the explanation. That means that my goal is to bring my audience to the same understanding and application of Scripture that I have, a goal that explicitly involves the conversion and progressive sanctification of

1. T. H. L. Parker, *John Calvin: A Biography* (Philadelphia: Westminster, 1975), 89.

those who hear. Thus, an exposition with an evangelistic and theological emphasis is implied in the goal.

Every sermon begins with the selection of the text. In my case it begins generally with the selection of a biblical book. The norms of selection include my understanding of Scripture. That is, it is unwise to attempt an explanation of a work of which I have a very limited understanding. Another norm is the spiritual maturity of the congregation, as the elders and I perceive it. In other words, what are the perceived needs of the body of believers? What biblical teaching would be helpful for us in our growth? Still another norm is the current state of the evangelical world with its interests and challenges.

After a consideration of these things, I choose a book of Scripture to expound. Then, following the selection of the book come the steps in preparation of the individual messages. First, I read the text in the original language. Those who have learned Greek, Hebrew, and Aramaic should not neglect them. Carlyle once brusquely blurted out, when asked about the neglect of the languages by the ministers of his day, "What! Your priests not know their sacred books!"[2]

Of course, this is not meant to discourage those who read only the English text. Those who read assiduously and carefully the English text in several good translations will find available to them almost all the help they need for careful exposition.

Second, I consult the available materials supplementary to the Bible: general reference works, dictionaries, grammars of the original languages when necessary, commentaries, systematic theologies particularly when theological ideas are in the passage, and yes, sermons! Every preacher should, if possible, obtain and use a good library. One may preach well without one, but hardly ever exceedingly well.

Careful study of the grammar and syntax of the sermon text is fundamental to clarity. Luther said, "The science of theology is nothing else but grammar exercised upon the words of the Holy Spirit." Fairbairn, the renowned Scottish theologian and preacher, reiterated Luther's claim, "He who is no philologian is no theologian; he who is no grammarian is no divine."

A word about commentaries should not be necessary, but is. I believe strongly in heavy reading of commentaries and, in fact, any exegetical and expository material that might enhance my understanding of the text. I cannot understand why some counsel young men to avoid such material and confine themselves to the text alone. To my mind that is a form of arrogance, the equivalent of affirming that we do not need the wisdom of those who have gone before us, who were also taught by the same Spirit of God to whom we look for insight (cf. John 16:12–15).

2. Bruce M. Metzger, "Grammars of the Greek New Testament," in *Tools for Bible Study IV*, ed. Balmer H. Kelly and Donald G. Miller (Richmond: John Knox, 1956), 52.

Third, in my reading I search for an accurate understanding of the author's argument, his flow of thought, and his intent in writing. A simple appreciation of the diverse types of literature in the Bible is necessary here. In Paul and the epistolary literature, careful attention to the connectives is essential.

Fourth, further effort must be expended to locate the author's theme in the section in view. John Stott calls this "the dominant thought,"[3] while others use such expressions as "the big idea." To reduce the passage to one simple proposition, as Charles Simeon recommended, is a helpful practice.

Fifth, at this point I am ready to attempt an initial outline of the section, gathering my thoughts around the theme, or the dominant thought, and paying attention to the transitional sentences, clauses, or phrases. My outlines are analytically constructed for clarity of thought.

Sixth, with a view to the presentation of the material in the pulpit, I make a selection of the key sentences, phrases, and words that I expect to give special treatment in the sermon. The norms of the selection may be doctrinal importance, critical importance for substantiating my understanding of the flow of the author's thought, or simply the striking practical application found in the terms. I make sure that these matters are represented plainly in my outline.

Seventh, I single out the points requiring illustration and work on finding them. The Bible itself is, without doubt, the finest source of illustrations, but due to my teaching field and experience, I use many illustrations drawn from the history of the Christian church and its doctrinal development. Thus, to my mind every preacher should have, read, and study histories of Christian doctrine. Further, the biographies of the great saints not only are edifying and instructive, but also afford excellent illustrative material. Since I incline to the theology of the Reformers, the lives of the Reformers, such as Luther, Calvin, Zwingli, and those who have followed in that tradition particularly appeal to me and provide illustrative material harmonious with the content of my preaching.

Eighth, at this point I usually make out a new outline of the message, being sure to have in it the important points, the transitional sentences that one must use in moving from one section of the outline, or message, to another. The illustrations should also be penciled in.

Ninth, at this point I work on the introduction and the conclusion to the message. I find it best to wait until the body of the sermon outline is finished before introducing it. This avoids the tendency to twist the body of the sermon to the introduction and conclusion. The introducing of the sermon is one of the most difficult exercises, especially if one has

3. John R. W. Stott, *Between Two Worlds: The Art of Preaching in the Twentieth Century* (Grand Rapids: Eerdmans, 1982), 224.

preached to one congregation for many years, as I have. The finding of new ways to introduce old themes is not easy. I find my greatest help, beyond the reflection upon the text and sermon materials themselves, in constant reading. My reading includes the Christian periodicals, the national newspapers and periodicals, relaxing novels, and as much of the important national and international literature as I have time for. The contemporary nature of the content of such literature usually provides useful illustrative material.

I find that I frequently introduce messages against the background of contemporary life, contemporary church life, and historical Christianity from the Reformed perspective of the doctrine of sovereign grace. For example, in the exposition of the First Epistle of John, one of its great themes is the fact that the divine life cannot be divorced from moral excellence (2:3–6). The present moral crises in contemporary life, as well as in contemporary evangelical church life, afford telling examples of the failure of which John speaks.

Further, John's doctrinal tests that touch the person and work of Christ (1 John 1:5–2:2, 18–19, 22–23; 4:2; etc.) may be illustrated from the long history of ecclesiastical debates over the person of Christ and his atoning work. In fact, ample opportunity is afforded by the background of the letter to instruct congregations in historical theology as the biblical text is being expounded. An introduction touching upon significant historical and theological questions is an excellent setting against which to expound Scripture. A brief discussion of the attempts of contemporary theologians to deny the penal satisfaction of Christ enlightens exposition of 1 John 2:1–2 or 4:9–14. Of course, one must do a bit of reading in contemporary theology, but then that, too, is rewarding for both preacher and congregation!

My conclusion is usually in the form of an observation upon the theme that I have expounded that merits further application. If the text contains the basis of a legitimate evangelistic appeal, and most passages do, then I like to end on that note, for we always have lost unbelievers in the audience. Substantial theology, wedded to an earnest evangelistic appeal, results in a healthy ministry. That, at least, is my aim.

Tenth, at this point I type my final outline on paper of a size to fit in the Bible I take into the pulpit (usually three small pages, five by seven inches). I also type out the illustrations I will use, particularly if they are taken from books, articles, or magazines, with documentation for use when, or if, the message is preached again. If I simply put in my notes, "Illustration: Man and dog," that may clearly mean something to me now, but several years later the sense will probably be gone forever.

It is probably superfluous to stress the fact that the preparation of a sermon must take place first and last in the preacher's heart. Calvin himself said of the minister of the Word, "It would be better for him to break his neck going up into the pulpit, if he does not take pains to be the first to follow God."[4]

The final step in preparation for preaching, and perhaps the most important, is earnest petition for divine blessing on the message. I never feel properly prepared if I have not spent time with the Lord, asking him to give enlightenment, conviction, regeneration, and faith as the passage is preached. Luther said that theologians are made by *oratio, meditatio,* and *tentatio,* or prayer, meditation, and trial. The same may be said of the preacher, and first place is given to prayer.

4. Parker, *John Calvin,* 95.

# The Lord of Creation
# and Redemption

Who is the image of the invisible God, the firstborn of every creature: For by him were all things created, that are in heaven, and that
are in earth, visible and invisible, whether they be thrones, or
dominions, or principalities, or powers: all things were created by
him, and for him: And he is before all things, and by him all things
consist. And he is the head of the body, the church: who is the
beginning, the firstborn from the dead; that in all things he might
have the preeminence. For it pleased the Father that in him should
all fulness dwell; And, having made peace through the blood of his
cross, by him to reconcile all things unto himself; by him, I say,
whether they be things in earth, or things in heaven. [Col. 1:15–20
KJV]

The claims of Jesus Christ for himself are, to say the least, astounding.
Listen to some of them. He claimed heavenly origin: "Ye are from
beneath; I am from above: ye are of this world; I am not of this world"
(John 8:23).

He claimed a unique relationship to God. To Philip he said, "He that
hath seen me hath seen the Father" (John 14:9). Think what this
means. The character of Jesus is the character of God, the holiness of
Jesus the holiness of God, the wrath of Jesus the wrath of God, the love
and compassion of Jesus the love and compassion of God, and the cross
of Jesus the revelation of both the justice of God and the self-sacrificing
love and grace of God.[5]

He claimed numerous divine prerogatives. He asserted a unique
knowledge of God, a knowledge of God that is divine, maintaining, "All
things are delivered unto me of my Father: and no man knoweth the
Son, but the Father; neither knoweth any man the Father, save the Son,

5. Cf. Robert Law, *The Emotions of Jesus* (New York: Scribner's, 1915), 11.

and he to whomsoever the Son will reveal him" (Matt. 11:27). He claimed supreme authority: "All power is given unto me in heaven and in earth" (Matt. 28:18). He claimed an absolute oneness with the Father, sinlessness, the power to forgive sin, to quicken the dead, to send the Holy Spirit, to be the only way to God, to have a life so valuable as to be a ransom for man (cf. Ps. 49:7), and to confer eternal life to his own (John 10:28–29).

Alfred Noyes felt bound to say of Jesus' statement, "Heaven and earth shall pass away, but my words shall not pass away" (Matt. 24:35). "The values of that utterance—subjected to the coldest standards of literary criticism—are not human. The voice of the Eternal is in it, before whom even the suns and universes dissolve like a shadow, and all the ages of time are but a moment."[6]

Modern criticism, to explain the picture of Christ as seen in the Gospels, often has claimed that the figure of Christ was created by the church. To this A. E. J. Rawlinson responded, "If it was Christianity that created the figure of the Christ of the Gospels, what was it that created Christianity?"[7]

Viewed by comparison with some of the Lord's own claims for himself, the claims that Paul the apostle makes of him in his letter to the Colossians do not seem out of order at all. Paul claims that the Lord Jesus Christ is the Lord of creation and Lord of redemption. These claims, he believed, if carefully considered, would deliver the Colossian believers from many false conceptions of spiritual truth. Specifically, the heresy of Gnostic Judaism, to which they had been exposed by false teachers, would be seen in its baleful light. Jesus Christ only an angelic emanation from the supreme God? The one who made all those astonishing claims? On the face of the matter, the babble of the philosophers of Asia Minor was nonsense. New believers, however, are susceptible to nonsense, as a look at the Christian church today and the things that find credence within it show.

Paul believed that to know Christ is to be delivered from spiritual error and chaos; therefore, he confronted the errorists in Colosse frankly and frontally with one of his greatest statements concerning Christ. Often called by scholars "The Great Christology," Colossians 1:15–20 is a striking presentation of the person and work of the Second Person of the eternal Trinity, the Lord Jesus Christ.

We owe the passage to the heresy which was on the verge of infecting the little church that met in Philemon's house in the city of Colosse in Asia Minor. The name given to the heresy, "Gnostic Judaism," simply

6. Alfred Noyes, *The Unknown God* (London: Sheed and Ward, 1934), 354.
7. A. E. J. Rawlinson, *The New Testament Doctrine of the Christ* (London, New York, Toronto: Longmans, Green, 1926), 10.

says that it contained elements traceable to Judaism and later Gnosticism. Thus, in one respect we can be thankful for the heresy, because the church of Jesus Christ would be impoverished substantially if it did not possess this significant testimony to the preeminence of its Redeemer.

We turn now to "The Great Christology" and Paul's stirring defense of the lordship of Christ over the physical creation and the spiritual creation, the church. Sharing with his readers and spiritual brethren and sisters his own deep experiences of grace, strongly desiring that they avoid the pitfalls and perils of false teaching, under the burden of the Spirit's guidance he exalted the Lord Jesus Christ as the solution to the ferment in Colosse.

## Christ the Lord of the First Creation

*The essential basis of his lordship* (v. 15a). New Testament scholars have speculated that the passage we are studying may have been part of an early Christian hymn, or credal statement, that antedated Paul's epistle. The question remains a moot one, but what is not moot is the remarkable status given by Paul to Jesus Christ in the passage. This tribute to God's beloved Son begins by speaking of him as "the image of the invisible God" (v. 15). The word *image*, and sometimes also its diminutive form, was used for a portrait in Greek. Two ideas were associated with it: the idea of representation and the idea of manifestation.[8] It suggests a likeness that is not accidental (such as one automobile resembling another), but one derived from an archetype, or original pattern, which in this case is God. Furthermore, the word, especially in the light of the emphatic adjective describing God, "the invisible," contains the notion of manifestation. Jesus of Nazareth is the revelation of the unseen God; he is the great and final theophany. God is Christ-like—can we say less or more?

When Philip asked Jesus, "Lord, shew us the Father, and it sufficeth us," the Lord replied, "Have I been so long time with you, and yet hast thou not known me, Philip? He that hath seen me hath seen the Father . . ." (John 14:8–9). When the Pharisees asked Jesus, "Where is thy Father?" he replied, "Ye neither know me, nor my Father: if ye had known me, ye should have known my Father also" (John 8:19). He is, indeed, the perfect likeness and manifestation of God. It is simply heretical to deny, as do the cults, the orthodox doctrine of the deity of Christ.

The present tense, "is," implies that he is always and everywhere the manifestation of God (cf. John 1:18). Was it Lord Byron who said, "If God is not like Jesus Christ, then God *ought* to be like Jesus Christ"?

8. J. B. Lightfoot, *Saint Paul's Epistles to the Colossians and to Philemon* (London and New York: Macmillan, 1890), 143, 144.

*The economic basis of his lordship* (v. 15b). Paul continues his description of Christ, speaking of him as "the firstborn of every creature" (literally, firstborn over all creation, NIV). The words might seem at first glance to teach that Christ is part of the creation, or a created being. That, of course, is not true for several reasons.

First, it is inconsistent with the context (cf. vv. 16–17), which states that he existed before all things. In fact, the context states that he is the Creator himself. Jesus of Nazareth was no newcomer at Bethlehem.

In the well-known controversy in the ancient church between the followers of Arius, who denied the eternal sonship of Christ and, thus, his deity, and the followers of Athanasius, who affirmed Christ's deity, the Arians drew attention to the word *firstborn*, as found here, suggesting that it denoted that Christ was less than deity. Athanasius, however, drew attention to verse 16, where Paul writes, "In him were all things created," and tellingly went on to say, "But if all the creatures were created in him, he is other than the creatures, and is not a creature but the creator of the creatures."[9] The point was well made.

Second, it is inconsistent with the rest of the New Testament, which often affirms his uniqueness and responsibility for creation (cf. John 1:3).

Third, the word Paul uses, "firstborn," has two connotations in biblical usage: priority, and sovereignty. In view of the statement of verse 18, that he has become preeminent in all things, it seems probable that Paul has the thought of sovereignty primarily in view. The use of the word in the Greek Old Testament confirms this, for in Psalm 89, which is strongly messianic, the psalmist says of Christ, "Also I will make him my firstborn, higher than the kings of the earth" (Ps. 89:27, LXX).[10] Paul, then, effectively counters any claim of the heretics that Christ was only an angelic emanation from God and part of the creation. He is creation's Lord.

Fourth, there was a Greek word in usage that meant "first-created," but it is significant that both the Old and New Testaments did not use it in the passages referring to the Messiah, the Lord Jesus Christ.

Fifth, a final fact makes it impossible to understand "firstborn of every creature" as saying our Lord was a created being. That is the fact that throughout Scripture he is set forth as man's Savior. If he were a created being, in no way could he be our Savior. Only God can save sinners. Thus, the saving experience of every Christian is a testimony to the deity of the Lord Jesus.

9. Saint Athanasius, *Orationes contra Arianos* 4.2.62, in *A Select Library of Nicene and Post-Nicene Fathers of the Christian Church*, 2d series, ed. Philip Schaff and Henry Wace (Grand Rapids: Eerdmans, 1971).

10. The thought of sovereignty is also found in the Hebrew word *bekor*, used by the psalmist.

*The explicit proof of his lordship* (vv. 16–17). In verses 16 and 17 the apostle writes, "For in him were all things created, in the heavens and upon the earth, things visible and things invisible, whether thrones or dominions or principalities or powers; all things have been created through him and for him; and he is before all things, and in him all things consist" (ASV). Two great works of our Lord are described in the verses, and they are the foundation of his lordship over the creation.

First, Paul states that Christ is the Creator of the universe. In fact, he expands the concept to include his work as architect, builder, and goal of the universe. The "for" (literally, because) introduces the reason Paul is able to say that Christ is sovereign over the whole creation. Three prepositional phrases delineate his relation to the universe. The first is found in the opening clause, "In him were all things created." The first phrase, "in him," has been rendered in some versions "by him" (cf. KJV, NIV), but since that idea of agency is found very clearly in the second phrase, "by him," later in the verse, it seems better to render the earlier phrase, "in him."

What would the phrase *in him* say that is not found in the later phrase *by him*?[11] It might indicate that Paul was looking at the Lord Jesus as the architect of the universe. Bishop Lightfoot suggested this, saying that he is the place where the eternal ideas have their abode.[12] This illuminating contribution to Pauline though may be set forth most clearly by an illustration.

Several steps are involved in the construction of a substantial building. First, at the owner's request, an architect designs the building, preparing plans and specifications in accordance with the expressed desires of the owner. Then the plans are submitted for bids by builders or contractors, and a builder is secured to erect the structure. After the completion of the edifice, it is occupied by the owner and devoted to its intended use. Our Lord is not only the builder of the universe; he is also its architect and owner. All things have been created *in him* (the plans for the creation abode eternally in his mind), by him (he acted as builder), and for him (the creation belongs to him and is to reflect his glory as the scene in which the eternal counsel is to be brought to its glorious fruition).

Before the indescribable majesty of the eternal Christ we are constrained to respond in reverence and awe, "How great thou art!"

---

11. Technically, the sense would be local, which is permissible grammatically (cf. 1:17; Acts 17:28).

12. Lightfoot, *Saint Paul's Epistles,* 148, 149; cf. Martin Dibelius, *An die Kolosser, Epheser, und Philemon,* rev. D. Heinrich Greeven, 3d ed. (Tübingen: J.C.B. Mohr [Paul Siebeck], 1953), 12.

Second, the thought now passes from creation to preservation, and the apostle states that Christ is the sustainer of the universe (v. 17). "All things hold together in him" is the way he puts it. This is the second proof of his lordship over the whole creation. By virtue of his preexistent person and power he continues to exercise sovereignty over all the cosmic powers of the universe.

The clause, "And he is before all things," reminds one of the statement Christ made in the days of his flesh. Speaking to the Jews of his day in support of his claim, "Your father Abraham rejoiced to see my day: and he saw it, and was glad" (John 8:56), Jesus declared, "Verily, verily, I say unto you, Before Abraham was, I am" (v. 58). It was a clear expression of his preexistence.

The word rendered "consist" in the King James Version (NIV, NASB, "hold together") marks him out as sustainer of the universe and its unifying principle of life. In Platonic and Stoic philosophy the word was used to describe the marvelous unity of the entire world, but for Paul it is Christ and his Word who is the unifier of the universe that he brought into being. "He is," as Lightfoot long ago declared, "the principle of cohesion in the universe."[13]

There is an expression commonly used that comes to mind when I think of Christ as the principle of cohesion in the universe. It is the word *unglued*. For children it is a common word, for when dolls are broken, they are often glued back into good condition for further use. They may, however, become unglued.

In Charleston, South Carolina, where I lived, antique furniture is very common and prized by the people there. My family has always liked antiques, particularly the Early American ones. Now antiques are not always very strong, and growing children learn that quite early in life. We have all rushed in to dinner a bit tardy—in Charleston at about two o'clock in the afternoon—for the principal meal of the day, and have fallen into our chairs only to hear the telltale crack of broken expensive antiques and the sharp voice of parental disapproval. Often such pieces must be glued again, at least in part, and for them to come unglued is not uncommon.

Now, however, we use this word to describe people. They "come unglued," by which we mean that they become upset, unnerved, demoralized, reduced to jelly, or something like that, over an unpleasant happening! This is the opposite of Paul's word *hold together*. Our Lord's mighty power is the reason the whole world does not come unglued, is not reduced to chaos or nothingness again. Daniel describes him as "the God in whose hand thy breath is" (Dan. 5:23). Every breath that we draw is under his sovereign direction. In fact, the only breath of which

13. Lightfoot, *Saint Paul's Epistles*, 154.

we can be sure is the one we are drawing at this very moment. If, then, our trust is in him who prevents the universe from disintegrating by his sovereign control, what need is there to push the panic button?

The practical significance of this truth is almost beyond comprehension. Every twinkling of the eye, every beat of the heart, every thought of the human mind is dependent upon his sovereign beneficence. His arm upholds the universe and, if his omnipotent power were withdrawn, all things would fade into their original nonexistence.[14] What light this throws upon that experience of the disciples with the Lord when, crossing the Sea of Galilee after a busy day of ministry and with their weary leader asleep in the stern of the frail vessel, a lashing storm arose and churned the little sea into wet fury. Within a few moments the experienced fishermen were terrified by the intensity of the storm. Anxiously and somewhat peevishly they turned to their sleeping companion and brusquely roused him, exclaiming, "Master, carest thou not that we perish?"—quite unaware that there is no sinking with the Savior aboard. Jesus arose, rebuked the wind, and said to the sea, "Hush! Be still!" In the dead calm that followed, he reproved the disciples with words they would surely remember for the rest of their days, "Why are ye so fearful? how is it that ye have no faith?" (Mark 4:40). Awestruck, they could only murmur to one another, "What manner of man is this, that even the wind and the sea obey him?" What light Paul's words throw upon their experience! If he is the principle of cohesion in the universe, it is no wonder that he said to them what he said. And if he is the One in whom all things consist, and if he has pledged himself to us, then we have safe and certain passage through the storms and plagues of life.

In the light of the things Paul has been saying, how remarkable and wonderful is the incarnation! As the devout old Scottish commentator, John Eadie, said, "That the creator and upholder of the universe should come down to such a world as this, and clothe Himself in the inferior nature of its race, and in that nature die to forgive and save it, is the most amazing of revelations."[15] And yet, as the professor added, it is "most glorious truth; truth sealed with the precious blood of Calvary."

The God of Genesis 1 is the babe of Matthew 1 and 2. The one of whom Isaiah said, "Who hath measured the waters in the hollow of his hand, and meted out heaven with the span, and comprehended the dust of the earth in a measure, and weighed the mountains in scales, and the hills in a balance" (Isa. 40:12) is the same person of whom Paul said, "For I determined not to know any thing among you, save Jesus Christ, and him crucified" (1 Cor. 2:2).

14. John Eadie, *A Commentary on the Greek Text of the Epistle of Paul to the Colossians* (Edinburgh: T. and T. Clark, 1884), 57.

15. Ibid., 58.

The same God of whom Jeremiah said, "But the LORD is the true God, he is the living God, and an everlasting king: at his wrath the earth shall tremble, and the nations shall not be able to abide his indignation" (Jer. 10:10), is he of whom John wrote, "And the Word was made flesh, and dwelt among us" (John 1:14), and "Jesus wept" (11:35), and also, "After that he poureth water into a bason, and began to wash the disciples' feet, and to wipe them with the towel wherewith he was girded" (13:5).

And the one of whom Ezekiel wrote, "And above the firmament that was over their heads was the likeness of a throne, as the appearance of a sapphire stone: and upon the likeness of the throne was the likeness as the appearance of a man above upon it" (Ezek. 1:26), is the same one of whom John wrote in his Gospel, "But one of the soldiers with a spear pierced his side, and forthwith came there out blood and water" (John 19:34).

And, finally, he who warned ancient Israel and said, "Take ye therefore good heed unto yourselves; for ye saw no manner of similitude on the day that the LORD spake unto you in Horeb" (Deut. 4:15), says at length to his own, "Behold my hands and my feet, that it is I myself: handle me, and see; for a spirit hath not flesh and bones, as ye see me have" (Luke 24:39).[16]

## Christ the Lord of the New Creation

*His lordship declared* (v. 18a). The apostle's words that begin the eighteenth verse, "And he is the head of the body, the church," affirm his lordship. The Greek text is rather emphatic, for the pronoun *he* is represented in the original text by an intensive pronoun. In the light of this, the clause may be rendered, "And he, and no other, is the head of the body, the church," a rendering that excludes other pseudo-lords of the church.

Paul's thought now moves from sovereignty over the cosmos to sovereignty over the church. The word *head* asserts Christ's inseparability from the church, but it also excludes his identity with it. As his body, the church is united with him. He, however, is not the church; he is the church's head, owning and controlling the body. That is why the church is commonly called "the body of Christ," but never "the body of Christians." It is his church, and we, the members, are to be submissive to him, just as the apostle elsewhere says that a wife, although she is united to her husband, is to be submissive to him (cf. Eph. 5:22–23).

What does this clause say of present-day church life? Well, it says surely that the head of the church is not in Rome, or Nashville, or Louisville, or in any other locale where denominational headquarters

16. At the reading of Eadie's comments at this place one can easily detect my dependency upon him.

are located. The head is in heaven! We do not need a Giovanni Battista Montini or a Robert Runcie as our head. We have a sovereign head, whose nature, thoughts, and purposes toward us are divine. We need not revere Peter's bones in Rome, for we worship the Lord Jesus Christ, universally sovereign and saving.

*His lordship proved* (v. 18b). "That in all things he might have the preeminence" reveals the divine intent in Christ's work. He is sovereign over the first creation, because he created it and sustains it. He is sovereign over the new creation, the church, because he has accomplished the church's redemption. His redeeming work enabled him to add a new facet to his preeminence. He was preeminent over the creation; he has now become preeminent in all things, material and spiritual.

His preeminence may be illustrated by the experience of Peter on the Mount of Transfiguration. After ascending the mountain with Peter, James, and John, Jesus was transfigured before them. His face shone as the sun, and his raiment was white as the light. Moses and Elijah appeared to the astonished apostles, who had just awakened from sleep and had seen Christ's glory. The representatives of the Law and the Prophets talked with our Lord about his death that he should accomplish at Jerusalem.

The experience was so shocking and terrifying to Peter that he began to babble, not realizing what he was saying (Luke 9:33). He rashly suggested that three tabernacles be built on the mountaintop, one for our Lord, one for Moses, and one for Elijah. While Peter was still speaking, a voice from the Father in heaven interrupted him, saying, "This is my beloved Son: hear him" (Luke 9:35).

The clause *while he thus spake,* has always intrigued me. What did Peter intend to add to his suggestion about building the three tabernacles? Is it possible that he intended to say, "and three more, one for James, one for John, and one for me"? We'll never know the answer to that question, but the suggestion is one that suits what we know of Peter.

The Lord in heaven did not think much of Peter's babbling, for he interrupted the apostle with words of divine wisdom, "This is my beloved Son: hear him." Put in our language, it might be something like this, "Peter, this is my beloved Son, please shut up and listen to him!" At any rate, one can see that the Father is jealous for his Son's glory and will not permit anyone to be placed upon the same level, not even a Moses or an Elijah. In all things he must have the preeminence.

There was a day in the history of Joshua and the children of Israel when the same lesson was taught them. Israel was before Jericho, and Joshua, the captain of the Lord's hosts, was out doing some reconnoitering around the city, preparing for the assault to capture it. As he was engaged in his work, he saw a man "over against him with his sword drawn in his hand." Joshua went over to him and said, "Art thou for us, or for our adversaries?"

That was surely a natural question, and Joshua expected an explicit answer in terms of the two alternatives. The answer that came, however, was unexpected, for the "man" said, "Nay; but as captain of the host of the LORD am I now come." Well, one does not answer an either/or question with a no. In this case, however, the following words fully explained the situation to the leader of Israel. Again, to put the answer in our words, it was something like this, "No, General Joshua, I have not come to serve under you in your army, nor under the Jerichoites in theirs. I have come to take over your army as general. Your rank is now that of lieutenant general!"

The answer was certainly one that Joshua understood. Evidently there was something in the demeanor of the "man" and in the tone and sense of his words that convinced Joshua that he was in the presence of someone who was more than a man. The Word of God says, "And Joshua fell on his face to the earth, and did worship, and said unto him, What saith my lord unto his servant?"

The captain of the Lord's host replied, "Loose thy shoe from off thy foot; for the place whereon thou standest is holy." The words concluding the section are striking. "And Joshua did so" (Josh. 5:13–15). In this way the great leader of the Lord's people learned the identity of the real Captain of the Lord's host. Joshua had experienced a theophany, an appearance of God before the time of the incarnation. Most evangelical scholars regard the divine person to have been the Second Person of the Trinity, our Lord Jesus Christ. Thus, Joshua learned that preparation and ordination by Moses to the task of leading Israel were not enough. Subordination to him who has the preeminence is fundamental to success in the work of the Lord. He must always have the preeminence.

### The Ground of His Primacy in Redemption

*In his person* (v. 19). In the nineteenth verse the apostle writes, "For it pleased the Father ["the Father" is supplied by the translators] that in him [that is, in Christ] should all fulness dwell." The "for," opening the verse, identifies the ground of Christ's primacy in redemption. All saving fullness and power reside in him. That is, he is the only saving mediator between God and men by virtue of his cross and resurrection. Contrary to the heretics' claims of a hierarchy of angelic mediators emanating from God, Christ being at best only one of them, Paul contends that Christ is the covenant head of God's people, "a Prince and a Saviour" (Acts 5:31), in whom alone redemption is found. He stands officially before God the Father as the royal high priest, the sole mediator between God and man.

*In his work* (v. 20). In the final verse of the section Paul describes our Lord's official work in more detail under the figure of reconciliation, a reconciliation touching not only individuals, but the whole universe.

Reconciliation is the finished work of God by which he brings men and the creation from the position and attitude of enmity toward him to an attitude and status of amity by the cross. We are all familiar with the association of reconciliation with persons. But here Paul expands the concept to touch "all things," including things in heaven and things on the earth.

In what sense can heaven itself be the object of Christ's reconciling work? Whatever the passage means, one thing is sure: Paul does not teach universalism, that is, that all persons or intelligences shall be saved. He does not say that reconciliation extends to things under the earth (cf. Phil. 2:10).

But what about the text? He does say that God has reconciled "all things" to himself, including things in the heavens. Some statements in Job may bear on this question. There we read, "Behold, He puts no trust in His holy ones [=angels?], and the heavens are not pure in His sight" (Job 15:15 NASB). Again, we read, "If even the moon has no brightness, and the stars are not pure in His sight" (25:5 NASB).

The answer to the problem is probably to be found in Paul's words in Romans 8:18–23. Here the apostle sees man and the creation linked together, and he envisions the universe as disturbed by man's sin in Eden (cf. Gen. 3:17–19). Elsewhere Paul states that the church shall judge angels, which indicates that the angelic world is involved in the defilement of the fall (cf. 1 Cor. 6:3). Answering to this, the reconciling work of the Son of God, the representative mediator, is destined to restore the whole creation to its divinely determined order. When man's reconciliation according to the divine program for the ages is completed, then that reconciliation shall be extended to the entire physical creation. Just as sin and creation's disorder and curse occurred in history, so shall redemption and the creation's reconciliation occur in history. The curse shall be replaced by the glorious day when "the wilderness and the solitary place shall be glad for them; and the desert shall rejoice, and blossom as the rose" (Isa. 35:1; cf. Eph. 1:10).

The significance of this in the Colossians' situation is patent. The angels, far from being true objects of worship (2:18), are themselves in need of the effects of the Savior's ministry!

Paul traces the means of the accomplishment of this mighty and telling work of reconciliation to "the blood of his cross" (v. 20). That is the instrument by which alone God deals with our sin, and with our hearts also. In the one case, sin is expiated and God is propitiated, and God's love is righteously freed to offer salvation to men. In the other case, he woos and wins our believing response as the Holy Spirit brings home to us the saving efficacy of the blood of Christ and his loving claims. He reconciles the rebel! Isaac Watts put it this way,

> Was it for crimes that I have done,
> He groaned upon the tree?
> Amazing pity, grace unknown,
> And love beyond degree!

I conclude with an obvious and urgent question that arises from a section in which our Lord has been pictured as the architect, builder, and sustainer of the cosmos, as well as the reconciler of the saints by the blood of his cross. The vast cosmos, sustained by him, yields complete allegiance to him. My question is this, "Will those who hear the good news of his saving cross respond by trust in him?" And then, "Will the new creation, the redeemed church, respond to its head and creator as the old creation does to him"? As the winds and waves obeyed him in that storm on the little lake when he shouted, "Hush! Be still!" will our hearts so respond and melt into the deep calm of eternal peace with God?

While we sturdily affirm our belief that Christ is preeminent in all things, is he really preeminent in our lives—in you and in me? Or, to put it in the words of the Heidelberg Catechism, "But what doth it help thee now, that thou believest all this?"

Pastor Theodore Monod used to illustrate the necessity and reasonableness of giving oneself to the will of God like this. Let us imagine a man passing out of a meeting, who sees a person in front of him drop a piece of paper. He picks it up and discovers that it is a banknote. Let us suppose it is a hundred-dollar bill. He hesitates, wondering how to deal with the situation, but then says to himself, "I will give the person who dropped it ten dollars and keep ninety dollars." His conscience, however, interposes and objects. So he decides, "I will give him ninety dollars and keep ten dollars." Again his conscience is aroused and objects. Finally, with a sigh the finder says, "Then I will do the grand and glorious thing. I will consecrate the entire hundred dollars to the man who lost it." But anyone who heard the man's conversation with himself would say, "That's not a grand and glorious thing to do, but a mere matter of ordinary honesty to give the man what was his own."

That's what personal commitment to the Lord comes down to. If by his grace we have come to see ourselves as offenders against God's law

and guilty of condemnation and eternal death, and if we have been ran-
somed and reconciled to God through the blood of the cross, then to
give ourselves to him is not a great and grand thing, but a mere matter
of common honesty. May God in his immeasurable grace enable us to
respond in faith and trust and common honesty to him who has loved
us and loosed us from all our sins in his blood.

# 11

## Walter C. Kaiser, Jr.

Walter C. Kaiser, Jr., is academic dean, senior vice president of education, and professor of Old Testament and Semitic languages at Trinity Evangelical Divinity School, where he has been since 1966.

He is a popular conference speaker and the author of numerous books. Among them are *Toward an Exegetical Theology: Biblical Exegesis for Preaching and Teaching, The Old Testament in Contemporary Preaching,* and *Toward an Old Testament Theology.* His Ph.D. degree is from Brandeis University.

# Keeping a Finger on the Text

Preparation for the delivery of the sermon is not an incidental or optional part of the preaching process. In many ways it is so determinative that without it the sermon usually commands little or no respect.

Spurgeon made this point in a delightful way in his lectures to his students. He told them what happened one time after the Bishop of Lichfield had lectured on the necessity of earnestly studying the Word of God as preparation for preaching. A certain vicar demurred at having this added burden placed on his ministry by his lordship, "for," said he, "often when I am in the vestry I do not know what I am going to talk about; but I go into the pulpit and preach, and think nothing of it." Spurgeon reminded his class that his lordship replied to the misguided vicar, "And you are quite right in thinking nothing of it, for your churchwardens have told me that they share your opinion!"

The hard work in preaching is found in the preparation. It is not easy. It requires time, self-discipline, rigid scheduling, good planning, and just plain hard work. The process must begin long before the time comes to preach on the text chosen, for the planning usually takes place at two different levels: the long-range planning for the general series and the immediate planning which tackles the individual units for each weekly message.

## Personal Preparation

I usually begin to plan about one or two years in advance for each new series of messages I intend to use at weekend services and summer Bible conferences. Since I am engaged in a rather vigorous academic schedule throughout the school year, and since I prefer to use a different series for each of the six or eight Bible conferences at which I speak each year, I must plan well in advance. The pastor likewise will find it advantageous to anticipate at least one year in advance the sermons that will best meet the needs of the congregation.

But where does one start? How can the preacher keep coming up with new materials, since all of us have such limited amounts of knowledge and only so many themes that we are especially adept at handling?

I have followed the practice of selecting a new book of the Bible or, if the biblical book I choose is especially long, I confine myself to a particular section of that book. Limiting one's selection to a biblical book or to a section of a book saves the interpreter from wasting valuable time fretting over what to preach on each Lord's Day. A series, generally, will cover at least twelve Sundays, allowing for interruptions to recognize special holidays or special days in the church calendar.

There is more to choosing a biblical book than just taking the next one in the canonical order, or deciding on a mere whim, coupled, perhaps, with the added inducement of a newly published commentary on that book. Each biblical book represents God's address to us on one or more key issues. The better one understands both the overall unifying theme of divine revelation and how each book contributes to that theme, adding its own individual subthemes, the more capable one will be in matching biblical books with the great issues of our day.

Great preaching will not ignore the fact that men and women need to hear the Word of God against the backdrop of the major ills, dilemmas, and questions of our own day. Therefore, it is as crucial for the preacher to be a student of the times as to be a student of Scripture. Only when a good match has been made between current questions and their biblical answers will preaching be effective, relevant, and challenging.

I have found that my college training in liberal arts has greatly helped me to get a handle on the philosophical, ethical, moral, cultural, aesthetic, economic, religious, and political issues of the day. I recommend that those who lack this preparation read the *Great Books* series published by Britannica, or participate in a Great Books Reading Club in their community. The same recommendation is appropriate for those who received a good liberal-arts education and who wish to continue to expand their own thinking by interacting with the sources of much modern Western thought.

Another way to keep abreast of contemporary thought is to form your own reading club from four to six members of your congregation or friends in the community. These individuals would help decide what are the great opinion-making books, plays, and cultural events currently in vogue. Each member would volunteer to read one of these books or attend a particular event and review it for the benefit of the whole group. The awareness gained by following one of these suggestions might shape much of the preaching plan for the coming year.

## Moving from the Text to the Sermon

As a seminary student I was greatly influenced by the analytical method of Bible study taught by my New Testament professor, Dr. Merrill C. Tenney of the Wheaton Graduate School of Theology.[1] In his Greek New Testament courses, I began to compose block diagrams which kept together whole phrases, clauses, and even short sentences in the biblical text. Based on the assumption that a paragraph has only one major idea, these diagrams provided a visual flow of the thought pattern of each paragraph.

I adopted this approach as my own because I was deeply convinced that there was a famine in the land of genuine expository preaching. Almost all evangelical preachers, of course, describe their own method of preaching as expository preaching. However, I prefer to define expository preaching as follows:

> Expository preaching is that method of proclaiming the Word of God in which both the *shape* and the *content* of the message arise from the passage itself. Since a paragraph by definition deals with a single idea, the smallest

1. See Merrill C. Tenney, *Galatians: The Charter of Christian Liberty,* rev. ed. (Grand Rapids: Eerdmans, 1957), for a full description of his Bible study method. This approach was pioneered to some extent by William Jenkyn, *An Exposition Upon the Epistle of Jude* (Edinburgh: Nichol, 1863), and Henry Parry Liddon, *Explanatory Analysis of Saint Paul's Epistle to the Romans* (London: Longmans, Green, 1899). I incorporated it in my book, *Toward an Exegetical Theology: Biblical Exegesis for Preaching and Teaching* (Grand Rapids: Baker, 1981).

unit of the biblical text which can be expounded in an expository sermon is a paragraph. Thus, in an expository sermon based on a single paragraph, each main point in the outline reflects some aspect or component—drawn from the paragraph—of the idea found in the topic sentence. When an expository sermon is based on several paragraphs, each main point in the outline reflects the idea embodied in the topic sentence of one of these paragraphs.

Once I have chosen the biblical book or section of a book, I design a title for the sermon series that relates the theme of the book (or section) to concerns people face today. For example, in a time of worldwide political and economic uncertainty, I might prepare an expository series on the Book of Daniel, entitled "Our International Unrest and the Triumph of the Kingdom of God." In a time of national distress or personal tragedy, I might turn to the Book of Lamentations and preach on "Finding Hope in the Face of Adversity" or "Coping with Grief."

Next, I divide the book or section of the book into its proper pericopes, that is, the teaching blocks that reflect all that the writer has said on a particular topic. A pericope might extend to a full chapter or, in some rare cases, to several chapters. I now identify the number of paragraphs each teaching block has. Unless I am dealing with narratives, proverbs, or legal texts, each paragraph will be represented by a major point in my sermon outline, while my subpoints will reflect the development of thought within that paragraph.

The movement from the theme or topic sentence (which defines what that paragraph is all about) to the main points of the sermon is a process I have described elsewhere as "principlizing." To principlize is to set forth the biblical author's arguments, claims, and statements in ways that are timeless and relevant to the current needs of the church and society (contextualization).

I have found it best to keep the following rules in mind as I attempted to principlize: Never use the past tense of the verb in a major point in the sermon; never use any proper names of persons or places except the names of God and Christ; and never use any third person pronouns but use instead the first person plural—"we," "us," and "our." These rules will prevent the message from becoming a mere description of an ancient historical situation and urge us on in bridging the gap between the "then" and the "now."

### Applying the Sermon to the Listener

One of the most critical moves in preaching is to convince the listeners that they should act upon the truth which they are hearing. Each must be convinced that the scriptural truth being taught is indeed relevant to that individual's situation and demands some kind of personal response to God before the service of worship is over.

I usually prefer to make the connections between the text and the need for personal response as I move through each major point of the sermon, rather than waiting until the conclusion to do this. The connections we make may be of various kinds: (1) cause and effect—Given this cause, should it not produce this effect or result in us? (2) ethical—Why am I living this way when God's Word demands a totally different lifestyle? (3) apologetical—Why am I holding this grudge against God? or, Why do I think that there is no way some of the principles taught in Scripture can apply to anyone who is living and operating in the real world?

We must, as ambassadors of high heaven, press the case made in the text to the point of decision. I ask myself as I go through my sermon preparation, What does this text demand of me and of my hearers today? How must I change? What must I repent of and confess to God? What have I failed to say, do, or think, or failed to influence others to do or believe that is distinctive, or even unique, to this text? What sort of corrections, modifications, and new commitments are demanded of me and those to whom I preach if we are going to escape condemnation for being mere hearers of God's Word, and not doers of it?

Some of our applications are so broad, so general, they can fit a thousand different texts. We must learn to particularize the challenge, the summons, the invitation of each text in terms of its own distinctive emphasis as it bears upon the lives of people today. I have found it best to plan these specific applications in advance and to include them in the notes which I will use in the pulpit. All too often, in the rush to cover the material while staying within the allotted time, we lose our train of thought and do not aim our summons to personal response as sharply and succinctly as we should. Naturally, this is the point where we reveal most clearly whether we have prayed enough over this sermon, and whether the Spirit of God first got hold of us before we issued the call to others. People can detect these things in our tone of voice, in the passion and conviction with which we issue our challenge to them, and in the earnestness with which we plead with them to do exactly what God is urging us to do in the text we have undertaken to expound.

## Reflecting on the Process of Sermonizing

The temptation is all too convenient for us preachers, whatever our age and our store of theological knowledge, to stop reading, studying, and growing—and so to stagnate. Once this sad state of affairs has set in, it usually happens that no matter how many new texts the preacher attempts to expound, eventually every one takes on the same shopworn shape. The same theological content is read into every text, while the text's true teaching often is unnoticed. When the preacher is not growing, we can be sure that the listeners will not grow either.

The best antidote to dry seasons is the habit of reading widely and constantly, studying the biblical text continually and intensively, and maintaining a highly particularized prayer life. This is not to say that there are no additional factors that also affect this equation and are just as real and necessary to the growing process. No matter what we do, however, there still may be some dry seasons, but our Lord can use even these to shape us if we faithfully follow the practices mentioned here.

I have found it personally helpful to study a new biblical book, or sections of a book, or even several different books every year. I try to read regularly as many newsweeklies, newspapers, and book reviews in the Sunday paper and in professional journals as I can. During the course of each year I also read best-selling novels that have some message their authors are seeking to get across, as well as several serious books both in my own field and in the field of general culture. My hope is to develop out of all this reading a cultural apologetic which is alert to where the masses are, as well as to where biblical studies and the church are going.

# Our Incomparably Great God

You who bring good tidings to Zion,
     go up on a high mountain.
You who bring good tidings to Jerusalem,
     lift up your voice with a shout,
lift it up, do not be afraid;
     say to the towns of Judah,
     "Here is your God!"
See, the Sovereign LORD comes with power,
     and his arm rules for him.
See, his reward is with him,
     and his recompense accompanies him.
He tends his flock like a shepherd:
     He gathers the lambs in his arms
and carries them close to his heart;
     he gently leads those that have young.

Who has measured the waters in the hollow of his hand,
     or with the breadth of his hand marked off the heavens?
Who has held the dust of the earth in a basket,
     or weighed the mountains on the scales
     and the hills in a balance?
Who has understood the mind of the LORD,
     or instructed him as his counselor?
Whom did the LORD consult to enlighten him,
     and who taught him the right way?
Who was it that taught him knowledge
     or showed him the path of understanding?

Surely the nations are like a drop in a bucket;
     they are regarded as dust on the scales;
     he weighs the islands as though they were fine dust.
Lebanon is not sufficient for altar fires,
     nor its animals enough for burnt offerings.
Before him all the nations are as nothing;
     they are regarded by him as worthless
     and less than nothing.

To whom, then, will you compare God?
What image will you compare him to?
As for an idol a craftsman casts it,
and a goldsmith overlays it with gold
and fashions silver chains for it.
A man too poor to present such an offering
selects wood that will not rot.
He looks for a skilled craftsman
to set up an idol that will not topple.

Do you not know?
Have you not heard?
Has it not been told you from the beginning?
Have you not understood since the earth was founded?
He sits enthroned above the circle of the earth,
and its people are like grasshoppers.
He stretches out the heavens like a canopy,
and spreads them out like a tent to live in.
He brings princes to naught
and reduces the rulers of this world to nothing.
No sooner are they planted,
no sooner are they sown,
no sooner do they take root in the ground,
than he blows on them and they wither,
and a whirlwind sweeps them away like chaff.

"To whom will you compare me?
Or who is my equal?" says the Holy One.
Lift your eyes and look to the heavens:
Who created all these?
He who brings out the starry host one by one,
and calls them each by name.
Because of his great power and mighty strength,
not one of them is missing.

Why do you say, O Jacob,
and complain, O Israel,
"My way is hidden from the LORD;
my cause is disregarded by my God"?
Do you not know?
Have you not heard?
The LORD is the everlasting God,
the Creator of the ends of the earth.
He will not grow tired or weary,
and his understanding no one can fathom.
He gives strength to the weary
and increases the power of the weak.
Even youths grow tired and weary,
and young men stumble and fall;
but those who hope in the LORD
will renew their strength.

They will soar on wings like eagles;
    they will run and not grow weary,
    they will walk and not be faint. [Isa. 40:9–31 NIV]

The Wall Street crash of October 1987, the international unrest in the Middle East, the complicated issue of apartheid in South Africa, the civil wars in several Central American nations—disquieting news of developments like these are enough to throw many into a deep state of depression. To what can a person cling in such troubled times as these? Will everything be lost? Is nothing safe and reliable?

Times like these remind us more forcefully than ever that the Christian church needs a new view of God. Our God, indeed, is too small—to borrow the familiar words from J. B. Phillips—if we allow ourselves to be more impressed by events around us, however horrendous, than by the greatness of our God. For, as Isaiah 40:9–31 tells us, our God is infinitely greater than all the perplexing problems of our day.

Like a thunder peal which reverberates against the mountainsides, so this text announces with unbounded joy its comforting message in verse 9: "Say to the towns of Judah, 'Here is your God!'" Who, since George Frederic Handel wrote the *Messiah,* could hear these words and not repeat them in the grand cadences of that great oratorio?—"Say unto the cities of Judah, 'Behold your God!'" (KJV).

There is our main theme: a new look at our incomparably great God. First proclaimed to Judah more than seven hundred years before Christ, this good news must now be announced to the whole world. We will therefore paraphrase the text like this: "Say to the cities of America; yes, say to the cities of Africa, Asia, Europe, indeed the whole world, 'Behold your God!'" For here is the one for whom the people of all nations should be longing, as, indeed, many now are.

Our God exhausts every attempt ever made to compare him to anything. In verses 12–13 of our text, he is seen to be incomparably great in three respects: in his power, in his person, and in his provision or pastoral care. These three areas of incomparability are suggested in the three strophes of this magnificent passage: verses 12–17, 18–24, and 25–31. Moreover, the last two strophes (in poetry a strophe functions as a paragraph does in prose) are marked off in verses 18 and 25 by the rhetorical device of repeating the same question in almost identical form. This question serves as a heading for each of the last two strophes.

Before we come to the main burden of this passage, we must examine verses 10–11, which function much like an overture in an opera. These two verses also contain an early statement of the three areas of God's incomparability, as they point to his power: "his arm rules for him" (v. 10a); his person: "his reward is with him" (v. 10b); and his pastoral care: "He tends his flock like a shepherd" (v. 11). With the refrains of this grand overture still ringing in our ears, we now turn to the development of the first comparison.

## Our God Is Incomparably Great in His Power

In order to establish the proper perspective, the prophet begins by asking five questions which deal with God's omnipotence. In these questions five natural phenomena are measured with five measuring devices. These phenomena head the list of things which may tend to frighten us and tempt us to put their power ahead of God's. Isaiah wants us to understand that the infinite power of God is equal to our present need for guidance. Indeed, if the awareness of God's power were more deeply seated in our souls, we would not be so alarmed and disturbed by every calamity.

How trifling in bulk are the seven seas!—just a handful of water in comparison to God's greatness! How minuscule in distance is the spread of the heavens!—just the span of a man's hand in comparison to God's greatness! How meaningless in volume is the dust of the earth!—just a third of a bushel in comparison to God's greatness! And how trivial are the mountains and the hills!—all easily balanced on a scale in comparison to the greatness of God!

Nothing in nature poses any threat to the living God. There is no reason why anyone should ever be intimidated by any display of brute force or power, for God's power has always exceeded every power in the natural world in the past, and by that same power he continues to regulate his world in the present.

What is ascribed to God's power must also be said of his goodness and wisdom. Verses 13–14 ask five more questions about God's wisdom and goodness in the exercise of his power. None of us taught the Lord anything, neither did he go to any of our schools for his understanding. Nothing can "regulate" or put a damper on his Spirit, says Isaiah in verse 13, using a form of the same verb he had used in verse 12 for "marking off" the heavens with the span of a man's hand.

Why, then, do we tend to fear the accumulated wisdom of the academy or of all the scientists? If one should take all the largest state-of-the-art computers and hook them up to one another, they still would be no match for God's wisdom.

But some will whine, "It's not nature or modern intelligence that I fear; it's nations. There is no telling what they are liable to do in this day and age."

This attitude is anticipated in verse 15. Instead of setting forth the greatness of God in a detached and abstract way, Isaiah shows that God is the governor of the nations as well.

In three fast-moving similies, the nations are exposed for what they are—a drop in the bucket. Not actually, of course, but in comparison to the greatness of God. Listen carefully and you too will be able to hear how much the power of the nations adds up to. "Plink." That's it! *The preceding,* as they like to say in those radio-alert messages, *was a message from one of the most powerful nations of our day*—"Plink." Only a drop in the bucket and as dust on the scales.

Our God governs the world. Therefore, we must be careful not to exalt nations and the persons who govern them, and in so doing take a diminished view of the power of God. He is in charge and he can sovereignly rule and overrule as he pleases. No one can prevent him from doing so.

About this time we are ready to surrender all our mistaken notions and fears and, like those to whom the summons of verse 9 was first addressed, to announce from the mountains, figuratively speaking, that no one compares to God. In fact, our idea of God is so large that we are ready to build a model of his greatness.

Using the fabled majesty of the cedar forest of Lebanon and the renown that same area had for raising prime cattle, Isaiah in verse 16 mocks the proffered models as being far too inadequate to represent the greatness of God. We can get the picture if we imagine an American prophet saying that his idea of the magnificence of God would be expressed by cutting down all the giant redwood trees of California and stacking them ten miles high over an area fifty by fifty miles square, then offering on top of this mammoth altar all the long-horned cattle in Texas as a sacrifice to him. Surely that would be enough to show how great God is.

But the model would not be adequate. The effort would be puny in comparison to the greatness of our God. It would be only peanuts (with apologies to a former president of the United States) in comparison to the might and power of God. Verse 17 concludes with this reminder: "Before him all the nations are as nothing." And what is true of the nations is equally applicable to all of us and to all those persons and things that we tend to put in the place of God.

## Our God Is Incomparably Great in His Person

God, however, is much more than force or power. He is a living person. This fact is stressed fourteen times in the New Testament. Thus David went out against Goliath the giant armed only with a slingshot and an announcement to Goliath that he came against him in the name of the living God (1 Sam. 17:45; cf. v. 36). That God was alive was an idea that apparently had never entered Goliath's head. But, when he was struck with this idea, he lay dead on the ground. He was, as some say in another connection today, "stoned."

In verses 18–20 Isaiah talks about idols. Surely no moderns are into this perversion! When did you last see someone take a bowl of Wheaties and go out into the back yard and offer it to a molten, stone, or wooden idol: "Here goddy! Here goddy!" So why stop to discuss these verses?

The reason is that idolatry is, indeed, our cup of tea. Any time you or I make any person, any goal, any institution, or anything else equal to or higher than the living God in our loyalties or priorities, we have immediately succumbed to idolatry. That is the essence of idolatry: giving to anyone or anything else the loyalty and devotion we should render to God.

Isaiah has a field day as he teases about how ridiculous all this effort of making a god really is. Such non-beings should be coated with gold to give them some value. And, of course, they should have some silver jewelry, for that is what real, live people wear, don't they? "Oh, you are too poor to go to all that expense?" interjects Isaiah in verse 20. "Well, then, be sure to examine carefully the wood you are going to use for a deity. It would be horrible to have your god come down with termites, wouldn't it? And one thing more," adds Isaiah with what must now be gales of laughter, "Nail your god down, for it would be devastating to have your god fall over and come unglued" (much as the god Dagon did in the Philistine temple).

Our God is such a real and living person that all of the forces and interests we tend to raise up as his equal are as ridiculous as the blind, dumb, and deaf idols of the ancients. Why are we so tempted to treat these things as if they are more real and more important than God? Every time we give first place to our jobs, our leisure activities, our life goals, our worries, or our friends, we show that our view and estimation of God are greatly inadequate.

God is not only incomparably great in his person in relation to lifeless idols; he is incomparably great in his personal relation to princes and rulers (vv. 21–24). Even those who have been raised up to positions of authority are not exempt from the common lot of mankind—death. Some scarcely have begun to rule when suddenly they are swept off this earth. Then why are we so taken up with all their pronouncements and intimidated by all their show of power and strength?

It is God himself who gives life, appoints persons to positions of leadership over the nations, and determines their time in office, despite what those who plot military coups think or how populaces vote! This is because God is a living person and no one can restrain his power or upstage his program. The authority of God is superior to that of all rulers, governors, and dictators.

### Our God Is Incomparably Great in His Pastoral Care

Once more in verse 25 the prophet repeats the question he had asked in verse 18. In verse 28 he repeats the question he had asked in verse

21. Why does the prophet linger so long and repeat so much on a subject—especially one which holds so few, if any, subtleties? Why does a preacher today fall into the same pattern, protracting a message which is already abundantly clear in its central announcement?

It is because we tend to be more intimidated and frightened by all the empty masks of our day than we are encouraged by all the promises of God. We are bombarded constantly day after day by the spirit of modernity with its little innuendoes and catchy commercials that run directly counter to all the promises of the eternal God. Thus it is well for us to make sure that we are truly facing the question of God's incomparability with all its realism and relevance.

If we do not believe that God really is concerned about little people like ourselves, then we should go outside for a lesson from the stars. "Lift up your eyes and look to the heavens: Who created all these?" Isaiah asks (v. 26). Not only did God create these stars, but he maintains them and he knows each one by name. Why, then, do we not believe that he knows us? It is a scientifically established fact that the number of stars in the heavens exceeds the number of people on this planet by an astronomically large figure.

That ought to settle the question of whether you and I count in God's sight or not. If his providential care of the stars is so exacting and so individualized that he knows every one of them by name, and not one of them is missing because of his great power, how dare we ever think that he is so transcendent and so far removed from us that in our littleness we are beyond his concern, and our troubles too trifling to attract his attention?

God's pastoral care is equal to the challenge of our moments of despondency as envisioned in verse 27. It is as if God says, "I know what you are thinking. You say, 'It's not fair! God doesn't seem to know about my difficulties, and my rights are disregarded by him!'" Why do we think that is true? Didn't God know that was how Israel felt? Doesn't he know that is how we sometimes feel ourselves? And don't his care and his provision extend all the way to the very depths of our despondency? He is the incomparably great God.

In fact, God's pastoral care for us exceeds in strength the boundless energy of those who are in the prime of life. He is not overcome by the fainting and weariness known to mortals. He never tires from neglect to take food nor exhausts his capacity to do more work. The young children who seem to have boundless energy and the young men who are called up to serve their country alike will fall exhausted. But God never grows weary or weak. He is changeless and eternal. He never rests from his work of doing good, and nothing can restrain him from showing kindness to all those to whom he wishes to show it. He gives power to the faint and helps those who have fallen (vv. 28–30).

Where, then, must we go if we are to receive such help from such an unwearied God? We must go in faith to him. "Those who hope in the LORD," declares verse 31, "will renew their strength." This word *hope* is not a passive word, suggesting that one must take one's chances and hope for the best. Instead, it is one of the strongest Old Testament words for belief and trust. It suggests a robust confidence that God is exceedingly great and able to do above all that we ask or think. The men and women who have this confidence are the ones who soar on wings like eagles, who run and do not grow weary, who walk and do not faint.

The strength of God is made perfect in our weakness, taught the apostle Paul in 2 Corinthians 12:9. Paul was only applying to believers what Isaiah says about our Lord in verses 28 and 29. That is the point of our whole study of this passage. We twentieth-century Christians are all too often unable to stand against the evil forces that are so rapidly changing the world around us, because we have not yet learned who God really is, nor do we have any idea how incomparably great are his power, his person, and his pastoral care for hurting, frightened, and tired people.

Our hearts need to sing with the psalmist, "The LORD is my light and my salvation—whom shall I fear? The LORD is the stronghold of my life—of whom shall I be afraid?" (Ps. 27:1).

It is high time that the church got up on a high mountain and loudly proclaimed, "You cities of Europe, Africa, Asia, America, and you islands of the sea, Take one long, steady look at our God! Behold, he will come again. Behold, he now rules and reigns! We are silly not to factor in his presence and his power, for he is the mightiest of all sovereigns in heaven and on earth!"

We rejoice with the hymn writer who paraphrased the apostle Paul's words in 1 Timothy 1:17 this way:

> Immortal, invisible, God only wise,
>     In light inaccessible hid from our eyes,
> Most blessed, most glorious, the Ancient of Days,
>     Almighty, victorious, Thy great name we praise.

# 12

## J. I. Packer

J. I. Packer is professor of systematic and historical theology at Regent College, Vancouver, British Columbia. In addition, he serves as a senior editor of *Christianity Today,* shares a team ministry at St. John's Anglican Church in Vancouver, and is a popular conference speaker.

Packer has more than forty-five books to his credit. Among them are *Knowing God, Evangelism and the Sovereignty of God, God's Words, Keep in Step with the Spirit,* and the *New Dictionary of Theology,* which he coedited with Sinclair Ferguson and David Wright. He received his B.A., M.A., and Ph.D. degrees from Oxford University.

# Speaking for God

### Defining the Sermon

Before we can think about preparing sermons, we must know what a sermon is; so I shall start by offering a definition. Not all will endorse it: a theological liberal couldn't, and my guess is that many evangelicals, who could, don't and won't. (If my guess is wrong, no one will be happier than I am—nor, I think, more surprised!) I will state the definition, however, as plainly as I can, and my readers shall judge for themselves what acceptance it merits.

First, let me focus the definition. An institutional definition of a sermon would describe it as a hortatory monologue delivered from a pulpit to people in pews as part of a liturgical program. A sociological definition would highlight the expectations that sermons seek to fulfill and the responsibilities that they are thought to impose. A homiletical definition would view the sermon as didactic communication, put over by means of a special rhetorical technique. Such definitions certainly have their place, but at this moment I am on a different track. The definition I offer—the definition with which I live, which commands my conscience, and guides me in preparing specific messages—is theological (that is, trinitarian and theocentric) and functional (that is, centering on intention and effect).

This definition, or concept, was given me in embryo during the winter of 1948–49, when I was privileged on Sunday evenings to sit under the preaching of the late D. Martyn Lloyd-Jones at Westminster Chapel in London, England. Yehudi Menuhin has written of how overwhelmed he was the first time he played Beethoven's Violin Concerto under Furtwaengler, by reason of the power with which the great conductor recreated Beethoven's music all around him. Well, that was how I felt that winter as I heard Dr. Lloyd-Jones preach the gospel of Christ from the Gospel of Matthew, opening up Matthew 11 with magisterial weight and passion in some twenty discourses.

Since then I have lived, worshiped, and preached under an ineffaceable sense of the authority of what Dr. Lloyd-Jones was doing. It is only in recent years, however, that I have been able to verbalize it to myself and others in a way that seems to me anything like adequate to the reality. And even so, my definition may not communicate all that from my standpoint it expresses, for preaching is ordinarily caught by contact rather than taught by rote. If my readers, preachers though they themselves may be, have never experienced such preaching as I encountered forty years ago, they may well miss much of the meaning of my words. Nonetheless, I hope that my definition will in fact strike some sparks.

A sermon is an applicatory declaration, spoken in God's name and for his praise, in which some part of the written Word of God delivers through the preacher some part of its message about God and godliness in relation to those whom the preacher addresses. This definition grounds a particular view of the preacher's task on a particular view of the nature of Scripture. Fuller explanation is needed on both these points, and it is convenient to take them in reverse.

### The Nature of Scripture

Holy Scripture, the inspired Word (message) of the living God, may truly be described as God preaching—preaching, that is, in the sense of instructing, rebuking, correcting, and directing every reader and hearer for the furthering of faith, praise, holiness, and spiritual growth. God preaches thus in and through all the various stories, sermons, soliloquies, schedules, statistics, songs, and supplications that make up the individual books of the canon. All that Bible writers tell us about God and man, God himself tells us; for the sacred text is not just man's witness to God, but is also, and indeed primarily, God's own witness to himself, given us in this human form. Everything in Scripture teaches something of the Father's plan, something of the ministry and majesty of the Son as fulfiller of it, and something too about the gift and glory of eternal life, and the way to set forth God's praise. Furthermore, it teaches it as from God himself. The approach to Scripture followed by preachers in the older Reformational-Puritan-Pietist-Evangelical tradition, from Luther to Lloyd-Jones, was determined by the clarity with which they grasped this truth, and it is our own urgent need to get back on this wavelength. Only as God himself is perceived to be preaching in our sermons can they have genuine spiritual significance, and God will be perceived to speak through us only as we are enabled to make plain the fact that it is really the Bible that is doing the talking.

### The Role of the Preacher

Since the Triune God—the Father and the Son, through the Spirit—already preaches to us in every part of the Bible, the human preacher's task resolves into becoming a mouthpiece and sounding board for the divine message that meets him in his text. It is not for the preacher to stand, as it were, in front of and above the Bible, setting himself between it and the people and speaking for it, as if it could not speak for itself. Rather, his role is to stand behind and below it, letting it deliver its own message through him, and putting himself explicitly and transparently under the authority of that message, so that his very style of relaying it models response to it. From this standpoint preaching is, indeed, in Phillips Brooks's phrase, "truth through personality," and the preacher is, indeed, half of his sermon. Only as he manifests both the mentality of a messenger and the disposition of a disciple will the preacher communicate any sense of God speaking in what he says. Insofar as he fulfills these two roles his preaching will be genuinely prophetic: he will speak from God in his character as a servant of God. The Holy Spirit who enables him to do this will lead God's people to recognize God's authority in what he is saying. The form of authority that is acknowledged in Scripture as authentically moral and spiritual is the authority of God and so represent him. That is how it is here. The authentic authority of the pulpit is the authority, not of the preacher's eloquence, experience, or expertise, but of God speaking in Scripture through what he says as he explains and applies his text.

So the preacher, rather than the critical commentator or the academic theologian, is the true interpreter of Scripture; for the preacher is the person whose privilege it is to bridge the apparent gap between the Bible and the modern world by demonstrating the relevance of what Scripture says to the lives of those whom he addresses.

Interpretation means, among other things, bringing literary and artistic legacies to life and showing their significance for those who stand at a distance, temporal or cultural or both, from the producers of these materials. Biblical interpretation involves both grammatical-historical exposition of what the text meant as instruction for the writer's envisaged readership, and contemporary application of it at the level of principle to show what it means for us today and what response it (or, rather, God in it) is calling for. Commentaries and theologies are resources for this task, but only preachers can fully perform it; and they perform it fully only as they apply their text in a rational and realistic way. To pass on biblical content, unapplied, is only to teach, not to preach. A lecture, as such, is not a sermon. Preaching is teaching plus—plus, that is, application of truth to life. One's adequacy as a preacher, interpreting God's Word to God's people, is finally determined not by the erudition of one's exegesis but by the depth and power of one's application. This is the next matter that my definition of a sermon requires me to discuss.

### The Theory of Application

A largely forgotten part of the evangelical heritage with regard to preaching is the procedure sometimes called "discriminating application," which Puritan writers were the first to formulate. I offer now a functional analysis of application, formally and schematically viewed, which is essentially a restatement in modern terms of what this procedure requires. Three guidelines are involved.

Application should constantly focus on the unchanging realities of each person's relationship to God.

The most important question that anybody ever faces is the issue of one's relationship with God. Both exposition and application in preaching must center here. Within the Bible story, cultures and circumstances changed and the externals of worship and devotion took different forms at different times. The New Testament era saw the coming of God incarnate, the establishing of Christ's kingdom, the eschatological gift of the Spirit, the superseding of type by antitype and of ethnic Jewishness by a global outlook, and the new reality of life in Christ. But the basic elements in relating rightly to our holy, gracious Creator remained in essence the same from Genesis to Revelation, and are so still. These elements include faith, love, hope, obedience; humility, repentance, forgiveness, fidelity; thankful praise and trustful prayer; stewarding gifts, sanctifying one's activities, serving others, and resisting evil both in one's own heart and in the world outside. These are the unchanging realities that the preacher's elucidations of Scripture, whatever else they deal with, must regularly highlight and illustrate, and that his applications, one way and another, must regularly cover. The Bible is given us to teach us godliness. All our preaching ought to further that purpose.

Application should constantly focus on the person, place, and power of Jesus Christ.

The Bible in its entirety is witness to Christ and to the Father's plans involving him. By setting these before us it makes us "wise for salvation" through faith in him (2 Tim. 3:15). Central to application in preaching, therefore, is the task of systematically relating God's love in Christ to the whole wide range of needs and perplexities to which, as we say (with truth), "Christ is the answer." This requires us both to dwell on his mediatorial office as our prophet, priest, and king, and also to present his person as set forth in the Gospels, so that he will be known and trusted as the individual that he was and is, and will never be reduced to an unknown $x$ in soteriological equations. Yet, just as it would not be enough to require faith in the office and work of Christ without delineating his personal profile in this way, so too it is not enough to exhibit Jesus the man as our example and ignore the work of his saving lordship—which is a continuing defect, unhappily, of the North American liberal tradition. In application, both the compassionate wisdom of the man from Galilee dealing with various kinds of sinners, and the saving power of "Jesus! my Shepherd, Husband, Friend, / My Prophet, Priest, and King, / My Lord, my Life, my Way, my End," must be brought to bear together.

Application should constantly search the consciences of the hearers.

It is the preacher's responsibility to plan the applicatory part of his sermon to this end, so that the message is "homecoming" (Alexander Whyte's word) in a specific way to as many of his congregation as possible. In every congregation there are likely to be people in each of the following categories (which, as will be seen, are not entirely exclusive):

1. unconverted and self-satisfied, needing to be awakened and humbled;
2. concerned and enquiring, wanting to be told what being a Christian today involves;
3. convicted and seeking, needing to be guided directly to Christ;
4. young Christians who need to be built up and led on;
5. mature Christians, aging both physically and spiritually, who need to be constantly encouraged, lest they flag;
6. people in trouble, through moral lapses, circumstantial traumas, "losses and crosses" (a Puritan phrase), disappointment, depression, and other such afflictions.

It has been wisely observed that in every congregation there will be at least one broken heart. Just as homemakers who prepare meals try to ensure that there will be enough kinds of food to satisfy all who are there, so too we who prepare sermons must try to see that, over a period of time if not in each single message, applications are made that will be home-coming and health-giving, through God's blessing, to each of these classes of people.

There are basically four types of application, each of which can be developed from any Bible truth about God and man, and each of which may and should be made from time to time to all six sorts of people. (Not that all twenty-four specific applications could actually be developed in one sermon! My point is that they are there to be developed, as wisdom directs.) There is, first, application to our mind, where the logical form is: the truth presented shows us that we ought not to think thus-and-so (and if we have thought it up to now, we must stop thinking it); instead, we should think such-and-such. Second, there is application to our will, where the logical form is: the truth presented shows us that we ought not to behave thus-and-so (and if we have started, we must stop at once); instead, we ought to do such-and-such. Third, there is application to our motivating drives, where the logical form is: the truth presented shows us that if we are living as we should, we have very good reason to carry on, and if we are not living so, we have very good reason to change our ways. Fourth, there is application to our condition, where the logical form is: How do we stand in relation to the truth presented? Have we faced it, taken it to heart, measured and judged ourselves by it? How do we stand in relation to the God who speaks it to us? It is through these four types of application, whether made to us from the pulpit or by us to ourselves in private meditation, that Scripture fulfills to us its appointed function of correcting, rebuking, and training in righteousness (2 Tim. 3:16).

How the preacher will express and angle each type of application on each occasion is something that he must of necessity decide for himself in light of what truth he is applying, what he knows about those he is addressing, what was said to them in previous sermons, and a host of other factors. A good rule of thumb for pastoral sermons, however, is that half the message should be in essence instruction in biblical truth about God and man and half should be in essence specific application of that truth. Observing these proportions, it seems to me, one cannot go far wrong.

## Preparing the Sermon

How do I prepare my own sermons? The short answer is that I try to produce messages that conform to the specifications already set out. Being an academic without a stated pastoral charge, I often find myself preaching to congregations about which I know very little, but I sieve my material as best I can through my applicatory grid in hope of ensuring that I shall say something relevant and timely to as many as possible of the six types of people who I expect will be there.

Where do sermon messages come from? For most preachers, I think, and certainly for me, there are two main sources: first, the known needs of congregations, which suggest particular themes and passages on which to preach, and maybe even series of sermons; second, our own experience of being taught and disciplined by God, which leaves us with insights and wisdom that we find ourselves wanting to pass on. Sometimes a lectionary or prior church decision prescribes the passage on which one must preach. In that case, one will search it and meditate and pray over it, seeking in it an important truth with an application that one has the skill to handle. Sometimes the occasion (Christmas, Easter, a national crisis, or some other event) dictates one's theme; then one will seek a passage to expound and apply appropriately. I would add here that a rounded theological understanding of the will and ways of God, and of the nature, demands, and resources of the Christian life is a great help in enabling one to see what truth one is looking at in particular Bible passages. Calvin's *Institutes,* covering these themes in classical fashion, is one theological guide that has suggested to me many messages over the years.

What routines and resources do I use in preparing sermons? My method (which I share simply because I have been asked to, and without wishing to make rules for anyone else) is, so to speak, first to walk round my text, or whatever I suspect will be my text (for at first, I am not always sure about that), looking at it in its larger context (i.e., as part of the book from which it comes, and of the Bible as a whole), and scribbling possible schemes of points to teach, angles of interaction with life and its problems to pursue, and personal applications to develop. I find that I need to start this process several days before the message has to be produced, for getting an outline that seems right—that is, one that expresses my heart and that I see how to use in searching the hearts of others—often takes me some time.

Only when I think I have such an outline do I turn to the church's expository legacy of commentaries and homiletical materials, exploring it and drawing on it to fill out the scheme I already have. Ordinarily, reading others' work before my own outline is clear makes it harder, rather than easier, to settle in my mind what my message from the text is supposed to be. For the record (though I do not suppose I am typical in this), modern expositions do not help me half as much as does Matthew Henry, the Puritan, and modern printed sermons do not suggest to me half as much as do those of C. H. Spurgeon and the sermonic writings of J. C. Ryle. As for illustrations, whenever I can, I use Bible stories to illustrate Bible doctrine. Beyond this, I find that there are usually illustrations enough in everyday events. For me, at least, exotic illustrations turn preaching into a performance remote from life, so that sermon time ceases to be an encounter with God and becomes an entertainment break, and accordingly, I expend no effort in hunting for them.

How much preparatory writing do I do? As much as is necessary to ensure that I know my message and have words at my command to make all my points, both expository and applicatory, in a clear, pointed, weighty way that gives no offense other than the inescapable offense of the gospel itself. How much writing is needed to get to this point varies, I find, from preacher to preacher.

How much written material do I take with me into the pulpit? As much as I need to be exact, as well as free and spontaneous, in the way that I speak. This, for me, means a half-sheet of paper, with skeletal notes in abbreviations of my own devising, for each half-hour of talk. Some preachers need less; some need more. Some need to have a complete script with them, not to read word for word, but to give them confidence as they speak, knowing that should words suddenly fail to come spontaneously they can drop their eyes to the script and find there what they need to start the flow again.

Furtwaengler, whom I mentioned earlier, was always thorough in his orchestral rehearsals, describing them as his preparation for improvising at the performance. In the same way thorough preparation equips the preacher to be spontaneous in the pulpit. Fumbling spontaneity, which indicates insufficient preparation, is always a depressant, but controlled creativity, carrying the sense that the person knows what he is doing even though he is doing some of it on the spur of the moment, generates a sort of communicative electricity that keeps people on the edge of their seats. So it was when Furtwaengler played Beethoven, Brahms, and Bruckner. So it was when Dr. Lloyd-Jones preached, as I can testify. So I pray, over and over, that it will be each time I preach. I hope that you who read this do the same.

This goal, no doubt, was what W. H. Griffith-Thomas had in view when he offered young preachers his formula for sermon preparation: "Think yourself empty; read yourself full; write yourself clear; pray yourself keen; then into the pulpit, and let yourself go!" But Thomas's sprightly words are not to be heard as sanctioning the frivolity of exhibitionist exuberance. Preaching is too serious a business for that, since the glory of God and the issues of eternity are bound up with it; and the act of preaching is spiritually demanding. "It is easy," said Charles Simeon, nearly two centuries ago, "for a minister to preach in the pulpit, and even to speak much good matter; but to preach is not easy—to carry his congregation on his shoulders as it were to heaven; to weep over them, pray for them, deliver the truth with a weeping, praying heart; and if a minister has grace to do so now and then, he ought to be very thankful." One can only agree; and I wish to make Simeon's words my own exit line.

It remains simply to say that the following sermon was first prepared when I was given the passage to preach on; that Henri Blocher's *In the Beginning* (Downers Grove: InterVarsity, 1984) gave me most help in focusing its style, and so getting a fix on the points it was written to make; that the applicatory questions jumped at me like a tiger; and that as written it is somewhat shorter than when I have preached it.

# Babel!

Now the whole world had one language and a common speech. As men moved eastward, they found a plain in Shinar and settled there.

They said to each other, "Come, let's make bricks and bake them thoroughly." They used brick instead of stone, and tar for mortar. Then they said, "Come, let us build ourselves a city, with a tower that reaches to the heavens, so that we may make a name for ourselves and not be scattered over the face of the whole earth."

But the LORD came down to see the city and the tower that the men were building. The LORD said, "If as one people speaking the same language they have begun to do this, then nothing they plan to do will be impossible for them. Come, let us go down and confuse their language so they will not understand each other."

So the LORD scattered them from there over all the earth, and they stopped building the city. That is why it was called Babel—because there the LORD confused the language of the whole world. From there the LORD scattered them over the face of the whole earth. [Gen. 11:1–9 NIV]

"They said, 'Come, let us build ourselves a city, with a tower that reaches to the heavens, so that we may make a name for ourselves and not be scattered over the face of the whole earth'" (v. 4). "From there the LORD scattered them over the face of the whole earth" (v. 9). Do you hear the echo? Do you see the irony? God brought upon these people the very thing they had aimed to avoid! This, in fact, is his regular way of judging human pride and folly, which is what he is doing here.

Do not be misled by the fact that this tale is told in a way that makes it sound like folklore and legend rather than history. All history from such early times is narrated in a half-poetic sort of prose. What we are being told here is how the great city of Babylon was first founded, and what its name really means. Babylonians used to explain the name as *babili,* meaning "gate of God"; but *babel* (Babylon, that is) is shown here to be an echo of the Hebrew for "confused," a name given as a memorial of the act of God that turned mankind's common language into a confusion of tongues some time, it would seem, between 10,000 and 5000 B.C.

But what has the story to say to Christians at the end of the twentieth century? A great deal! It is, in truth, a mirror of the modern world, in which we see revealed what China, and Russia, and the United States, and Britain, and Canada, and all the younger nations are up to at this moment. It pictures for us, very vividly, what we nowadays call the power game.

Look at the story again. It describes a grandiose project undertaken by the settlers in the Fertile Crescent (the plain of Shinar), between the rivers Tigris and Euphrates, following the flood. The plan was to build a city with a huge skyscraper tower (what the Babylonians later called a ziggurat) in the middle of it. The tower was to make a statement: it was to tell all who ever chanced that way that this was a proud and strong community, not to be trifled with. Thus the building of the tower would help them to make a "name"—that is, a reputation—for themselves.

We still do it: Paris has its Eiffel Tower, and Washington, D.C., has its Washington Monument, and Toronto has the highest of the lot, the Canadian National tower. These towers are all gestures of national pride. So you need not wonder why, as a new Canadian, I felt much glee as I told you that the Canadian National tower is the highest! But we all need to face the fact that, as this story shows, in a fallen world national and civic pride is not, and never can be, an entirely innocent thing. Why not? Because it feeds into the power game, which is always to some extent vicious, as this first slice of Babylon's history is meant to make plain.

## A Mirror of the Modern World

I spoke of the Babel story as a mirror of the modern world. It is so in two respects.

First, it shows us the purpose of human pride in the world today. That purpose is power. Pride, said Augustine, was the original sin. Eve was betrayed into embracing the goal of being equal with God and independent of God. With the wisdom Satan promised that eating the forbidden fruit would bring, she and Adam would have power to get along without God, and that was what, in that mad moment of temptation, Satan got her to want. The passion for power, the craving to be on top and in charge, always starts, as it did in Eden, with a dislike of dependence in any form, and pride is the flame that sets this passion and this dislike ablaze. You see it today in world politics. Every nation wants its own independence, and maintains what we grimly call "forces" in order to secure and protect that independence. You see it equally in global economics. Every nation wants to develop to the point of self-sufficiency and independent wealth. And you see it in the way that individuals seek to manipulate and control and exploit other individuals in business, in the home, in the church—yes, even in the church—and in every social unit under the sun. Playing the power game, in which he who grabs the greatest amount of independence and domination wins, is standard behavior on the part of our fallen race.

Where power beckons and pride drives, moral corners get cut and misconduct of one sort or another results. Athletes take forbidden steroids in order to win races; politicians follow forbidden courses in order to win elections; and so on. If I just whisper here "Ben Johnson" and "Watergate," you will, I think, get the message. The pianist Gerald Moore wrote that his friend Walter Legge, the supreme British impresario of a generation ago, "told me that what he wanted most in life was power." Legge shared with Moore his two ambitions, to marry the most beautiful singer in the world and to manage the finest orchestra in the world, and in the estimate of Moore and others, as well as in his own, Legge succeeded in doing both those things. But in both connections he proved himself a tyrant and, as we would say, a pain in the neck. There is a pattern here: the pride that sparks off the quest for power produces a ruthless self-absorption that rides roughshod over other people, forgetting that they have rights and feelings, too. This is the negation of love and care and service, and it is a gross and grievous evil.

The Babel story highlights two further realities that result when pride, with its passion for power, is in the saddle. The first is unrest, which in its extreme can produce paranoia. The more power you have, the more you fear to lose it, the more you feel threatened by that possibility, and the more you are driven to hunt for more power yet, so as to protect what you have already. Empire-builders cannot stop once they have started. Did not John D. Rockefeller, the financial tycoon, when asked what he most wanted in life now that he was a multimillionaire, reply, "Just a little bit more"? You see this pattern of paranoid unrest in the settlers' resolve to build the city "so that we . . . not be scattered over the face of the whole earth." Who was going to scatter them? They were the only ones there! But the urge to protect themselves against they knew not what had taken hold of them, and they felt forced to increase the power they already had—just in case, as we say. So they set themselves to build.

Now appears the second reality that pride produces, namely, unrealism, leading to grandiose gestures of bravado and foolhardiness. The plan was to build "a tower that reaches to the heavens." In the plain of

Shinar the settlers had found clay for brick-making and bitumen (sticky tar) in open slime pits. Were their raw materials and technology adequate for the project? The comment in verse 3, "They used brick instead of stone, and tar for mortar," is there to tell us that their resources were not adequate at all. Imagine putting up a brick skyscraper with no proper mortar to hold the bricks together! But prideful dreaming had led them beyond the bounds of realism. For the moment they felt that nothing was beyond them: anything they desired they could do—which is the modern technological dream, too. How up-to-date this old story really is! Their euphoric conceit was detected by God and is reflected in his comment in verse 6: "If . . . they have begun to do this, then nothing they plan to do will be impossible for them"—that is, there is nothing of which they will not think themselves capable, and which they will not attempt. The foolhardy unrealism of pride overreaching itself in grandiose and harmful wildcat schemes is a further familiar misery mirrored here.

But look now at the second main thing that this story shows us, namely, the purpose of divine providence in the world today. That purpose, or at least the part of it that is highlighted here, is preservation of the present order of things until God's eternal plan for bringing sinners to faith in the Savior and so gathering and building his universal church has been completed. This world will certainly end, but it will be God, not man, who decides when. Until it pleases God to bring down the curtain, he will continue to block human schemes which, wittingly or unwittingly, threaten the stability of the planet. That is the significance of his blocking the building of Babel by making it impossible for members of the building team to communicate, so that they gave up the project and drifted away from the site, and so were scattered in precisely the way they had hoped not to be. God foresaw that had the Babel project succeeded, nothing could have stopped them, and the damage they might then do to his world would be vast. So he judged their pride by blocking their project. He was then preserving the world for Christ's first coming. Now he is preserving it for the appointed day of Christ's second coming, and until that day he will continue to block the world-threatening follies of fallen man.

In an age threatened, as ours is, by global ecological disaster through pollution, famine, nuclear calamity, destruction of the ozone layer, the greenhouse effect, and similar nightmares, this is a very steadying truth. It does not guarantee that the world will last much longer—who knows how soon God has planned that the Savior should return? It does not guarantee that Christ's appearing will not be ushered in by the kind of horrors I have just listed—indeed, the New Testament drops hints that seem to point the other way. But it does guarantee that the end of this world, like the end of your physical life and mine within it, will take place at the time and in the way that God wills, and not otherwise. Man proposes, but God disposes, and our times are in his hands. The possibilities of human perversity wrecking God's world on the grand scale through environmental and technological idiocies that are now within our power seem limitless, but God in his merciful providence will restrain the processes of destruction until his time to end all things arrives. Be reassured: the Judge is still on the throne!

## Three Heart-Searching Questions

Is this all that the story of Babel has to say to us? Indeed, no; three questions jump out of the story to search all our hearts. I shall put them to you in direct form, just as they present themselves to me.

First, Do you, and do I, embody the attitude of Babel? The Babel attitude, as we have seen, was a compound of pride, paranoia, and pursuit of power. Pride says: "I must be big, bigger than these others." Paranoia says: "I am being threatened; I must strengthen my position." Power, dancing like a will-o'-the-wisp before your mind, says: "Chase me! I'm worth catching! Now you're after me! That's good!" Do you recognize any part of this attitude to life in yourself? Are you building somewhere your own tower of Babel—your own focus of self-assertion, manipulation, and power-grabbing? What would those who know you best—your friends, your colleagues, your fellow church members, your own family—say about you if asked that question? Do not protest that there is nothing of the Babel spirit in your heart. If you told me that, I should not believe you.

Do you know about the shortest letter ever written to a newspaper? It was sent by G. K. Chesterton to England's *Daily Mail*, which had invited readers to send in their answers to the question, "What's wrong with the world?" Chesterton's letter ran: "Dear Sir, I am. Yours sincerely." Witty? Yes, and wise! The origin of the Babel that surrounds us in the world outside us is the Babel that operates in your heart and mine. We need not only to be forgiven for indulging the Babel attitude—we certainly need that!—but also to be changed inside, so that the Babel attitude will no longer control us and Babel behavior will no longer mark us.

Thank God, then, for Jesus Christ, the living Savior! Not only does he bring us forgiveness through his cross, but he also drains out of us the pus of pride (pardon that repulsive image, but I am talking about a repulsive thing), and implants in us by his Spirit a heart of obedience, love, and humility, like his own. Have you yet sought that change from him? Have you yet found it? Is it not high time you repented of your addiction to Babel behavior, and asked to be changed?

Now a second question: Do you, and I, experience the anathema of

Babel? An anathema is a curse, announcing a penalty. God inflicted his anathema on Babel by direct action. As verse 8 says, and verse 9 repeats for emphasis, he scattered the settlers into isolation and loneliness, in which each was cut off from the rest both geographically and by the language barrier. Today, we all live pretty much on top of each other in the human anthill, and there are few language barriers. Nevertheless, loneliness and the sense of isolation have become the great Western heartache, as all counselors know, and surrender to the spirit of Babel can only make it worse. I remember a fortune-cookie motto that read: "Confucius say: top of ladder nice place, but very lonesome." Oh, how true! Relationally, our Western world has rotted in recent years.

I do not think you will contradict me when I say that something of the bitterness of feeling isolated and alienated from those to whom we should be closest—colleagues, friends, spouse, children, parents—is known to us all.

But have you realized, I wonder, that a saving trust in Jesus Christ starts a solution to this particular agony? When we receive Jesus into our lives as Savior and Lord, he commits himself to be with us always, so that henceforth we are never really alone, even in dark moments when we feel we are. Thus the anathema of Babel begins to be reversed, for now we are sharing our life with Christ our companion. And the reversal goes further, as the next question shows.

Lastly, then: Do you, and I, embrace the alternative to Babel? What is that alternative? Scripture makes it very plain. Babel means pride, and paranoia, and the power game, and consequent alienation and isolation, which together continue to constitute God's scattering judgment on those who follow the Babel way. God's alternative—Babel in full reverse—is a new way of living enjoyed by those who receive Christ, the way of fellowship with God and fellow believers in humility and love.

This alternative broke surface on the day of Pentecost, when the Holy Spirit was poured out. The gift of languages, described at the start of Acts 2, is often viewed as the reversal of Babel, but the truer and deeper reversal is the lifestyle of the infant church pictured at the end of Acts 2. "All the believers were together. . . . Selling their possessions and goods, they gave to anyone as he had need. Every day they continued to meet together. . . . They broke bread in their homes and ate together with glad and sincere hearts, praising God . . ." (Acts 2:44–47). This way of living continued through the early centuries, when the pagans said in amazement, "See how these Christians love one another!" It should be continuing still in every church, for it is the authentic form of Christian living. Life in fellowship with Christians completes the reversal of Babel that life in fellowship with Christ begins.

Some congregations never seem to grasp that they are called to be, quite precisely, God's alternative to Babel—his alternative, that is, to the arrogant, manipulative, self-seeking, power-grabbing pattern of community life which is all that the secular world ever knows. Many congregations fail in practice to come up to the mark of being God's alternative to Babel. Does yours? Is the spirit of Babel banished from it? Do you help to keep that spirit out by your own prayers and actions? Are visitors to your church able to see that here are Christians who love each other? If our churches were more obviously God's alternative to Babel, fellowships of faith and love and hope and help whose members work as hard in serving their Savior as the builders of Babel once worked in the service of their own pride, Christianity would have more credibility in the world than it musters at the moment. When people see the alternative to Babel consistently lived out, as the first Christians in Jerusalem lived it out, they will surely take notice. I tell you frankly, I long to see that day!

So I ask you directly, as I close: Do you, as a servant of Jesus Christ, embrace God's alternative to Babel as the proper way of life for yourself and your church? Will you then set yourself to live it out consistently at home, and in the fellowship of the congregation, and wherever else you go? This is the ultimate challenge of the Babel story to New Testament Christians. May we all have ears to hear it. On that basis I say: God bless you all. Amen.

# 13

## Ray C. Stedman

Since 1950 Ray C. Stedman has pastored the Peninsula Bible Church in Palo Alto, California. He speaks frequently at conferences and has more than twenty-five books to his credit, including *Body Life, Authentic Christianity, Spiritual Warfare,* and expository studies of Job, Mark, and Romans. He earned his Th.M. degree from Dallas Theological Seminary.

# Declaring God's Word through Expository Preaching

The greatest contribution the church can make today to a troubled and frightened generation is to return to a consistent and relevant preaching of the Word of God! All Christians would agree that what is most needed in the present age is a loosing of the power of God among us, but what is often forgotten is that the proclamation of his Word has always been God's chosen channel of power. "He sent forth his word and healed them" (Ps. 107:20), the psalmist declares. And it is not so much preaching from the Bible that is needed, as it is preaching the Bible itself—in other words, expository preaching!

### What Is Exposition?

Exposition is preaching that derives its content from the Scripture directly, seeking to discover its divinely intended meaning, to observe its effect upon those who first received it, and to apply it to those who seek its guidance in the present. It consists of deep insight and understanding of the thoughts of God, powerfully presented in direct personal application to contemporary needs and problems. It is definitely not a dreary, rambling, shallow verse-by-verse commentary, as many imagine. Nor is it a dry-as-dust presentation of academic biblical truth, but a vigorous, captivating analysis of reality, flowing from the mind of Christ by means of the Spirit into the daily lives and circumstances of twentieth-century people.

I first came to understand and value expository preaching from the writings of G. Campbell Morgan, the prince of English expositors in the early decades of the twentieth century. I ran across his books while trying to teach an evening Bible study class of sailors at Pearl Harbor during World War II. I learned from him not only how to discover the patterns of thought development in a biblical passage, but how to organize those patterns into contemporary presentations that would touch directly upon the issues of life today. In forty years of preaching and teaching I have never been able to match Morgan's beauty of language and richness of literary allusions, but I have had him continually before me as a model to follow.

Other expository preachers have added touches of their own uniqueness to my learning process. Dr. Harry Ironside of the Moody Church of Chicago left his mark upon me through a summer spent with him as his chauffeur, secretary, and constant companion. From him I learned simplicity of style and warmth of illustration. Campbell Morgan's successor at Westminster Chapel, D. Martyn Lloyd-Jones, also greatly raised my appreciation of the Bible's relevancy and authority. I have been privileged also to know with some degree of intimacy men like J. Vernon McGee, Lewis Sperry Chafer, Richard Halverson, Stephen Olford, John R. W. Stott, Francis Schaeffer, and J. I. Packer. These all have, in one degree or another, taught me lessons of preaching power.

## Preparing to Preach

Upon coming to Palo Alto in 1950, I began immediately to preach through books of the Bible, working my way through Sunday after Sunday until I had finished the whole book. I have tried to keep an even balance between the New Testament and the Old, usually alternating from one to the other. This has great advantages over textual preaching in that it forces one to handle the difficult themes of Scripture as well as the more popular ones. Further, it keeps truth in balance since it follows the pattern of Scripture itself in mingling several themes in one passage, and thus makes possible the apostolic goal of "declaring the whole counsel of God." If a series grows so long it tends to weary the congregation, I do not hesitate to break it off in favor of another, but will come back later and finish the original series. Since for years now all my messages have been put into print, when a series is finally finished, it is a complete coverage of the biblical book and is available as a unit for private or group study.

My method of sermon preparation has evolved from this concept of preaching. Having chosen which book of the Bible I will preach through, taking into consideration the needs of the congregation, the level of doctrinal instruction they may not yet have attained, and the spirit of the times we are passing through, I then begin to read the book through several times in various versions. My objective is to create a general outline of the book as a guideline to my preaching. I note the broad divisions of the book and the major changes of subjects. What I want is a bird's-eye view of the whole. For instance, my division of the Gospel of John is very simple: The Prologue, 1:1–18; The Manifestation of the Messiah, 1:19–4:54; Growing Unbelief, 5:1–12:50; The Unveiling of the Church, 13:1–17:26; The Murder of the Messiah, 18:1–19:42; The New Creation, 20:1–21:25.

I then choose a section from the first division upon which to base my first message. The section should be short enough to be manageable in the time available (thirty to forty minutes) yet constitute a single main theme. Next I check out all textual and linguistic problems and read the historical background for customs or other features that need explaining or emphasizing. Then I begin work on a detailed exegetical outline of the passage. Outlining permits me to put textual truth into my own words, and yet reveals clearly the logical development of the author's thought. This outline is the backbone of my message. It may take several hours of work to produce, but it is essential in order to maintain clarity and faithfulness to the text.

## Where Commentaries Come In

After I have completed this outline, then (and only then) do I read commentaries or other men's messages on the passage. This reading constitutes a check upon my own exegesis, and permits me to make changes or add insights (with due acknowledgment) to my own work. At this point I have probably put eight to ten hours of work into my text, but have only reached the half-way point of preparation. The exegesis is now complete. I know what I am going to say, but I do not yet know how I am going to say it.

I turn then to the work of presentation. Here I begin to form what I call my preaching notes. They are based upon the exegetical outline I have made, but I must now select what to include and what to leave out. Here also I add the illustrations which will make the text stick in people's minds and hold their attention until the end is reached. I think through how best to introduce the passage, usually with a personal story or reference to some current event. I must choose which themes to enlarge upon and which only to touch upon and then pass on. My notes will reflect all this and lead me logically and climactically to my predetermined conclusion. <u>I will take these notes to the pulpit with me, but I try to know them so thoroughly that I need only the briefest glimpse from time to time to keep me on track.</u> I believe it is very important to maintain eye contact with my audience while I am preaching.

## The Preaching Experience

I try to have my preparation complete by Friday afternoon, or at the latest, Saturday morning. I need to let my notes alone for at least half a day before preaching, while I prepare my body and heart with rest and prayer and other work. Following this approach, through the years I have gained a growing sense of the grandeur of preaching. I have seen many examples of its power to transform both individual lives and whole communities. I have increasingly felt a divine compulsion to preach, so that I know something of Paul's words, "Woe to me if I do not preach the gospel!" (1 Cor. 9:16). But even more I feel a deeply humbling conviction that I could never be given a greater honor than the privilege of declaring "the unsearchable riches of Christ." I often hear in my inner ear the words of the great apostle, "This is how one should regard us, as servants of Christ and stewards of the mysteries of God" (1 Cor. 4:1). I can think of no greater work than that.

# A Father's Joy

But since we were bereft of you, brethren, for a short time, in person not in heart, we endeavored the more eagerly and with great desire to see you face to face; because we wanted to come to you—I, Paul, again and again—but Satan hindered us. For what is our hope or joy or crown of boasting before our Lord Jesus at his coming? Is it not you? For you are our glory and joy.

Therefore when we could bear it no longer, we were willing to be left behind at Athens alone, and we sent Timothy, our brother and God's servant in the gospel of Christ, to establish you in your faith and to exhort you, that no one be moved by these afflictions. You yourselves know that this is to be our lot. For when we were with you, we told you beforehand that we were to suffer affliction; just as it has come to pass, and as you know. For this reason, when I could bear it no longer, I sent that I might know your faith, for fear that somehow the tempter had tempted you and that our labor would be in vain.

But now that Timothy has come to us from you, and has brought us the good news of your faith and love and reported that you always remember us kindly and long to see us, as we long to see you—for this reason, brethren, in all our distress and affliction we have been comforted about you through your faith; for now we live, if you stand fast in the Lord. For what thanksgiving can we render to God for you, for all the joy which we feel for your sake before our God, praying earnestly night and day that we may see you face to face and supply what is lacking in your faith?

Now may our God and Father himself, and our Lord Jesus, direct our way to you; and may the Lord make you increase and abound in love to one another and to all men, as we do to you, so that he may establish your hearts unblamable in holiness before our God and Father, at the coming of our Lord Jesus with all his saints. [1 Thess. 2:17–3:13 RSV]

Real father-love is in short supply in our world today. What we see is a frightening increase of child abuse, of fathers actually attacking their own children. A simple little song, "Dear Mister Jesus," the tale of a child who remembers the abuse she suffered at her father's hand, has been played on radio stations all over the country. Sometime ago I read the sad story of a four-year-old boy who was beaten to death by his stepfather because he had wet his pants. When his body was dug up, a tiny cross was found clutched in his hand. It tears one's heart to think of fathers treating their children that way, but it points up the need we have today for father- and mother-love.

## A Father's Love

The passage from 1 Thessalonians is a great testimony to a father's love. The church, after all, is a family, and God is our great Father. No aspect of Christian faith warms my heart more than knowing that God is my Father. My father left home when I was only ten years old, and I have never since known a father other than my heavenly Father. But what a tremendous encouragement it has been to me to know that I have a Father who loves me. On one occasion when Jesus was informed that his mother and brothers were waiting for him, he said of those he was teaching, "These are my mother and my brothers and my sisters" (Matt. 12:49–50), thereby indicating that a spiritual tie is as rich and deep as a physical tie—and oftentimes more so.

In verse 17 of chapter 2, the apostle pours out his father's heart of concern for these new Christians whom he had left in Thessalonica. "But since we were bereft of you, brethren, for a short time, in person not in heart, we endeavored the more eagerly and with great desire to see you face to face; because we wanted to come to you—I, Paul, again and again—but Satan hindered us. For what is our hope or joy or crown of boasting before our Lord Jesus at his coming? Is it not you? For you are our glory and joy."

I wonder where the idea ever arose that Paul was stern and cold. You cannot read this letter without sensing the warmth of his heart and the depth of his love. At the time he wrote this letter, he was ministering alone in the city of Corinth. He was feeling the loneliness of that moment. Being far away from loved ones is very unpleasant. Forgetting the danger that had driven him from Thessalonica and the cruelty he had experienced there, Paul longed to be with these converts again. He even tried to go to see them but was prevented by satanic interference.

## Satanic Opposition

In this chapter we see three sources of opposition to the apostle: opposition from the state (v. 2); opposition from society (v. 14); and here, opposition from Satan. While these might look like three enemies, they were really one. Other Scriptures indicate that the state and society are often channels of the devil's attempts to hinder the spread of the good Word of God. This is what Paul was encountering here.

Have you ever experienced a frustrating time in your own life when again and again you tried to do something you knew was right and found it hard going? You met opposition and hindrance, perhaps even from your own family. That is satanic hindrance, the devil's psychological manipulation of minds to arouse opposition and plant obstacles in the path of those who seek to do what is good and right.

When my wife and I were in Northern Ireland a couple of summers ago, we spent some time in a wonderful church there. The young pastor and his wife were beginning to teach body life and spiritual warfare. It once had been a lifeless church, but now it was alive and growing, filled with youth and young couples. But while we were there we learned that the best friend of the pastor had suddenly turned against them. He began to spread lies and slanders about them throughout the congregation, upsetting the whole church. It was a terrible time of pain and suffering for them. We have since learned that God has cleared it all up. The pastor has been vindicated and the miscreant has been exposed. But what caused it? It was satanic opposition, the devil with his clever ability to work through people to stir up things.

The Bible is the only book that explains the persistence and malevolence of evil. Why do we struggle so in this life? What are we up against? Jesus told us that it is the devil. "He is a liar and a murderer," said the Lord. He deceives and he kills. The satanic mind is responsible for the murderous violence, the widespread deceit, and the false philosophies that confront us today. Paul himself tells us, "We are not contending against flesh and blood, but against the principalities, against the powers, against the world rulers of this present darkness" (Eph. 6:12). No other book tells you that it is not people who are your problem, but rather the spiritual forces of evil that prevail in the world.

In his writings Paul suggests three things we need to keep in mind about satanic opposition. First, and perhaps most important, it is permitted by God. We find this same teaching in the Book of Job, where we read that Satan had to come before God and get permission from him to afflict Job's body. This man lost everything—his family, home, and wealth; and he suffered terribly from boils which covered his whole body. But God allowed his suffering. The end of the book reveals what was accomplished by that suffering, but it was all hidden for the moment from Job's eyes. So, too, it is hidden from our eyes. But the Bible reveals to us that there is a malevolent power of evil at work in this world. There are demonic beings, master manipulators, who are able to lead people about, putting thoughts in their minds, and who can even plant obstacles in the path of the gospel.

God permits this satanic opposition, because he uses it for his own purposes. That is the second fact we must remember. Opposition is God's method of training. Affliction, suffering, pain, and heartache are often God's way of getting our attention. Many of you have gone through that. You paid little attention to him until you suffered a time of great heartache. Then you began to hear what he is saying to you. God uses opposition to train us, and beyond that, to give us an opportunity to overcome trouble, to rise above it.

The third thing to remember, as this passage makes clear, is that satanic opposition underscores the value of believers. Paul writes in verse 19, "For what is our hope or joy or crown of boasting before our Lord Jesus at his coming? Is it not you? For you are our glory and joy." Whatever else those words may mean, they are saying that Paul considered the spiritual maturing of these believers in Thessalonica and other places his most important work. He is saying, "I have invested my life in you and your growth into spiritually mature and wholly developed Christians. This is the most important thing in the world to me. When the Lord Jesus comes, I will glow with pride that you have achieved the changes in your life that I so greatly long to see."

## Marks of Maturity

My wife and I read every morning a fine devotional book which has been assembled from the writings of Dr. J. I. Packer. In a passage we read the other day, he quoted the words of a psychologist on the six marks of maturity. Americans love to take self-examinations, so here is one for you on what it means to be grown up, to be whole, balanced, sane, and able to cope with life.

The first mark of maturity is the ability to deal constructively with reality, to face facts, not to cover them up or call them something else, but to deal with life as it truly is. Mature people do not kid themselves.

The second mark is adapting quickly to change. We all experience change: in our physical bodies, at work, in the family, and elsewhere. I am amazed at how much some of you have changed through the years, while I remain exactly the same! Immature people resist change. It makes them nervous. But one mark of maturity is to adapt to change, because change is inevitable.

The third mark is freedom from the symptoms of tension and anxiety. The worried look, the frown, the ulcers, the palpitations of the heart—all come because a person is upset, anxious, and worried. Maturing means you have begun to see that God is in control of this world. He is working out purposes that you do not always understand, but you can accept them. He will take you through the deep water, not drown you in it. Maturity means you are learning to trust.

Fourth, maturity means to be more satisfied with giving than receiving. Some of you have learned that the joy of Christmas is not getting presents but giving them. To see the joy in someone else's face when that person gets something he either needs or wants—the pleasure that gives you is a sign you are growing up. You are discovering the true values of life.

The fifth mark of maturity is to relate to others with consistency, helpfulness, and mutual satisfaction. Maturity is learning to get along with other people; to cooperate with them; to be a help, not a hindrance; to seek the good of others, even at cost to yourself.

Finally, maturity is sublimating and redirecting anger to constructive ends. Maturity is the ability to use the adrenaline that anger creates, not to lose your temper and so add to the problem, but to correct an unpleasant situation, or to help change the nature of a difficulty. This is maturity, and this is what the apostle longed for in these believers at Thessalonica.

## Commitment Rewarded

Paul's concern, as this passage makes clear, demanded of him a very deep commitment:

"Therefore when we could bear it no longer, we were willing to be left behind at Athens alone, and we sent Timothy, our brother and God's servant in the gospel of Christ, to establish you in your faith and to exhort you, that no one be moved by these afflictions. You yourselves know that this is to be our lot. For when we were with you, we told you beforehand that we were to suffer affliction; just as it has come to pass, and as you know. For this reason, when I could bear it no longer, I sent that I might know your faith, for fear that somehow the tempter had tempted you [here is that satanic interference again] and that our labor would be in vain" (vv. 1–5).

Twice in this section the apostle says there came a time in Athens when he could "bear it no longer." That does not mean that he was anxious and fearful. Rather, he had not heard from these converts for so long that he felt he must take some action to find out what was going on in Thessalonica. At great deprivation to himself, he decided to send Timothy to them, while he remained alone in Athens and then went on to Corinth.

I spent the summer of 1960 in the Orient with Dr. Dick Hillis. I was scheduled to speak to six hundred Chinese pastors on the island of Taiwan. This was a difficult assignment, as my messages were to be interpreted into two different languages, Mandarin and Taiwanese. It is hard enough speaking through one "interrupter." When there are two, however, by the time one sentence has been interpreted both ways, you have forgotten what you just said! But I was comforted by the fact that Dick Hillis, a veteran missionary, was with me. The day before I was due to speak, he got a telegram saying that his mother in California was ill, and he had to return home. I have never forgotten the depression and loneliness that came over me when that happened. I am sure that is how Paul must have felt when he was left alone in Corinth, that cultured but degraded center of Roman life. He had to face the city by himself. But he was willing to do it in order that these Thessalonian believers might grow in their faith. So he sent Timothy to them.

Paul had three things in mind, he tells us. First, he wanted to establish them in faith, that is, to teach them the great realities on which their faith rested: the coming of Jesus, his life and ministry, his death upon the cross, his resurrection, the coming of the Holy Spirit, and thus the availability to them of a new resource in God that the world could know nothing about. The Thessalonians needed to be established in these truths, and that was Timothy's mission.

Secondly, these believers needed to be exhorted to steadiness and to not panic when things got tough. They should never forget that suffering and affliction could be surmounted. They had a spiritual resource to lean upon which they did not have before, so they did not need to fear. God would take them through every difficulty and use each one for their benefit.

Paul had already laid the foundation for this ministry of Timothy when he was with them. He had told them that the human race was contaminated with a terrible pollution that the Bible calls sin. As you know, the great plague of our day is AIDS, an acronym for Acquired Immune Deficiency Syndrome. I think that sin, too, can be written as an acronym. It stands for Self-Induced Neurosis. Sin is a problem that rises from within. Jesus said, "Out of the heart of men, proceed evil thoughts, adulteries, fornications, murders" (Mark 7:21 KJV). Sin is an internal contamination which we inherited. The bad news that comes with this fact is that "the wages of sin is death," as Paul wrote in Romans. Pain, suffering, anguish, and alienation—all forms of death; that is the bad news. But with it always comes good news: "The wages of sin is death, *but the free gift of God is eternal life in Christ Jesus our Lord*" (Rom. 6:23, emphasis added). We cannot evade the painful results of our sinful choices, but we can find love, joy, and peace even while we are working through our just deserts.That is good news! That is what Paul had taught the Thessalonians, and what Timothy needed to remind them of, so they would remain steadfast when afflictions struck.

The third reason Paul sent Timothy to them was that he himself needed to know the present circumstances of these believers. Timothy would bring back word, and now he had returned with such a good report that the apostle is filled with joy, as he reports in verses 6 through 9.

"But now that Timothy has come to us from you, and has brought us the good news of your faith and love and reported that you always remember us kindly and long to see us, as we long to see you—for this reason, brethren, in all our distress and affliction we have been comforted about you through your faith; for now we live, if you stand fast in the Lord. For what thanksgiving can we render to God for you, for all the joy which we feel for your sake before our God, . . ." (vv. 6–9).

To Paul's great relief, his work has not been in vain. It stood solid and sure. The Thessalonians' faith was intact; their love was evident; and, best of all, their trust in God was secure. They held cherished memories of the apostle and longed to see him. He is filled with thankfulness and joy at this good news. It is always the natural reaction of a father's heart when he receives good reports of his children. This is how the apostle John felt, as he tells us in his third letter: "No greater joy can I have than this, to hear that my children follow the truth" (3 John 4).

I can testify to the same thing. My wife and I have been observing a young man, near and dear to us, who is going through a possible disintegration of his marriage. It is a painful time for him. His home is broken, his children have been taken away, but that very suffering has made him aware of his own contribution to this problem. He is seeing himself in a new light and is recognizing his mistakes. Though our hearts ache for him, we are also filled with joy because we see that he has found a new plateau in his relationship with God. In the midst of his agony he is rejoicing. He has even told us he is glad this devastating tragedy has happened because it has brought him to his senses, and he has discovered the joy of knowing God. That is what Paul was feeling as Timothy reported on the trials and testings of the Thessalonians.

### How to Pray

The apostle closes this section with a wonderful revelation of how to pray about situations like this. He writes that he has been "praying earnestly night and day that we may see you face to face and supply what is lacking in your faith. Now may our God and Father himself, and our Lord Jesus, direct our way to you; and may the Lord make you increase and abound in love to one another and to all men, as we do to you, so that he may establish your hearts unblamable in holiness before our God and Father, at the coming of our Lord Jesus with all his saints" (vv. 10–13).

Do you ever wonder what to pray for when you, your family, or your friends are going through deep struggles and sorrow? Romans 8:26 reminds us that at times we do not know what to pray for as we ought but the Spirit helps us! That is God's promise to us. Here we have a good example of how the Spirit helped the apostle to pray for exactly what these people needed.

There are three things about prayer we may note in these verses. First, Paul prayed "earnestly." He did not get down beside the bed at night and say, "Bless my friends in Thessalonica." Many people pray like the man who said, "Bless me and my wife, our son John and his wife; us four and no more." But Paul prayed earnestly for these friends. He thought about what they were going through. He set the problem before God, reminding him of his promises. He took time to think deeply on the Thessalonians' needs.

He also prayed frequently: "night and day," he said. Morning and evening, while he was working on tents, or whatever he was doing, his lips were moving in prayer because his heart was concerned for his friends. They were seldom out of his thoughts and whenever he thought of them, he prayed.

Finally, he prayed specifically. He had some very definite things to ask for, five of them, actually, which he lists. First, he prayed that he might "see [them] face to face." He wanted to get back to Thessalonica, to have the joy of seeing these dear friends again; so he laid that request before the Lord. Second, he wanted to minister further to them that he and his helpers might "supply what [was] lacking in [their] faith." They needed to know a great deal more about the Christian view of life and of the world. When you understand how to look at the events of your life the way the Bible does, then you are being realistic. All the confusion and illusion disappear and you start seeing things the way they really are. Paul wanted to open their eyes to further truths from God.

Then he prayed to overcome the satanic hindrance. "May our God and Father himself, and our Lord Jesus, direct our way to you." Are you finding it difficult to get where you want to go? Here is how to pray. Simply ask God to open a way for you—physically or spiritually, as the case may be—to the goal you have in mind. Jesus said, "Ask, and it will be given you; seek, and you will find; knock, and it will be opened to you" (Matt. 7:7). That is how Paul prayed. He knocked on this closed door, asking that he might get back to Thessalonica. Later accounts reveal that God answered that prayer and he did return to these believers.

Fourth, Paul prayed that their love might increase. According to the New Testament, this is the true mark of a successful church. I meet frequently with pastors from all over the country, and many of them talk about success in the ministry and how to measure a successful church. But they often measure success by numbers, or the size and impressiveness of the church building. Some famous church buildings in this country are advertised all over the land, and people travel far just to see them. But in the New Testament, success is gauged by how much people learn to love one another, forgive one another, listen to one another, support and pray for one another, and reach out to those in need around them. That is what Paul asked for the Thessalonians.

Finally, the apostle prayed that these Christians would continue to live righteously until the Lord's return: "May he establish your hearts unblamable in holiness before our God and Father, at the coming of our Lord Jesus with all his saints." The second coming of Jesus is no further away for you and me than it was for these believers in Thessalonica, since it is no further away than the end of our life. He comes for us, if we know him, when we die. Paul was therefore praying that the rest of their lives might be marked by "unblamable" living. That does not mean sinlessness, as we have already seen. Unblamable means that they were dealing with what was wrong in their lives, not covering it up or pretending it was not there. They dealt with the sin in their own hearts with the spiritual resources that God provides, and thus were enabled to turn from evil and walk closer and closer with him.

Paul knew that Jesus Christ will some day enter into this world of time again. Scripture anticipates it. We are, perhaps, nearing it right now. It could occur before the end of this century. It is no further away than our own personal death, but it may occur even sooner than that. Paul wanted all believers to live in the expectation of the Lord's coming, so that at his return their lives would be acceptable to him.

I have observed that most Christians pray that God will prevent things from happening: some injury, death, suffering, or heartache. Unfortunately, some people teach us that we have a right to be kept from all trouble. But the New Testament tells us that afflictions are needed in our lives. God does sometimes grant our requests and removes problems—and it is not wrong to pray for this if we also understand that he has perfect freedom to say no. But what he tells us to pray for is not that these things will be prevented from happening, but that they will be used to our spiritual advantage.

The night before Jesus was crucified he said to Peter, his most troublesome disciple (the one who suffered most from hoof-in-mouth disease), "Simon, Simon, behold, Satan demanded to have you, that he might sift you like wheat, but I have prayed for you." What was it Jesus prayed for? He did not pray, "Do not let it happen. Stop Satan from getting hold of him." No, what he said was "I have prayed for you *that your faith may not fail*" (Luke 22:31–32, emphasis added). These words were uttered only a few hours before Peter denied his Lord. That denial was Satan sifting him. But Jesus had prayed, "Father, though Peter must go through anguish and heartache, I pray that when it happens, his faith will hold firm, that you will take him through it all, and use it for good in his life."

When we come to the close of a day, or of a year, our prayers ought to be like this. Anything can happen on the morrow or in the coming year: heartache, tragedy, joy, triumph. But let us pray that whatever happens, it will deepen our faith, increase our love, open our blinded eyes to truth and reality, and strengthen our spiritual stability in this troubled, rootless world in which we live.

# Select Bibliography

Adams, Jay E. *Preaching with Purpose: A Comprehensive Textbook on Biblical Preaching.* Grand Rapids: Baker, 1982.

____. *Pulpit Speech.* Reprint ed. Grand Rapids: Baker, 1976.

Bartow, Charles L. *The Preaching Moment: A Guide to Sermon Delivery.* Nashville: Abingdon, 1980.

Blackwood, Andrew W. *Biographical Preaching for Today.* New York and Nashville: Abingdon, 1954.

____. *Expository Preaching for Today.* New York and Nashville: Abingdon-Cokesbury, 1953.

____. *Preaching from the Bible.* Reprint. Grand Rapids: Baker, 1974.

____. *The Preparation of Sermons.* Reprint. Grand Rapids: Baker, 1980.

Broadus, John A. *On the Preparation and Delivery of Sermons.* 4th ed. Revised by Vernon L. Stanfield. New York: Harper and Row, 1979.

Brokhoff, John R. *As One with Authority: The Ministry of Preaching.* Wilmore, Ken.: Bristol, 1889.

Brooks, Phillips. *The Joy of Preaching.* Reprint. Grand Rapids: Kregel, 1989. Formerly published as *Lectures on Preaching* (1877).

Brueggemann, Walter. *Finally Comes the Poet: Daring Speech for Proclamation.* Minneapolis: Fortress, 1989.

Buttrick, David G. *Homiletic: Moves and Structures.* Philadelphia: Fortress, 1987.

Cameron, Nigel, and Sinclair B. Ferguson, eds. *Pulpit and People.* Edinburgh: Rutherford House, 1986.

Clowney, Edmund P. *Preaching and Biblical Theology.* Phillipsburg, N.J.: Presbyterian and Reformed, 1956.

Cox, James W. *A Guide to Biblical Preaching.* Nashville: Abingdon, 1976.

____. *Preaching: A Comprehensive Approach to the Design and Delivery of Sermons.* San Francisco: Harper and Row, 1985.

Craddock, Fred B. *Preaching.* Nashville: Abingdon, 1985.

Davis, Henry Grady. *Design for Preaching.* Philadelphia: Fortress, 1967.

Davis, Ozora S. *Principles of Preaching.* Chicago: University of Chicago Press, 1929.

Eslinger, Richard L. *A New Hearing: Living Options in Homiletical Method.* Nashville: Abingdon, 1987.

Fant, Clyde E. *Preaching for Today.* Rev. ed. San Francisco: Harper and Row, 1987.

Farmer, Herbert H. *The Servant of the Word.* New York: Scribner's, 1942.

Freeman, Harold. *Variety in Biblical Preaching: Innovative Techniques and Fresh Forms.* Waco: Word, 1987.

Garvie, Alfred Ernest. *The Christian Preacher.* Edinburgh: T. and T. Clark, 1920.

Greidanus, Sidney. *The Modern Preacher and the Ancient Text.* Grand Rapids: Eerdmans, 1989.

Gustafson, James M. *Treasure in Earthen Vessels.* Chicago: University of Chicago Press, 1985.

Hicks, H. Beecher, Jr. *Preaching Through a Storm.* Grand Rapids: Zondervan, 1987.

Howe, Reuel L. *The Miracle of Dialogue.* Greenwich, Conn.: Seabury, 1963.

Jensen, Richard A. *Telling the Story: Variety and Imagination in Preaching.* Minneapolis: Augsburg, 1979.

Jones, Ilion T. *Principles and Practice of Preaching.* New York and Nashville: Abingdon, 1956.

Kaiser, Walter C. *Toward an Exegetical Theology: Biblical Exegesis for Preaching and Teaching.* Grand Rapids: Baker, 1981.

Killinger, John. *Fundamentals of Preaching.* Philadelphia: Fortress, 1985.

Larsen, David L. *The Anatomy of Preaching: Identifying the Issues in Preaching Today.* Grand Rapids: Baker, 1989.

Lenski, R. C. H. *The Sermon: Its Homiletical Construction.* Reprint. Grand Rapids: Baker, 1968.

Lloyd-Jones, D. Martyn. *Preaching and Preachers.* Grand Rapids: Zondervan, 1972.

Logan, Samuel T., Jr., ed. *The Preacher and Preaching.* Phillipsburg, N.J.: Presbyterian and Reformed, 1986.

Lowry, Eugene L. *The Homiletical Plot: The Sermon As Narrative Art Form.* Atlanta: John Knox, 1980.

Marcel, Pierre C. *The Relevance of Preaching.* Grand Rapids: Baker, 1963.

Miller, Calvin. *Spirit, Word, and Story: A Philosophy of Preaching.* Dallas: Word, 1989.

Nichols, J. Randall. *Building the Word: The Dynamics of Communication and Preaching.* San Francisco: Harper and Row, 1981.

Nouwen, Henri J. *Creative Ministry.* Garden City, N.Y.: Doubleday, 1978.

Perry, Lloyd M. *Biblical Preaching for Today's World.* Rev. ed. Chicago: Moody, 1989.

Pitt-Watson, Ian. *Preaching: A Kind of Folly.* Philadelphia: Westminster, 1976.

_____. *A Primer for Preachers.* Grand Rapids: Baker, 1986.

Robinson, Haddon W. *Biblical Preaching: The Development and Delivery of Expository Messages.* Grand Rapids: Baker, 1980.

Spurgeon, C[harles] H. *Lectures to My Students.* Series 1, 2, 3, revised. Reprint. London: Marshall, Morgan and Scott, 1965.

Stevenson, Dwight E. *In the Biblical Preacher's Workshop.* Nashville and New York: Abingdon, 1967.

Stewart, James S. *Heralds of Christ.* New York: Scribner's, 1946.

Stibbs, Alan M. *Expounding God's Word: Some Principles and Methods.* Grand Rapids: Eerdmans, 1961.

Stott, John R. W. *Between Two Worlds: The Art of Preaching in the Twentieth Century.* Grand Rapids: Eerdmans, 1982.

# Index